MCSE Windows® 2000
For Dummies®

CW00924194

Server Services

- ✔ Windows 2000 DHCP supports scopes, superscopes, and the use of MADCAP for multicast IP addressing.
- ✔ Windows 2000 Server provides WINS for backward compatibility with down-level clients.
- ✔ Windows 2000 networks are built on DNS, and Microsoft DNS Server supports all the necessary DNS features for Windows 2000 clients, including dynamic DNS.
- ✔ DNS is configured based on zones. Various resource records, such as A, CNAME, and MX can be used to point to various network services or servers.
- ✔ Windows 2000 offers a wide variety of printer support and printer configuration features. Windows 2000 computers can automatically publish shared printers in the Active Directory.
- ✔ When sharing folders, you can manage inheritance from parent folders on the Security tab of the folder's Properties dialog box.
- ✔ Document caching can be set to automatic for documents and programs, or to manual for documents.
- ✔ A standalone Dfs does not provide any inherent fault tolerance, while an Active Directory-integrated Dfs does provide fault tolerance.

Server Tools

- ✔ Use the Add/Remove Hardware wizard to install non-plug-and-play devices and to troubleshoot devices that are not functioning properly.
- ✔ Use Performance Monitor, Task Manager, and MSINFO to manage and gain important information about your system.
- ✔ Use the Windows Backup utility to create and manage backup jobs.
- ✔ Use Windows Safe Mode options and the Recovery console to repair damaged systems.
- ✔ Disk quotas give you an easy way to manage user disk space usage on the Windows 2000 Server.

For Dummies®: Bestselling Book Series for Beginners

MCSE Windows® 2000 Server For Dummies®

System Configuration

- All Windows 2000 computers contain system state data, which includes such items as the registry and the COM + component database. Only domain controllers have a SYSVOL folder.
- Windows 2000 supports dynamic disks and an unlimited number of disk volumes. Configuration changes can be make without rebooting.
- Routing and remote access are an integrated part of Windows 2000 Server, supporting a wide variety of protocols and technologies, including Virtual Private Networking (VPN).
- Terminal Services can be deployed in either Remote Administration mode or Application Sharing mode, but not both on the same server.

Installation

- Always check the HCL for hardware compatibility. The HCL is available on Microsoft's Web site and on the installation CD-ROM.
- Windows 2000 Server supports NTFS, FAT, and FAT32.
- You can upgrade directly to Windows 2000 Server from Windows NT 3.51, Windows NT 4.0, and Windows NT 4.0 Terminal Server.
- You can run setup from the CD-ROM, from a network share, or by running WINNT or WINNT32.
- You can perform unattended installations using the Setup Manager wizard to create answer files.
- Sysprep and Syspart are drive image technologies that you can use for deploying Windows 2000 Server.

Permissions

- NTFS permissions for files are read, write, read & execute, modify, and full control.
- NTFS permissions for folders are read, write, list folder contents, read & execute, modify, and full control.
- Effective NTFS permissions are the combined total of NTFS permissions, with the exception of Deny, which overrides all other permissions.
- If you copy a file or folder on the same NTFS volume or a different NTFS volume, the file or folder inherits the permissions of the destination folder. If you move a file or folder within the same NTFS volume, the file or folder retains its permissions. If you move a file or folder to a different NTFS volume, the file or folder inherits the permissions of the destination folder.
- FAT or FAT32 volumes do not support any NTFS permissions.

For Dummies®: Bestselling Book Series for Beginners

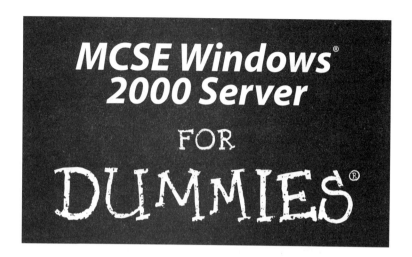

MCSE Windows® 2000 Server
FOR
DUMMIES®

by Curt Simmons

IDG Books Worldwide, Inc.
An International Data Group Company

Foster City, CA ◆ Chicago, IL ◆ Indianapolis, IN ◆ New York, NY

MCSE Windows® 2000 Server For Dummies®

Published by
IDG Books Worldwide, Inc.
An International Data Group Company
919 E. Hillsdale Blvd.
Suite 400
Foster City, CA 94404
www.idgbooks.com (IDG Books Worldwide Web site)
www.dummies.com (Dummies Press Web site)

Library of Congress Control Number: 00-101005

ISBN: 0-7645-0655-2

Printed in the United States of America

10 9 8 7 6 5 4 3 2 1

1B/QX/QY/QQ/IN

Distributed in the United States by IDG Books Worldwide, Inc.

Distributed by CDG Books Canada Inc. for Canada; by Transworld Publishers Limited in the United Kingdom; by IDG Norge Books for Norway; by IDG Sweden Books for Sweden; by IDG Books Australia Publishing Corporation Pty. Ltd. for Australia and New Zealand; by TransQuest Publishers Pte Ltd. for Singapore, Malaysia, Thailand, Indonesia, and Hong Kong; by Gotop Information Inc. for Taiwan; by ICG Muse, Inc. for Japan; by Intersoft for South Africa; by Eyrolles for France; by International Thomson Publishing for Germany, Austria and Switzerland; by Distribuidora Cuspide for Argentina; by LR International for Brazil; by Galileo Libros for Chile; by Ediciones ZETA S.C.R. Ltda. for Peru; by WS Computer Publishing Corporation, Inc., for the Philippines; by Contemporanea de Ediciones for Venezuela; by Express Computer Distributors for the Caribbean and West Indies; by Micronesia Media Distributor, Inc. for Micronesia; by Chips Computadoras S.A. de C.V. for Mexico; by Editorial Norma de Panama S.A. for Panama; by American Bookshops for Finland.

For general information on IDG Books Worldwide's books in the U.S., please call our Consumer Customer Service department at 800-762-2974. For reseller information, including discounts and premium sales, please call our Reseller Customer Service department at 800-434-3422.

For information on where to purchase IDG Books Worldwide's books outside the U.S., please contact our International Sales department at 317-596-5530 or fax 317-572-4002.

For consumer information on foreign language translations, please contact our Customer Service department at 1-800-434-3422, fax 317-572-4002, or e-mail rights@idgbooks.com.

For information on licensing foreign or domestic rights, please phone +1-650-653-7098.

For sales inquiries and special prices for bulk quantities, please contact our Order Services department at 800-434-3422 or write to the address above.

For information on using IDG Books Worldwide's books in the classroom or for ordering examination copies, please contact our Educational Sales department at 800-434-2086 or fax 317-572-4005.

For press review copies, author interviews, or other publicity information, please contact our Public Relations department at 650-653-7000 or fax 650-653-7500.

For authorization to photocopy items for corporate, personal, or educational use, please contact Copyright Clearance Center, 222 Rosewood Drive, Danvers, MA 01923, or fax 978-750-4470.

Use of the Microsoft Approved Study Guide Logo on this product signifies that it has been independently reviewed and approved in complying with the following standards: acceptable coverage of all content related to Microsoft exam number 70-215, entitled Installing, Configuring, and Administering Microsoft Windows 2000 Server; sufficient performance-based exercises that relate closely to all required content; and technically accurate content, based on sampling of text.

is a registered trademark under exclusive
license to IDG Books Worldwide, Inc.
from International Data Group, Inc.

About the Author

Curt Simmons, MCSE and MCT, is a technical trainer and author who has written almost a dozen high-level computing books, including several MCSE preparation titles. He has been working with Windows 2000 since beta 1. When not writing about Microsoft products, Curt spends his time with his wife and daughter — and in a perpetual state of remodeling his 100-year-old historical home. You can visit Curt on the Internet at `http://curtsimmons.hypermart.net`.

Author's Acknowledgments

I would like to thank Joyce Pepple for the opportunity to write this book. I especially owe a debt of gratitude to John Pont, one of the best editors to ever live on this planet. As always, I would like to thank my agent, Margot, for her tireless efforts on my behalf. A special thanks to Eric Kearsley and Sento Corp. for a very thorough technical review. Thanks also to Andy Simpson for writing the questions for the Dummies Test Engine on the book's CD. I also want to thank everyone in the Media Development and Production departments at IDG Books Worldwide for all their behind-the-scenes efforts. And of course, thanks to my wife, Dawn, who has to live with me and deal with my many "Windows 2000" moods!

ABOUT IDG BOOKS WORLDWIDE

Welcome to the world of IDG Books Worldwide.

IDG Books Worldwide, Inc., is a subsidiary of International Data Group, the world's largest publisher of computer-related information and the leading global provider of information services on information technology. IDG was founded more than 30 years ago by Patrick J. McGovern and now employs more than 9,000 people worldwide. IDG publishes more than 290 computer publications in over 75 countries. More than 90 million people read one or more IDG publications each month.

Launched in 1990, IDG Books Worldwide is today the #1 publisher of best-selling computer books in the United States. We are proud to have received eight awards from the Computer Press Association in recognition of editorial excellence and three from Computer Currents' First Annual Readers' Choice Awards. Our best-selling ...*For Dummies*® series has more than 50 million copies in print with translations in 31 languages. IDG Books Worldwide, through a joint venture with IDG's Hi-Tech Beijing, became the first U.S. publisher to publish a computer book in the People's Republic of China. In record time, IDG Books Worldwide has become the first choice for millions of readers around the world who want to learn how to better manage their businesses.

Our mission is simple: Every one of our books is designed to bring extra value and skill-building instructions to the reader. Our books are written by experts who understand and care about our readers. The knowledge base of our editorial staff comes from years of experience in publishing, education, and journalism — experience we use to produce books to carry us into the new millennium. In short, we care about books, so we attract the best people. We devote special attention to details such as audience, interior design, use of icons, and illustrations. And because we use an efficient process of authoring, editing, and desktop publishing our books electronically, we can spend more time ensuring superior content and less time on the technicalities of making books.

You can count on our commitment to deliver high-quality books at competitive prices on topics you want to read about. At IDG Books Worldwide, we continue in the IDG tradition of delivering quality for more than 30 years. You'll find no better book on a subject than one from IDG Books Worldwide.

John Kilcullen
Chairman and CEO
IDG Books Worldwide, Inc.

Eighth Annual
Computer Press
Awards ≥1992

Ninth Annual
Computer Press
Awards ≥1993

Tenth Annual
Computer Press
Awards ≥1994

Eleventh Annual
Computer Press
Awards ≥1995

IDG is the world's leading IT media, research and exposition company. Founded in 1964, IDG had 1997 revenues of $2.05 billion and has more than 9,000 employees worldwide. IDG offers the widest range of media options that reach IT buyers in 75 countries representing 95% of worldwide IT spending. IDG's diverse product and services portfolio spans six key areas including print publishing, online publishing, expositions and conferences, market research, education and training, and global marketing services. More than 90 million people read one or more of IDG's 290 magazines and newspapers, including IDG's leading global brands — Computerworld, PC World, Network World, Macworld and the Channel World family of publications. IDG Books Worldwide is one of the fastest-growing computer book publishers in the world, with more than 700 titles in 36 languages. The "...For Dummies®" series alone has more than 50 million copies in print. IDG offers online users the largest network of technology-specific Web sites around the world through IDG.net (http://www.idg.net), which comprises more than 225 targeted Web sites in 55 countries worldwide. International Data Corporation (IDC) is the world's largest provider of information technology data, analysis and consulting, with research centers in over 41 countries and more than 400 research analysts worldwide. IDG World Expo is a leading producer of more than 168 globally branded conferences and expositions in 35 countries including E3 (Electronic Entertainment Expo), Macworld Expo, ComNet, Windows World Expo, ICE (Internet Commerce Expo), Agenda, DEMO, and Spotlight. IDG's training subsidiary, ExecuTrain, is the world's largest computer training company, with more than 230 locations worldwide and 785 training courses. IDG Marketing Services helps industry-leading IT companies build international brand recognition by developing global integrated marketing programs via IDG's print, online and exposition products worldwide. Further information about the company can be found at www.idg.com. 1/26/00

Publisher's Acknowledgments

We're proud of this book; please register your comments through our IDG Books Worldwide Online Registration Form located at `http://my2cents.dummies.com`.

Some of the people who helped bring this book to market include the following:

Acquisitions, Editorial, and Media Development

Project Editor: John W. Pont

Acquisitions Editor: Joyce Pepple

Proof Editor: Dwight Ramsey

Technical Editor: Eric Kearsley

Permissions Editor: Carmen Krikorian

Associate Media Development Specialist: Megan Decraene

Editorial Manager: Constance Carlisle

Media Development Manager: Heather Heath Dismore

Editorial Assistant: Candace Nicholson

Production

Project Coordinator: Maridee V. Ennis

Layout and Graphics: Amy Adrian, Gabriele McCann, Jill Piscitelli, Brian Torwelle, Julie Trippetti, Brandon Yarwood

Proofreaders: Corey Bowen, John Greenough, Susan Moritz, Marianne Santy, Susan Simms

Indexer: Sharon Hilgenberg

General and Administrative

IDG Books Worldwide, Inc.: John Kilcullen, CEO

IDG Books Technology Publishing Group: Richard Swadley, Senior Vice President and Publisher; Walter R. Bruce III, Vice President and Publisher; Joseph Wikert, Vice President and Publisher; Mary Bednarek, Vice President and Director, Product Development; Andy Cummings, Publishing Director, General User Group; Mary C. Corder, Editorial Director; Barry Pruett, Publishing Director

IDG Books Consumer Publishing Group: Roland Elgey, Senior Vice President and Publisher; Kathleen A. Welton, Vice President and Publisher; Kevin Thornton, Acquisitions Manager; Kristin A. Cocks, Editorial Director

IDG Books Internet Publishing Group: Brenda McLaughlin, Senior Vice President and Publisher; Sofia Marchant, Online Marketing Manager

IDG Books Production for Branded Press: Debbie Stailey, Director of Production; Cindy L. Phipps, Manager of Project Coordination, Production Proofreading, and Indexing; Tony Augsburger, Manager of Prepress, Reprints, and Systems; Laura Carpenter, Production Control Manager; Shelley Lea, Supervisor of Graphics and Design; Debbie J. Gates, Production Systems Specialist; Robert Springer, Supervisor of Proofreading; Trudy Coler, Page Layout Manager; Troy Barnes, Page Layout Supervisor, Kathie Schutte, Senior Page Layout Supervisor; Michael Sullivan, Production Supervisor

Packaging and Book Design: Patty Page, Manager, Promotions Marketing

◆

The publisher would like to give special thanks to Patrick J. McGovern, without whom this book would not have been possible.

◆

Contents at a Glance

Cartoons at a Glance

By Rich Tennant

page 9

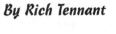

page 33

page 63

page 191

page 217

page 253

page 283

page 337

page 363

page 373

Fax: 978-546-7747
E-mail: richtennant@the5thwave.com
World Wide Web: www.the5thwave.com

Table of Contents

Introduction

· ·

*W*elcome to the world of Windows 2000 and the Windows 2000 exam track. If your goal is to tackle the Windows 2000 Server exam, you have come to right place. This book is exactly what you need for studying and mastering exam 70-215, Installing, Configuring, and Administering Microsoft Windows 2000 Server.

I don't mind telling you at the outset that Windows 2000 Server is no picnic, and if you want to pass the exam, you should plan on many hours of study and practice. The exam is designed to test your intellectual and hands-on knowledge of Windows 2000 Server. This book can help you master both, but you will have to study and keep your hands on a Windows 2000 server to ensure that you have the skills you need to pass the exam. Windows 2000 Server is a deep subject, but this book tells you what you need to know for the exam.

About This Book

This book is a complete resource for mastering exam 70-215. While writing this book, I focused solely on the exam objectives — after all, the test questions are developed from the objectives. Everything in this book focuses on preparing you for the exam.

As you study this book, you need to keep in mind exactly what the test covers — that is, the exam objectives listed in Microsoft's exam preparation guide. Chapter 1 explains the exam objectives and shows you how exam 70-215 fits into the Windows 2000 certification track. As you study, you will notice that every part and every chapter in this book focuses specifically on the exam objectives. With this approach, you can rest assured that you are studying information you are likely to see on the exam.

To help you pass exam 70-215, every chapter contains the following elements to keep your studies focused and on track:

- A concise listing of exam objectives covered in the chapter.
- A Quick Assessment question-and-answer section to help you gauge your current knowledge and skill before you begin studying the chapter.
- To-the-point, easy-to-read text so you can digest the exam content quickly and easily.

- ✔ Lab exercises that focus on configuration topics you are likely to see on the exam.
- ✔ A Prep Test at the end of each chapter so you can make certain you master the chapter's content.
- ✔ Concise tables and bulleted lists of important information that you need to memorize for the exam.

In addition to all these chapter tools, I also provide two full-length practice exams at the end of the book. The practice exams are designed to test you on the exam objectives you have studied in each chapter. In addition to all these test-preparation tools, the CD-ROM contains hundreds of practice questions and the Dummies Test Engine. You can use this tool to generate your own practice exams and even customize them as desired. The CD also contains demonstration and sample versions of test-prep software products for your review.

How This Book Is Organized

This book is divided into ten parts. The first part of the book helps you understand the exam objectives and key Windows 2000 technologies. Parts II through VIII exactly follow the divisions of exam objectives listed in Microsoft's exam preparation guide. This design keeps your studies focused squarely on the exam objectives. In other words, you can be certain you are not wasting your time studying information that you will not see on the exam. Part IX is the "Part of Tens," a place where you can gain some additional testing insight. Part X contains two practice exams and information about the CD that accompanies this book.

The following sections offer more details about what you can find in each part of the book.

Part I: Welcome to the World of Windows 2000

Part I explores the world of Windows 2000 and the Windows 2000 exam track. You can read all about the exam objectives in this part, as well as how the Windows 2000 Server exam fits into the Windows 2000 MCSE certification path. You also can review foundational Windows 2000 technologies and concepts.

Part II: Taking the Plunge: Installing Windows 2000 Server

The exam expects you to have hands-on experience as well as technical knowledge about installing Windows 2000 Server. In this part, you examine the installation processes for both attended and unattended installations. You also explore troubleshooting issues for failed installations.

Part III: Installing, Configuring, and Troubleshooting Access to Resources

For the exam, you need to know how to configure your server to meet the needs of your network clients and provide the services to keep your users happy. In this part, you explore the Windows 2000 networking technologies of DHCP, WINS, and DNS. You review how to install, configure, and troubleshoot each of these services. You also explore the new printing features in Windows 2000 so you can use your server as a print server. Then, you study all about shared file and folder management, including Web folders. Finally, you review Distributed File System (Dfs) and how to implement Dfs on your server and in your network.

Part IV: Configuring and Troubleshooting Hardware Devices and Drivers

In previous versions of Windows, hardware management was a serious pain. Windows 2000 greatly improves hardware management by providing a plug-and-play operating system and several new hardware management tools. In this part, you examine the installation and removal of hardware, hardware configuration, troubleshooting issues, and the management of hardware drivers.

Part V: Managing Windows 2000 Server

To ensure that your Windows 2000 server functions properly, you have to manage it so that it meets the performance needs of your network. In this part, you examine such issues as monitoring and optimizing system performance, managing processes, managing system state data and user data, and backing up and recovering data using Windows Backup.

Part VI: Managing, Configuring, and Troubleshooting Storage Use

In the past, hard-disk management was rather dull and didn't give you lots of options. Windows 2000 changes all that by providing various new hard-disk technologies, such as dynamic disks and volumes. In Part VI, you can study all about these issues, including fault-tolerance configuration, data compression, disk quotas, and troubleshooting hard-disk problems.

Part VII: Configuring and Troubleshooting Windows 2000 Network Connections

Windows 2000 provides rich support for networking components and options. In this part, you explore the exam topics that relate to networking connections. This part explores protocols and connections, remote access, and the implementation of Terminal Services. All of these topics are exam-specific and exam-important!

Part VIII: Implementing, Monitoring, and Troubleshooting Security

Windows 2000 Server provides many new security features, but you are tested on only a few of them during the Windows 2000 Server exam. In this part, you can review encrypting file system (EFS), local and system policies, the Security Configuration tool, and the configuration of auditing — all topics that you can find in Microsoft's list of exam objectives.

Part IX: The Part of Tens

You simply can't survive without the Part of Tens, a *For Dummies* tradition. In this part of the book, I offer ten exam-day tips to help you prepare for the exam, and I explore ten common questions and answers about the Windows 2000 Server exam. These topics give you a complete package to help you master exam 70-215.

Part X: Appendixes

In Part X, you find two full-length practice exams. Use these exams to test your knowledge and skills. You also find complete information about installing and using the CD that accompanies this book. Speaking of which . . . .

About the CD-ROM

The *MCSE Windows 2000 Server For Dummies* CD-ROM includes sample and demo versions of some great test-prep software, as well as the Dummies Test Engine, which can generate practice exams on demand to help you get ready for exam day.

Conventions Used in This Book

This book is designed to help you get the necessary exam content in the easiest manner. I hope this book makes your journey through the exam study much easier. To help you, watch for these features:

- The lab exercises are straightforward and quick. I don't say things like, "Click the Start Menu, then point to Programs, then point again to Administrative tools, then navigate to DNS." Instead, I use a command arrow to simply say something like, "Click Start⇨Programs⇨ Administrative Tools⇨DNS." This feature makes the labs much easier to read and follow.

- Another convention used is `monotype font`. When you see this font, you know you are looking at an exact URL you can access for more information about a particular subject.

- Tables and bulleted lists help you to digest information quickly and easily. When you see information in a table or a bulleted list, you need to memorize it!

- Finally, Prep Tests and the practice exams contain numerous questions designed to mimic the interface questions you are likely to see on the exam. (Read more about this question style in Chapter 1.) These questions simply ask you a question and then provide you with a picture of some portion of the Windows 2000 Server interface. You answer these questions by describing what you would do to configure that interface element.

How to Use This Book

The *MCSE...For Dummies* books are designed to help you make the most of your exam studies. So, to make the most of your exam studies, you have to make the most of the elements in this book. Make certain you take both the Quick Assessment and the Prep Test found in each chapter. These exercises test your mastery of the chapter's content and can help you find your exam strengths and weaknesses. Also, practice each lab on a test machine. I cannot overemphasize this point: There is no replacement for hands-on practice!

Pay careful attention to tables, bulleted lists, and the icons in each chapter. These elements give you important information and help you zero in on exam content. Finally, take the two practice exams in the appendixes at the end of the book and use the CD-ROM game and the Dummies Test Engine to get even more practice.

Icons Used in This Book

To help you with your studies, I use several icons, each of which appears in the margins next to key paragraphs. The icons help you pinpoint information that warrants close attention as you study. I use the following icons in this book:

The Tip icon points out some handy piece of information for getting the most out of Windows 2000 Server and an important piece of information you should keep in mind for the exam.

The Remember icon helps you target information that's worth remembering for the exam.

The Warning icon points out some potential problem or pitfall you may encounter when configuring Windows 2000 Server. Keep this warning information in mind for the exam.

When you see the Instant Answer icon, you know the text provides you with information that can help you respond correctly to a test question.

 Look for the Time Shaver icon to discover ways that you can save time as you study and practice for the exam.

Where to Go from Here

If you need to check your knowledge of Windows 2000 Server before you begin studying the rest of this book, be sure to check out the chapters in Part I. They can help you get your feet on solid ground. From there, begin studying each chapter, taking the Quick Assessment test at the beginning of the chapter so you can zero in on what you know and what you don't know. Make sure you take the Prep Test at the end of each chapter and perform each lab exercise found in the chapters so you'll have both the conceptual and hands-on knowledge you need for the exam. Finally, make certain you take the two full-length practice exams to test your knowledge.

Good luck!

Part I

Welcome to the World of Windows 2000

The 5th Wave — By Rich Tennant

©RICHTENNANT

$$(a+5)^9 =$$
$$\int x\, dx = \frac{\partial^{3/2}}{}$$
$$x \rightarrow$$
$$:= xe(\cdot x)$$

"It's part of my employer tuition assistance agreement with the 'Pizza Bob' corporation."

In this part . . .

Welcome to the world of Windows 2000 and the MCSE Windows 2000 Server exam. In this part, I tell you all about the Windows 2000 exam track and how you can get your Windows 2000 MCSE certification.

In Chapter 1, I explore the Windows 2000 exam track and the objectives for the Windows 2000 Server exam. I also offer some general observations about your Windows 2000 MCSE studies. Chapter 2 reviews Windows 2000 technologies to make certain that you have your feet on the ground before you begin studying for the Windows 2000 Server exam.

Chapter 1

The Windows 2000 Server Exam

In This Chapter

▶ Checking out the Windows 2000 exam track

▶ Reviewing the objectives for the Windows 2000 Server exam

▶ Deciding whether you are ready

*T*he release of Windows 2000 brings numerous changes in the Microsoft Certified Professional (MCP) program. In particular, all current Microsoft Certified Systems Engineers (MCSEs) must update their current certification to Windows 2000, and all new MCSE candidates must follow the new Windows 2000 exam track.

In this chapter, I explore the overall requirements of the Windows 2000 exam track, and then I focus your attention on exam 70-215, Installing, Configuring, and Administering Microsoft Windows 2000 Server — the exam for which this book helps you study. Exam 70-215 is one of the core exams required for earning certification as a Windows 2000 MCSE.

Exploring the Windows 2000 MCSE Track

Before you take a look at the Windows 2000 Server exam, you need to understand how exam 70-215 fits into the entire Windows 2000 MCSE track and what other Windows 2000 exams you need to pass in order to obtain your MCSE credentials. The following sections show you the required and elective exam options.

Checking out the Windows 2000 core exams

To earn certification as a Windows 2000 MCSE, candidates need to pass the following exams:

- Exam 70-210, Installing, Configuring, and Administering Microsoft Windows 2000 Professional
- Exam 70-215, Installing, Configuring, and Administering Microsoft Windows 2000 Server
- Exam 70-216, Implementing and Administering a Microsoft Windows 2000 Network Infrastructure
- Exam 70-217, Implementing and Administering a Microsoft Windows 2000 Directory Services Infrastructure

Until December 2001, current MCSEs certified on Windows NT 4.0 can take exam 70-240, Microsoft Windows 2000 Accelerated Exam for MCPs Certified on Microsoft Windows NT 4.0. This accelerated, intensive upgrade exam replaces the four core exams (70-210, 70-215, 70-216, and 70-217) with one exam.

Rounding out the Windows 2000 core exams

In addition to the four core exams that I list in the preceding section, all MCSE candidates must pass one of the following exams:

- Exam 70-219, Designing a Microsoft Windows 2000 Directory Services Infrastructure
- Exam 70-220, Designing Security for a Microsoft Windows 2000 Network
- Exam 70-221, Designing a Microsoft Windows 2000 Network Infrastructure

Taking your pick of the Windows 2000 elective exams

In addition to the four core exams and the one additional core exam (see the previous sections in this chapter), MCSE candidates must pass two elective exams that are not scheduled for retirement. The following electives are available as I write this book:

- ✔ Exam 70-013, Implementing and Supporting Microsoft SNA Server 3.0, or exam 70-085, Implementing and Supporting Microsoft SNA Server 4.0

- ✔ Exam 70-018, Implementing and Supporting Microsoft Systems Management Server 1.2, or exam 70-086, Implementing and Supporting Microsoft Systems Management Server 2.0

- ✔ Exam 70-019, Designing and Implementing Data Warehouses with Microsoft SQL Server 7.0

- ✔ Exam 70-027, Implementing a Database Design on Microsoft SQL Server 6.5, or exam 70-029, Designing Databases with Microsoft SQL Server 7.0

- ✔ Exam 70-026, System Administration for Microsoft SQL Server 6.0 or 6.5, or exam 70-028, Administering Microsoft SQL Server 7.0

- ✔ Exam 70-056, Implementing and Supporting Web Sites Using Microsoft Site Server 3.0

- ✔ Exam 70-076, Implementing and Supporting Microsoft Exchange Server 5, or exam 70-081, Implementing and Supporting Microsoft Exchange Server 5.5

- ✔ Exam 70-078, Implementing and Supporting Microsoft Proxy Server 1.0

- ✔ Exam 70-088, Implementing and Supporting Microsoft Proxy Server 2.0

- ✔ Exam 70-079, Implementing and Supporting Microsoft Internet Information Server 4.0 by Using the Internet Explorer Administration Kit, or exam 70-080, Implementing and Supporting Microsoft Internet Information Server 5.0 by Using the Internet Explorer Administration Kit

- ✔ Exam 70-219, Designing a Microsoft Windows 2000 Directory Services Infrastructure

- ✔ Exam 70-220, Designing Security for a Microsoft Windows 2000 Network

- ✔ Exam 70-221, Designing a Microsoft Windows 2000 Network Infrastructure

- ✔ Exam 70-222, Upgrading from Microsoft Windows NT 4.0 to Microsoft Windows 2000

If two versions of the same product exist, only one exam will count toward the MCSE. For example, exam 70-013 and exam 70-085 cover SNA Server 3.0 and SNA Server 4.0, respectively. You cannot take both of these exams for your two electives — only one will count.

Before taking any elective exam, make sure Microsoft has not scheduled that exam for retirement. The retirement status of exams changes over time, so check www.microsoft.com/trainingandservices for the latest list of retired exams before taking any electives.

Examining the Windows 2000 Server Exam

Exam 70-215 is a required core exam for the Windows 2000 MCSE track. Before you begin studying for your Windows 2000 Server exam, you should take a look at the exam objectives. The list of exam objectives details the job skills you must master to pass the exam.

When I first read the Windows 2000 Server exam objectives, I was a bit surprised. The Windows 2000 Server exam focuses on installing, implementing, supporting, and troubleshooting Windows 2000 Server as a member server in a Windows 2000 network. You will not be tested on domain controllers and integration with the Active Directory. You can expect to see exam questions that focus on various member server roles, such as file and print server, Web server, distribution server, and terminal server. You can read more about this issue in the section "Understanding the exam scope" later in this chapter.

Some MCSE candidates mistakenly believe that the Windows 2000 Server exam will not be difficult because it does not test your knowledge of domain controllers and the Active Directory. This is not at all the case, so study carefully and intelligently!

Like all things in the Microsoft world, exam objectives for the Windows 2000 Server exam — as well as all other exams — may change. Check www.microsoft.com/trainingandservices for updates to exam objectives.

In the following sections, I list the Windows 2000 Server exam objectives, and then I make some general comments about the objectives and the exam itself.

Reviewing the objectives for exam 70-215

The following sections in this chapter provide a complete list of the job skills you must master to pass the Windows 2000 Server exam, based on the list of exam objectives in Microsoft's exam preparation guide. As you study this book, you will see that its structure closely follows Microsoft's list of exam objectives. I organized the book in this way to help you review and study for the exam. With this part and chapter design, you can be certain that you are studying exam objective content that you need to know.

Installing Windows 2000 Server

✔ Perform an attended installation of Windows 2000 Server.

✔ Perform an unattended installation of Windows 2000 Server:

- Create unattended answer files by using Setup Manager to automate the installation of Windows 2000 Server.

- Create and configure automated methods for installation of Windows 2000.

✔ Upgrade a server from Microsoft Windows NT 4.0.

✔ Deploy service packs.

✔ Troubleshoot failed installations.

Installing, configuring, and troubleshooting access to resources

✔ Install and configure network services for interoperability.

✔ Monitor, configure, troubleshoot, and control access to printers.

✔ Monitor, configure, troubleshoot, and control access to files, folders, and shared folders:

- Configure, manage, and troubleshoot a standalone Distributed file system (Dfs).

- Configure, manage, and troubleshoot a domain-based Distributed file system (Dfs).

- Monitor, configure, troubleshoot, and control local security on files and folders.

- Monitor, configure, troubleshoot, and control access to files and folders in a shared folder.

- Monitor, configure, troubleshoot, and control access to files and folders via Web services.

✔ Monitor, configure, troubleshoot, and control access to Web sites.

Configuring and troubleshooting hardware devices and drivers

✔ Configure hardware devices.

✔ Configure driver signing options.

✔ Update device drivers.

✔ Troubleshoot problems with hardware.

Managing, monitoring, and optimizing system performance, reliability, and availability

✔ Monitor and optimize usage of system resources.

✔ Manage processes:
- Set priorities.
- Start and stop processes.

✔ Optimize disk performance.

✔ Manage and optimize availability of system state data and user data.

✔ Recover systems and user data:
- Recover systems and user data by using Windows Backup.
- Troubleshoot system restoration by using Safe Mode.
- Recover systems and user data by using the Recovery Console.

Managing, configuring, and troubleshooting storage use

✔ Configure and manage user profiles.

✔ Monitor, configure, and troubleshoot disks and volumes.

✔ Configure data compression.

✔ Monitor and configure disk quotas.

✔ Recover from disk failures.

Configuring and troubleshooting Windows 2000 network connections

✔ Install, configure, and troubleshoot shared access.

✔ Install, configure, and troubleshoot a virtual private network (VPN).

✔ Install, configure, and troubleshoot network protocols.

✔ Install and configure network services.

✔ Configure, monitor, and troubleshoot remote access:
- Configure inbound connections.
- Create a remote access policy.
- Configure a remote access profile.

✔ Install, configure, monitor, and troubleshoot Terminal Services:
- Remotely administer servers by using Terminal Services.
- Configure Terminal Services for application sharing.
- Configure applications for use with Terminal Services.

✔ Configure the properties of a connection.

✔ Install, configure, and troubleshoot network adapters and drivers.

Implementing, monitoring, and troubleshooting security

✔ Encrypt data on a hard disk by using Encrypting File System (EFS).

✔ Implement, configure, manage, and troubleshoot policies in a Windows 2000 environment:

- Implement, configure, manage, and troubleshoot local policy in a Windows 2000 environment.

- Implement, configure, manage, and troubleshoot system policy in a Windows 2000 environment.

✔ Implement, configure, manage, and troubleshoot auditing.

✔ Implement, configure, manage, and troubleshoot local accounts.

✔ Implement, configure, manage, and troubleshoot account policy.

✔ Implement, configure, manage, and troubleshoot security by using the Security Configuration Tool Set.

Understanding the exam scope

After you look through the exam objectives, you may be wondering what happened to the objectives concerning domain controllers and the Active Directory. Well, you won't find any specific references to those topics in the list of exam objectives.

The Windows 2000 Server exam tests your skills as an administrator of member servers in an Active Directory environment. On this exam, you will not see questions related to configuration or administration of domain controllers because all Windows 2000 domain controllers run the Active Directory. Exam 70-217, Implementing and Administering a Microsoft Windows 2000 Directory Services Infrastructure, focuses on domain controllers and the Active Directory. The Windows 2000 Server exam focuses on the Windows 2000 member server and its configuration and administration in an Active Directory environment. To perform successfully on this exam, you must have expert knowledge on not only the member server itself, but also its use in an Active Directory enterprise.

Don't worry; this book guides you through these issues to help you keep focused on the exam objectives and the information you need for the test.

What is the exam like?

The Windows 2000 Server exam, like all other Windows 2000 exams, uses a number of different testing technologies to test your skills. You may see any and all of the following testing technologies on the Windows 2000 Server exam:

- **Standard question and answer (Q&A):** Microsoft certification exams may contain standard multiple-choice questions in which you read a question stem and then choose the best answer(s) from a provided list. Standard Q&A questions may be simple questions, questions with multiple answers, or even complex scenario questions.

- **Adaptive technologies:** Some Microsoft exams contain adaptive technologies. Adaptive exams begin with an easy question, and then increasingly become more difficult as you answer questions correctly. If you do not answer questions correctly, the exam offers easier questions. The exam continues only long enough for the computer to determine whether your skill levels pass or fail. Therefore, an adaptive exam does not have a certain question count. Typically, these exams are fairly short, with some giving you only 15 questions before determining your score.

- **Select-and-place:** Microsoft is using a new exam technology called *select-and-place.* The select-and-place questions test your ability to synthesize information and develop a solution to a problem. Typically, these questions present you with a scenario, and then a graphical interface provides a simulation in which you configure the solution by dragging and dropping appropriate answers and data. These questions gather information about your overall knowledge of configuration and troubleshooting — and they can be quite difficult.

- **Case study:** Some Microsoft exams include a new case-study question format. You read a case and then make decisions or recommendations based on the case details. As you can imagine, the case-study questions test your ability to pull information together and make logical decisions. Like the select-and-place questions, these exam questions can be quite difficult.

- **Simulations:** Microsoft exams include simulations, which typically present a portion of the operating system interface and ask you how to configure some item. These simulation questions are designed to test your hands-on knowledge of the operating system and how to configure it for various tasks.

You can download samples of these testing technologies from Microsoft so you can see how they work. I highly recommend that you get the downloads before taking the exam so the different questions do not surprise you on exam day. Go to www.microsoft.com/mcp to get the test sample downloads.

Gathering tips for successful study

I want you to pass the Windows 2000 Server exam. After all, that's why I wrote this book — to help you prepare for the exam. This book covers everything you need for studying and passing exam 70-215. In order to accomplish your goal, you need to use this book and your study time wisely.

At the beginning of each chapter, I tell you which exam objectives that chapter covers. Then, I focus on the relevant information to help you study for the Windows 2000 Server exam. This book covers every exam objective, and every chapter contains Quick Assessment and Prep Test questions to make certain that you master the chapter's content. You'll also find two full-length exams at the back of the book and an extensive exam question pool on the CD-ROM. In short, this book has all you need to tackle exam 70-215 and strategically plan your exam study.

Watch out for Instant Answer icons throughout the book. These icons flag tricky information that may appear on the exam. Also, any time you see a table in the book, you need to memorize it. I use the table format for information that you need to memorize.

This book does not try to teach you how to use Windows 2000 Server; it is designed to help you study for the test. This book covers information that appears on the exam — and nothing more. If you are just starting out with Windows 2000 Server, you need another book and some learning time with the operating system before beginning this book.

As you study the book, use a highlighter or take notes to mark information for later review. By doing so, you greatly conserve study time, and you develop a list of information you can quickly review on exam day.

This book contains hundreds of practice questions. At the beginning of each chapter, you can find a Quick Assessment test to check your knowledge. And at the end of each chapter, you find a Prep Test to check your mastery of the chapter's content. Additionally, the appendixes at the end of the book include two full-length sample exams, and the CD-ROM contains hundreds of additional practice questions. Take advantage of these resources and use the practice questions to help you prepare for the exam!

Are You Ready?

Are you ready to study for the exam? This is an important question to ask yourself before you begin. Remember, this book is designed to help you study for the exam, so it expects you to come to the table with some Windows 2000 skills. Microsoft expects you to have hands-on knowledge of Windows 2000

Server before taking the exam, and in order to be successful, you must spend time working with the operating system and learning how to use it. This book, or any other book for that matter, is no substitute for hands-on, practical experience.

If you have the hands-on experience you need, then you're ready to begin your study. To increase your chances for success, block out time each day for intensive study and preparation.

Successful MCSE candidates study carefully and intelligently. To be successful on the exam, expect to put in some serious preparation hours before you take the exam. Are you ready? It's time to get started!

Chapter 2

Exam Prep Roadmap: Windows 2000 Networking Basics

● ●

In This Chapter

▶ Exploring Active Directory terms and concepts

▶ Understanding Windows 2000 domains

▶ Reviewing Windows 2000 server roles

▶ Examining the Windows 2000 networking interfaces

● ●

*T*he release of Windows 2000 certainly threw a learning curve at IT profes-
sionals who are used to Windows NT technologies and networking concepts. The Windows 2000 Server exam expects you to have a firm
understanding of a member server's place in a Windows 2000 Active
Directory environment. And to gain that understanding, you must master
some fundamental Windows 2000 networking concepts.

This chapter is your Windows 2000 networking primer. It reviews the founda-
tions of Windows 2000 networking and shows you the basic networking interfaces on your member server.

If you feel confident in your knowledge of Windows 2000 networking basics,
you can skip this chapter.

Tackling the Active Directory

The Windows 2000 Server exam does not test you directly on the Active
Directory because this exam focuses only on member servers. (Only domain
controllers run the Active Directory.) However, the exam does test your
knowledge of the role a Windows 2000 member server plays in an Active
Directory environment. To help you get your feet on the ground, this section
gives you a crash course in Active Directory technologies.

Taking a look at the Active Directory

The Active Directory is Microsoft's answer to directory services. The Active Directory organizes information about real network objects — users, shares, printers, applications, and so on — so users can find the resources they need. Thanks to the Active Directory, users do not have to keep track of which server holds which resource, or where a particular printer resides. The Active Directory lists the information, is completely searchable, and provides a standard folder interface so users can find what they need on the network. In short, the Active Directory organizes resources so users can easily find and use them.

The Active Directory also provides a single point of administration for network administrators. Instead of requiring you to manage multiple servers that hold multiple resources, Windows 2000 Server keeps all the directory information in the Active Directory and replicates it to all Windows 2000 domain controllers. Consequently, you can administer resource access, security permissions, user and group accounts, and all network resources from one central location.

Understanding domains and domain controllers

If you have worked with Windows NT at all, you are familiar with the concepts of domains and domain controllers. A *domain* is a logical grouping of users, computers, and resources. In actuality, the domain is a security boundary that enables administrators to control the resources in that domain and keep unauthorized users out of the domain. The Active Directory is built on the domain concept. The Active Directory uses domains to establish security and administrative boundaries.

Domain controllers are the servers that control or manage the domain. Unlike Windows NT, Windows 2000 does not use primary domain controllers (PDCs) and backup domain controllers (BDCs); instead, all domain controllers simply act as peers.

Through trust relationships, Windows 2000 Server replicates the Active Directory using *multimaster replication*. In other words, all domain controllers are responsible for maintaining the Active Directory and replicating changes to other domain controllers.

Windows 2000 automatically configures the Active Directory trust relationships between domain controllers through the Kerberos V5 security protocol, which is the primary security protocol in Windows 2000. Kerberos trust relationships are *transitive*. For example, if DomainA trusts DomainB, and DomainB trusts DomainC, then DomainA trusts DomainC. The transitive nature of the trust relationships is a feature of Kerberos and is not available in Windows NT.

Exploring the Domain Name System (DNS) and the Active Directory

Domain Name System (DNS) is the most widely used directory namespace in the world. Each time you use the Internet, you are finding Uniform Resource Locators (URLs) by using DNS. DNS takes a URL such as www.microsoft.com and resolves the URL into a TCP/IP address, such as 131.107.2.200. Computers must have the TCP/IP address to communicate on the Internet, and users find the URLs more understandable. DNS exists to resolve the two types of addresses.

The Active Directory is integrated with DNS, and the naming schemes used in the Active Directory are DNS names. For example, tritondev.com is a valid DNS name and can also be used as a Windows 2000 domain name.

With DNS as the locator service in the Active Directory, the local area network becomes more seamless with the Internet and intranets. For example, you can use tritondev.com as either an Internet name or a local area name, and kpeters@tritondev.com can serve as both an Internet e-mail address and a user name in the local network. With this structure, you can find items on your network in the same manner as you find them on the Internet.

Windows 2000 also supports Dynamic DNS (DDNS), a new addition to the DNS standard. DDNS can dynamically update a DNS server with new or changed values. (Before the development of DDNS, new or changed values required a manual update of the DNS server.) Because name records can be dynamically updated, true Windows 2000 networks no longer need to use Windows Internet Name Service (WINS). However, Windows 2000 supports WINS for down-level (backward) compatibility. You can find more details about WINS in Chapter 6 and DNS in Chapter 7.

Understanding LDAP (Lightweight Directory Access Protocol)

DNS is the namespace used in the Active Directory, and you access the Active Directory via LDAP (Lightweight Directory Access Protocol). To understand LDAP, you need a brief history lesson.

The X.500 standard is a directory specification that introduced DAP (Directory Access Protocol) to read and modify the directory database. DAP is an *extensible* protocol; it can handle directory requests and changes, as well as directory security. However, DAP places much of the processing burden on the client computers and is considered to be a high-overhead protocol.

LDAP, which is not defined within the X.500 specification, was developed to overcome the weaknesses of DAP. LDAP is an *open* standard. Anyone who wants to develop a directory service can use it. In contrast to DAP, LDAP is not restricted to X.500 directories, and it is not a client-based service. Instead, the LDAP service runs on the server, and the information is returned to the client.

The Active Directory is not an X.500 directory, but it supports the X.500 information model. However, systems using the Active Directory don't face the high overhead associated with implementing DAP and the X.500 standard. Instead, Windows 2000 and its Active Directory provide an LDAP-based directory that supports high levels of interoperability.

LDAP is widely supported on the Internet. If you have used newsgroups or searched the Web from a search engine, you probably used LDAP. The Active Directory directly supports this open standard so users can find the resources they need.

Checking out Active Directory terminology

The Active Directory has a hierarchical structure. Several components make up the structure, and of course, they all have their own terms and meanings. This section reviews the major Active Directory components that make up the hierarchy.

You don't need to worry about these terms for the Windows 2000 Server exam, but I provide basic definitions here to give you a complete picture of the Active Directory and its structure.

Object

An Active Directory *object* represents a physical object of some kind on the network. Common Active Directory objects include users, groups, printers, shared folders, applications, databases, and contacts. Each of these objects represents something tangible on the network.

Organizational unit

As its name implies, an *organizational unit* (OU) helps you organize your directory structure. An OU is a container designed to hold resources and even other OUs. For example, you could have an accounting OU that contains other OUs, such Accounting Group A and Accounting Group B. Each of those OUs can contain objects belonging to that OU, such as users, groups, computers, and printers.

OUs, like domains, can serve as a unit of administration and security. One of the major goals of Windows 2000 is to reduce the number of domains in network environments. Using Windows 2000's organizational units, many environments that had multiple domains under Windows NT can now have one domain with multiple OUs.

Domain

By definition, a *domain* is a logical grouping of users and computers. In practice, a domain is more than a logical grouping — it is a security boundary of a Windows 2000 or NT network. Each domain can have its own security policies and can establish trust relationships with other domains. The Active Directory comprises one or more domains.

Tree

The hierarchy of the domain, organizational units, and objects is called a *tree*. The term *endpoints* refers to objects within the tree, and the OUs in the tree structure are *nodes*. You can think of the tree's branches as OUs or containers and the leaves as objects. An object is the natural endpoint of a node within the tree.

Domain trees

A *domain tree* exists when several domains are linked by trust relationships and share a common schema, configuration, and global catalog. Windows 2000 trust relationships are based on the Kerberos security protocol, which automatically generates transitive trust relationships among all domain controllers in all trees.

A domain tree also shares a contiguous namespace. A contiguous namespace follows the same naming DNS hierarchy within the domain tree. For example, assume that `tritondev.com` is the root domain of a domain tree. `Namerica.tritondev.com` shares a contiguous namespace with `tritondev.com`, but `namerica.tritonprod.com` does not share a contiguous namespace.

Forest

A *forest* is one or more trees that do not share a contiguous namespace. The trees in the forest do share a common schema, configuration, and global catalog, but the trees do not share a contiguous namespace. All trees in the forest trust each other through Kerberos transitive trusts and are still viewed as one unit in terms of resources. For example, `tritondev.com` and `tritonprod.com` can be two different trees within one forest. `Tritondev.com` and `tritonprod.com` are both individual trees because they do not share a contiguous namespace. However, because of the Active Directory forest structure, these two trees can be connected so that users can access resources in the various domains in each tree.

Understanding Windows 2000 Server Roles

Only two main server roles exist in Windows 2000: domain controllers and member servers. Windows 2000 does not have PDCs and BDCs. All domain controllers act as peers and replicate directory information through multi-master replication. Rather than rely on one master replicator server, all domain controllers are responsible for replicating data.

Here's the simplest way to distinguish the two server roles: Domain controllers run the Active Directory, and member servers do not. In fact, the act of installing the Active Directory on a server promotes the server to domain controller status, and removing the Active Directory from a domain controller demotes the server to member server status. You cannot have a domain controller that does not have the Active Directory installed. Unlike Windows NT, you can promote or demote servers as many times as you like without reinstalling the operating system.

Here are some of the major characteristics of domain controllers:

- They perform all Active Directory tasks, such as adding, removing, and configuring users, groups, computers, and OUs.

- They are typically managed by members of the Enterprise Admins group.

- Domain controllers replicate Active Directory data through multimaster replication in transitive trust relationships.

- In mixed Windows 2000 and NT environments, they perform *operations master* roles, such as the Schema Master, Infrastructure Master, and PDC Emulator.

In contrast, here are some of the characteristics of member servers:

- Member servers provide standard support services, such as WINS, Dynamic Host Configuration Protocol (DHCP), Remote Access Service (RAS), print server services, and terminal server services.

- They do not have the Active Directory installed and cannot perform any Active Directory functions such as adding new users and groups.

- Typically, you use member servers for specific purposes (such as print and file servers) and to help remove network loads off domain controllers.

You can have a mixed Windows 2000 and NT environment that has Windows 2000 servers and NT servers. Typically, you upgrade all PDCs and BDCs to Windows 2000, and other NT servers can function as member servers until you upgrade them. This environment is called *mixed mode*.

Because NT servers look for a domain controller, upgraded PDCs perform PDC Emulator roles so they appear as PDCs to down-level servers. After you upgrade all servers to Windows 2000, you can switch the domain to native mode. Changing from mixed mode to native mode is an Active Directory operation.

Where Did It Go? Finding and Using Windows 2000 Server Networking Interfaces

One of the learning curves that network administrators face after upgrading to Windows 2000 involves figuring out how to perform basic tasks. Most configuration locations and common tools you used in NT have changed somewhat or have moved to an entirely different location. This learning curve can easily lead to administrators throwing their hands in the air and saying things like, "I only need to configure a protocol! Where is it?" In this section, I point out the major locations and functionality of networking components in Windows 2000 so you can review finding and using them.

Adding and removing services and components

Windows 2000 Server gives you two ways to add or remove networking services and components. First, you can use a new tool called Configure Your Server. This tool, which looks like a Web page, provides a graphical way to manage your server services and learn about the services that you install. Lab 2-1 shows you how to add or remove services using the Configure Your Server tool.

Lab 2-1	Using the Configure Your Server Tool

1. **Click Start**⇨**Programs**⇨**Administrative Tools**⇨**Configure Your Server.**

   The Configure Your Server tool opens, as shown in Figure 2-1.

2. **Click the desired link in the left pane to expand it.**

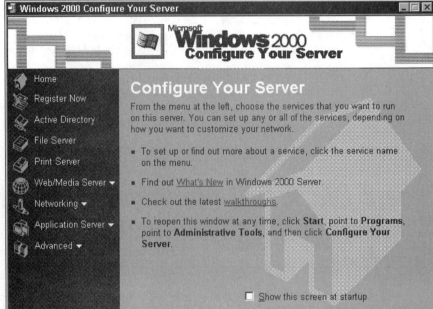

Figure 2-1:
The
Configure
Your Server
tool pro-
vides a
Web-based
interface to
install
server
services.

3. **Under the desired link, select the service you want to install or unin-stall. Then, follow the instructions that appear in the right pane to begin the process of installing or uninstalling the selected service.**

   For example, in Figure 2-2, I expanded the Networking link and then selected DHCP. To start the installation, click the Start link.

   Rather than use the Configure Your Server tool, you can use Control Panel's Add/Remove Programs tool to add or remove services and components. You'll find no difference in the results you get from using Configure Your Server or Add/Remove Programs — it is simply a matter of choice.

Using Add/Remove Programs does have one advantage: You can add or remove several components at the same time. Lab 2-2 shows you how to use Add/Remove Programs to add or remove services or components.

Lab 2-2	Using Add/Remove Programs

1. **Click Start➪Settings➪Control Panel.**

2. **Double-click Add/Remove Programs.**

3. **In the Add/Remove Programs dialog box, click Add/Remove Windows Components, as shown in Figure 2-3.**

Figure 2-2:
Selecting
the service
that you
want to
install.

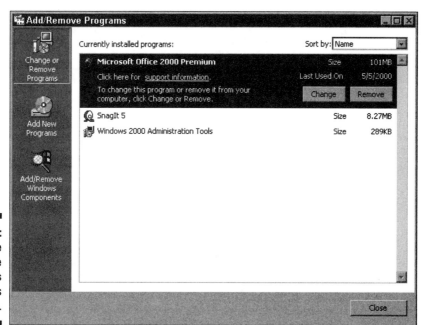

Figure 2-3:
Click the
Add/Remove
Windows
Components
button.

4. **In the Windows Components wizard, select the desired category, such as Network Services, and then click Details, as shown in Figure 2-4.**

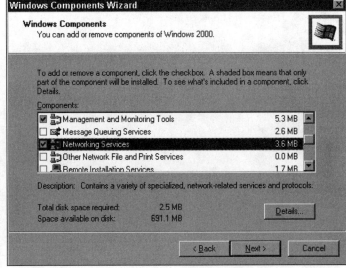

Figure 2-4:
Click the
Details
button to
see a list of
compo-
nents.

5. **In the services list that appears, click the appropriate check box to add a desired service, or clear the check box next to a service that you want to remove. Click OK.**

6. **Click Next.**

   Windows 2000 Server installs or removes the selected components.

7. **Click Finish to complete the wizard.**

Using My Network Places

In Windows 2000, My Network Places replaces NT's Network Neighborhood. In My Network Places, you have a few more options than in Network Neighborhood. You can open My Network Places and browse the network, including the Active Directory domains and OUs. As you begin to browse the network through the Entire Network icon, you can also perform searches for printers, computers, people, or files and folders.

In addition to browsing, you can add a network place by using the Add Network Place wizard. As shown in Figure 2-5, the wizard enables you to add a shared folder, Web folder, or FTP folder that automatically appears in My Network Places.

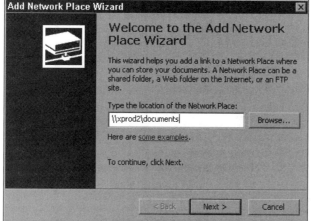

Figure 2-5:
Using the
Add
Network
Place
wizard.

Simply enter the desired location, click Next, and then click Next again to add the Network Place.

In addition to using the basic functionality of My Network Places, you can right-click My Network Places on the desktop and then click Properties to open the Network and Dial-up Connections folder. In this folder, you may see several connections, depending on the configuration of your server, such as your local area connection and dial-up connections. By using the Make New Connection wizard, you can create and configure various networking connections, such as modem or ISDN, Virtual Private Network (VPN), and direct connections.

You can right-click any connection and then click Properties to adjust settings for that connection. For your LAN connections, you see a General tab that enables you to install and remove clients, services, and protocols, as shown in Figure 2-6. You use this Properties dialog box to configure TCP/IP, file and print sharing, and other related components that I explore in later chapters.

Accessing Administrative Tools

As in Windows NT, you can access the administrative tools in Windows 2000 by clicking Start⇨Programs⇨Administrative Tools or by opening the Administrative Tools folder in Control Panel.

In Windows NT, each administrative tool has its own interface. For example, you use two different interfaces to configure WINS and DHCP. In Windows 2000, all administrative tools function as Microsoft Management Console (MMC) snap-ins.

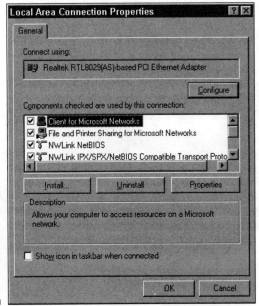

Figure 2-6:
Configuring
the
properties
for a
connection.

The MMC is a basic GUI interface that looks a lot like Windows Explorer. The MMC itself does not have any functionality; you use the MMC to load different snap-ins. The snap-ins are administrative tools — for example, DHCP Manager, WINS Manager, and RAS — that load into the MMC. Although you may have a slight learning curve, the end result is that all Windows 2000 administrative tools have the same look and feel. You have to master only one interface instead of a different one for each tool. The MMC is easy to use, and you can master it with about an hour of hands-on experience.

Part II
Taking the Plunge: Installing Windows 2000 Server

The 5th Wave   By Rich Tennant

"Can't I just give you riches or something?"

In this part . . .

As you know, installing a server can be a bumpy ride. Compared to its predecessors, however, Windows 2000 offers a greatly improved and much more stable installation process. The chapters in this part of the book tell you what you need to know for the exam questions that involve the installation of Windows 2000 Server.

In Chapter 3, you review the Windows 2000 hardware requirements and the steps for performing an attended installation. In Chapter 4, you examine unattended installations and how to create answer files in Windows 2000.

Chapter 3

Installing Windows 2000 Server

▶ Upgrading from Microsoft Windows NT 4.0

▶ Performing an attended installation of Windows 2000 Server

▶ Deploying service packs

▶ Troubleshooting failed installations

*I*f you are like me, you always have a few butterflies in your stomach when you begin a new server installation. Windows 2000 certainly offers an easier, more intuitive installation process than Windows NT Server 4.0 does, but you still need in-depth knowledge of the steps for installing the server software and troubleshooting any problems that you may encounter. You can expect to perform both tasks as an IT professional, and you can also expect exam questions on these topics.

For the exam, you need to understand everything that happens during a typical installation. To help you prepare for the installation-related questions on the exam, this chapter reviews the following tasks:

✓ Upgrading from Windows NT

✓ Performing an attended installation

✓ Troubleshooting installation problems

Quick Assessment

Upgrading
from
Microsoft
Windows
NT 4.0

1 Upgrading Windows NT 4.0 domain controllers to Windows 2000 domain controllers automatically launches the _____ installation wizard.

2 You can upgrade directly from Windows NT 3.51, Windows NT 4.0, or _____ to Windows 2000.

3 You cannot upgrade directly from versions of Windows NT earlier than 3.51 or Windows _____ to Windows 2000 Server.

Performing
an
attended
installation
of Windows
2000

4 If you need to make installation floppy disks, you can create them on any Windows computer using the _____ executable on the Windows 2000 installation CD-ROM.

5 When installing Windows 2000 as an upgrade to Windows NT 4.0 over a network share, connect to the network share and run _____.

6 During an attended setup, installation enables you to select the type of file system you want to use, with the preferred one being _____.

7 During an attended installation, if you choose typical network component installation, Setup automatically installs Client for Microsoft Networks, File and Print Sharing for Microsoft Networks, and _____.

Deploying
service
packs

8 Service packs typically provide operating system updates and _____.

Trouble-
shooting
failed
installations

9 One of the more common installation problems is incompatible _____.

10 If you believe an installation failure has occurred due to hardware or drivers, try using the _____ option.

Answers

1 *Active Directory.* See "Upgrading from Windows NT to Windows 2000."

2 *Windows NT 4.0 Terminal Server.* Study "Upgrading from Windows NT to Windows 2000."

3 *9x.* See "Upgrading from Windows NT to Windows 2000."

4 *MAKEBOOT.* Examine "Running Setup."

5 *WINNT32.EXE.* Review "Running Setup."

6 *NTFS.* See "Performing an Attended Installation."

7 *TCP/IP.* Read "Performing an Attended Installation."

8 *Fixes.* Study "About those Service Packs."

9 *Hardware/Drivers.* See "Troubleshooting Failed Installations."

10 *Safe Mode.* See "Troubleshooting Failed Installations."

Getting Ready for Installation

Thorough, careful planning helps to ensure a successful installation. Although you may be tempted to start the installation right away, you should first perform several planning actions in order to ensure that you have a successful and painless installation.

The following sections tell you about the planning actions you should perform. You need to know these tasks for the exam, and they apply to both a clean (new) installation and an upgrade.

Examining hardware requirements

No matter whether you plan to do an upgrade or a clean installation, before you ever attempt a Windows 2000 installation, make certain that your server meets the Windows 2000 hardware requirements.

Table 3-1 lists the installation hardware requirements recommended by Microsoft. Memorize them for the exam. For your work, however, remember that these are bare minimum requirements. You actually need much better hardware if you expect your server to function in a desired manner. But for the exam, you need to know the minimum requirements published by Microsoft.

Table 3-1	Windows 2000 Minimum Hardware Requirements
Component	*Requirement*
Processor	Pentium 133 MHz processor or higher
RAM	64MB minimum and 128MB or more recommended
Hard Disk	Partitions large enough to support the setup process (2GB is usually the minimum, but with the size and low cost of hard drives, your existing hard drive probably is large enough)
Resolution	VGA or higher
Keyboard	Standard keyboard
Mouse (optional)	Standard mouse
CD-ROM	For installation, at least 12X or faster
Network Card	For network installations, a NIC compatible with Windows 2000

To figure out whether you have Windows 2000-compatible hardware, you can check the Hardware Compatibility List (HCL).

Checking hardware compatibility

Before attempting an installation, you need to make certain that your hardware is compatible with Windows 2000.

Fortunately, Windows 2000 is a plug-and-play operating system, so hardware issues do not pose as much of a problem as they did in previous Windows versions. Better safe than sorry, however, so check out the Hardware Compatibility List (HCL) on your installation CD-ROM or at `www.microsoft` `.com`. For legacy devices, make certain you have your installation disks ready and check the HCL for Windows 2000 compatibility.

Even though the HCL may not list a particular device, you should not assume that the device does not work with Windows 2000 — perhaps Microsoft simply has not tested the device. If you do not find your device on the HCL, visit the hardware vendor's Web site to find out more information about compatibility with Windows 2000.

Make a decision about a file system

Windows 2000 supports File Allocation Table (FAT), File Allocation Table 32 (FAT32), and NT File System (NTFS). Before beginning the installation, determine which file system you want to use on the server. Of course, the file system of choice is NTFS. NTFS in Windows 2000 is an enhanced version that supports the security features of the Kerberos protocol. Without NTFS, you have very limited security on your system. Also, many configuration options require NTFS. FAT and FAT32 are provided for backward compatibility, but you do not need them unless you plan to dual-boot your server with Windows 9*x* (which probably isn't going to happen). In short, use NTFS.

Perform a backup

If you are upgrading to Windows 2000 from a previous version of Windows, you should perform a complete backup in case you run into problems during the installation. By doing a complete backup, you protect all your data and your current operating system.

Also, uncompress any DriveSpace or DoubleSpace volumes before upgrading to Windows 2000. Do not upgrade to Windows 2000 on a compressed drive unless you compressed the drive with the NTFS compression feature. As in any installation, if you have disk mirroring in effect on your system, disable it before beginning the installation.

Check your applications

Before installing Windows 2000, make certain that any applications currently installed on your system are compatible with Windows 2000. The README.DOC file on your installation CD-ROM provides a list of compatible applications. Read this file so you can avoid any surprises with your applications after the installation is complete. Also, check your application versions against compatibility information on each vendor's Web site.

Upgrading from Windows NT to Windows 2000

In many networking environments, you will upgrade Windows NT 4.0 servers to Windows 2000 servers rather than perform a clean installation. Upgrading preserves your major settings, keeps your data intact, and enables you to migrate the user and group accounts from Windows NT domain controllers to Windows 2000 and its Active Directory.

If your Windows NT 4.0 Server is a primary or backup domain controller, the Windows 2000 setup process first installs the server software and then automatically launches the Active Directory installation process, which upgrades the server to a Windows 2000 domain controller and migrates your user and group accounts into the Active Directory.

You can upgrade directly from Windows NT 3.51, Windows NT Server 4.0, and Windows NT 4.0 Terminal Server to Windows 2000. You cannot upgrade directly from versions earlier than NT 3.51. If you have an earlier version of NT, you must first upgrade to at least Version 3.51 before you can perform a direct upgrade.

You cannot upgrade Windows 95 and 98 to Windows 2000 Server. If you want to install Windows 2000 Server on a Windows 95 or 98 computer, Setup will delete the older operating system and begin a fresh installation.

Aside from these issues, the upgrade process works the same as a clean installation, and an upgrade involves essentially the same planning steps as a clean installation. For more information about preinstallation planning, see the section "Getting Ready for Installation," earlier in this chapter.

Running Setup

You have a few different options for starting the Windows 2000 Setup program.

You need to memorize these options for the exam:

- **Starting Setup directly from the CD-ROM:** If you are upgrading from an earlier version to Windows 2000, simply insert the CD-ROM into your CD-ROM drive and click Yes to begin the installation. On a blank machine that supports booting from a CD-ROM, you can also start the installation this way.

- **Starting Setup from a network share:** If you are installing Windows 2000 Server from a network share, connect to the share and change to the I386 folder. From a computer running MS-DOS or Windows 3.*x,* run WINNT.EXE. From a computer running Windows 9*x,* Windows NT 3.51, Windows NT 4.0, or Windows 2000, run WINNT32.EXE.

- **Starting Setup on a computer running MS-DOS:** To start Setup on a computer running MS-DOS, insert the installation CD-ROM into the CD-ROM drive. At the command prompt, access your CD-ROM drive letter, change to the I386 folder, and run WINNT.EXE.

- **Starting Setup from floppy disk:** On a blank machine that does not support booting from the CD-ROM drive, you need to make a set of installation floppy disks to start the installation. On any computer running any version of Windows, put the Windows 2000 installation CD-ROM in the CD-ROM drive, choose to browse the CD, open the BOOTDISK folder, and then double-click MAKEBOOT. A command window appears. Follow the instructions. You need four blank, formatted floppy disks, which MAKE-BOOT numbers 1, 2, 3, and 4, respectively.

Performing an Attended Installation

After you determine how you will start Setup (see the preceding section in this chapter), you simply need to start the installation process and follow the instructions that appear on-screen.

For the exam, you need to know what occurs during an attended installation. Review Lab 3-1, which walks you through an attended installation. Of course, you should have some hands-on experience installing the server software before taking the exam. Use Lab 3-1 as a guide for your practice sessions.

Lab 3-1	Performing an Attended Installation

1. **Insert installation Disk 1 and turn on your computer.**

   Setup inspects your system's hardware configuration and begins loading necessary setup files.

2. **When prompted, remove Disk 1, insert Disk 2, and press Enter.**

   Setup continues to load necessary setup files and then prompts you to insert Disk 3.

3. **Load the setup files from Disks 3 and 4, as directed by the on-screen prompts.**

   After reading the final disk, Setup asks whether you want to install Windows 2000, repair a Windows 2000 installation, or quit.

4. **Press Enter to continue the installation.**

5. **Read the licensing agreement that's displayed and then press F8 to continue.**

6. **Select a partition on your hard disk for the installation and press Enter.**

   Depending on your disk configuration, Setup may need to format your disk or partition.

7. **If so, select either NTFS or FAT and then press Enter.**

   Setup creates a list of files that it needs to copy to your hard disk for installation and then it automatically begins the file-copy process.

   After Setup completes the file-copy process, your computer automatically reboots.

   Remove any floppy disks from your disk drive before the system reboots.

   After the system reboots, Setup launches a GUI interface and the setup process continues.

8. **Click Next on the Welcome screen.**

   Setup detects and installs hardware devices on your system. This process takes several minutes, and your screen may flicker during the detection.

   After hardware detection, Setup displays a window in which you can customize Regional settings as desired.

9. **Use the customize buttons to adjust the settings, or click Next to continue.**

10. **In the resulting Personalize Your Software dialog box, enter your name and organization and then click Next.**

11. In the Licensing modes dialog box, select either the Per Server radio button or the Per Seat radio button. If you select Per Server, enter the number of concurrent connections. Each connection must have its own Client Access License (CAL). Make your selections and then click Next.

12. Enter the desired computer name, enter and confirm the administrator password (limited to 256 characters), and then click Next.

    The Windows 2000 Setup Components dialog box appears.

13. Select the components you want to install and click Next. (You can also install these components later.)

14. Enter your country, area code, and the number used to access an outside phone line (if applicable). Click Next.

15. Adjust the date and time settings so they are correct for your time zone. Click Next.

    Setup automatically installs network components and then prompts you to choose either typical settings or custom settings.

16. Make your selection and click Next.

    If you choose typical settings, Setup installs network connections for Client for Microsoft Networks, File and Print Sharing for Microsoft networks, and TCP/IP with automatic addressing.

17. Click the appropriate radio button if your server is a member of a workgroup or domain. If it's a member of a domain, enter the domain name in the dialog box that's displayed. Click Next.

    Setup builds a file list and continues installing components. This process may take several minutes.

    Setup performs the final tasks of installing Start menu items, registering components, saving settings, and removing temporary setup files.

18. Click Finish to complete the installation.

    Windows 2000 automatically reboots.

Troubleshooting Failed Installations

As you know, many problems can arise during an installation that can leave you very frustrated. Fortunately, Windows 2000 has a relatively stable setup process.

On a general troubleshooting note, you can find the cause of many setup problems in drivers and hardware that are not compatible with Windows 2000. Incompatible drivers or hardware can halt Setup during the hardware detection phase. Make sure you plan your installation and check the HCL before you run Setup.

During installation, you may receive STOP errors. A STOP error message identifies a problem that has stopped the installation.

For the exam, you need to know the most common STOP errors and how you should handle them:

- **STOP Message IRQL_NOT_LESS_OR_EQUAL:** This STOP message occurs when a device driver is using an improper memory address. If you can start Windows, check the system log for more detailed information, and remove any new hardware and device drivers that may be causing the problem.

- **STOP Message KMODE_EXCEPTION_NOT_HANDLED:** This message is caused by kernel mode exceptions, which may result from various events. Typically, you can attempt to troubleshoot this problem by making certain you have enough disk space for the installation, removing unnecessary or new device drivers, using a standard VGA driver, and making certain your system BIOS is current. If you can boot Windows, try using the Last Known Good Configuration by pressing the F8 key at startup. See Chapter 15 for more information about Safe Mode options.

- **STOP Message FAT_FILE_SYSTEM or NTFS_FILE_SYSTEM:** This error message occurs due to a heavily fragmented drive, file I/O problems, disk mirroring, or the operation of some antivirus software. Run **CHKDSK /f** to check the hard drive for corruption and then restart the computer. You can also use the Last Known Good Configuration option by pressing the F8 key at startup.

- **STOP Message DATA_BUS_ERROR:** This error is caused by a parity error in the system memory. Try restarting the computer in Safe Mode (see Chapter 15). You can also try disabling memory caching in the BIOS.

- **STOP Message NO_MORE_SYSTEM_PTES:** This error occurs because a driver is not cleaning up properly. Remove any recently installed software and hardware devices and try running Setup again.

- **STOP Message INACCESSIBLE_BOOT_DEVICE:** This error occurs during the initialization of the I/O system, and most typically is caused by a boot-sector virus. Run a virus-scan program to check for a boot-sector virus.

About Those Service Packs

The exam expects you to know about service packs. From time to time, Microsoft releases service packs in order to update portions of the Windows 2000 operating system and to provide fixes for portions of the operating system that may not be functioning properly. You can purchase service packs on CD-ROM at a minimal cost or you can download them from microsoft.com for free.

For the exam, just remember the purpose of service packs and keep in mind that an effective, timely rollout of service packs to your Windows 2000 servers is very important to keep your operating systems up to date.

Prep Test

1 Before attempting a Windows 2000 Server installation, which resource should you check to make certain your computer's hardware is compatible with Windows 2000?

A ○ README.DOC

B ○ HCL

C ○ LCH

D ○ HLC

2 Which file system supports the new security features provided by the Kerberos protocol?

A ○ FAT

B ○ FAT32

C ○ NTFS

D ○ KER32

3 The minimum amount of RAM for systems running Windows 2000 Server is 64MB, but Microsoft recommends at least _____.

A ○ 98MB

B ○ 128MB

C ○ 164MB

D ○ 198MB

4 You need to install Windows 2000 on a computer running MS-DOS. After switching to your CD-ROM drive, what do you need to run?

A ○ WINNT

B ○ WINNT32

C ○ SETUP

D ○ SETUP32

5 When you're upgrading previous versions of Windows to Windows 2000, on which operating systems can you run WINNT32.EXE? (Choose all that apply.)

A ❑ Windows NT 4.0

B ❑ Windows 3.1

C ❑ Windows 9x

D ❑ Windows NT 3.51

6 You notice that during a particular portion of setup, your screen flickers several times. At what setup stage does this occur?

A ○ File copy
B ○ Networking component installation
C ○ Automatic reboot
D ○ Hardware detection

7 During which phase of setup is the Setup program most likely to lock up?

A ○ Drive format
B ○ Registry configuration
C ○ Hardware detection
D ○ Networking component installation

8 Which tool can you use to resolve disk problems that have generated a FAT_FILE_SYSTEM or NTFS_FILE_SYSTEM error?

A ○ CHKDSK
B ○ Defragmenter
C ○ FDISK
D ○ CLNDSK

9 You receive a NO_MORE_SYSTEM_PTES STOP message. What is the most likely cause of this problem?

A ○ Device driver
B ○ Boot-sector virus
C ○ Corrupt memory
D ○ I/O errors

10 What operating system updates and fixes are released by Microsoft on a periodic basis?

A ○ Repair Pack
B ○ Service Pack
C ○ GEN Pack
D ○ None of the above

Answers

1 *B. HCL.* You should check the Hardware Compatibility List, which is available at `www.microsoft.com/hcl` and on your installation CD-ROM, to make certain your hardware is compatible with Windows 2000. *Review "Getting Ready for Installation."*

2 *C. NTFS.* The new NTFS in Windows 2000 supports the advanced security features of the Kerberos protocol, the primary authentication protocol in Windows 2000. *Read "Getting Ready for Installation."*

3 *B. 128MB.* Microsoft recommends that all systems running Windows 2000 Server have at least 128MB of RAM. *Study "Getting Ready for Installation."*

4 *A. WINNT.* On a computer running MS-DOS, access the CD-ROM drive at the command prompt and run WINNT to start the installation. *See "Running Setup."*

5 *A, C, D. Windows NT 4.0, Windows 9x, and Windows NT 3.51.* All these systems and Windows 2000 support WINNT32.EXE. *Study "Running Setup."*

6 *D. Hardware Detection.* During the hardware detection phase of setup, your screen may flicker for a few moments. This is a normal part of the installation process. *Study "Performing an Attended Installation."*

7 *C. Hardware Detection.* Setup is most likely to experience problems during the hardware detection phase. You can reduce the likelihood of this occurring by checking the HCL before beginning setup to make certain that all your hardware devices are compatible with Windows 2000. *Study "Troubleshooting Failed Installations."*

8 *A. CHKDSK.* You can run CHKDSK to attempt to fix a corrupt hard drive that prevents installation to continue. *Study "Troubleshooting Failed Installations."*

9 *A. Device Driver.* A device driver that does not clean up properly may cause this error. *Study "Troubleshooting Failed Installations."*

10 *B. Service Pack.* Microsoft periodically releases service packs to update the operating system and to resolve problems. *Study "About Those Service Packs."*

Chapter 4

Performing Unattended Installations

● ●

Exam Objectives

▶ Creating answer files by using Setup Manager to automate the installation of Windows 2000 Server

▶ Creating and configuring automated methods for installation of Windows 2000

● ●

*A*s with any software installation, you can manually install Windows 2000 by sitting at the machine and answering the prompts that Setup displays. In large environments, however, this installation method becomes impractical; you simply have too many computers to perform manual setups. Fortunately, Windows 2000 enables you to perform *unattended setups.* An unattended setup does not require any intervention from you. After you initiate the process, Setup performs its job automatically.

For the exam, you need to know how to configure and run unattended setups. The process is not too difficult, but you can expect some tricky exam questions. This chapter reviews unattended setups and their configuration, focusing on the following tasks, which you must know for the exam:

✔ Performing unattended installations

✔ Creating answer files

✔ Using other installation options

Quick Assessment

Creating
answer files
using Setup
Manager

1   In an unattended installation, Setup uses a(n) _____, which automatically provides the input that the user would give during a manual installation.

2   When using unattended installations over a network, you need to create a(n) _____ folder.

3   The WINNT _____ setup parameter enables you to copy all source files to your local hard disk.

4   The WINNT32 _____ setup parameter enables you to create a temporary folder within the folder that contains the Windows 2000 files.

5   You can create an answer file either _____ or by using Setup Manager.

6   You can find Setup Manager on both the Windows 2000 CD-ROM and the Windows 2000 _____.

7   By default, answer files are named _____.

8   You can create drive images by using the _____ utility.

Creating
and
configuring
automated
methods for
installation
of Windows
2000

9   If the master computer's hardware differs from the target computers' hardware, you can use the _____ utility.

Answers

1 *Answer file.* See "Preparing for Unattended Installations."

2 *Distribution.* Study "Preparing for Unattended Installations."

3 */makelocalsource.* See "Preparing for Unattended Installations."

4 */copydir.* Examine "Preparing for Unattended Installations."

5 *Manually.* Review "Creating an Answer File."

6 *Resource Kit.* See "Creating an Answer File."

7 *UNATTENDED.TXT.* Read "Creating an Answer File."

8 *Sysprep.* Study "Using Other Setup Methods."

9 *Syspart.* See "Using Other Setup Methods."

Preparing for Unattended Installations

By using an unattended installation, you can roll out Windows 2000 to multiple computers without having to physically sit at those computers and answer setup questions. To prepare for an unattended installation, you have to complete two basic tasks:

- ✔ Creating a distribution folder
- ✔ Reviewing setup switches

A *distribution folder* is a network share that holds the setup files. With this network share, you can perform unattended installations to the computers on your network.

You can create the network share on any computer on your network. Simply create a folder named i386 and then copy the contents of the Windows 2000 installation CD-ROM to the shared folder. Depending on your needs, you may also choose to create a OEM subfolder within the i386 folder. You can use the OEM subfolder to store any additional subfolders needed to satisfy the Microsoft OEM requirements and your own installation needs.

In addition to creating the distribution folder that holds the setup files, you should review the setup switches that are available for both WINNT.EXE and WINNT32.EXE. (See Chapter 3 for more information about WINNT and WINNT32.)

Here's the syntax for WINNT.EXE:

```
WINNT [/S[:sourcepath]] [/T[:tempdrive]] [/I[:inffile]] [/X]
      [/C] [/U[:answer_file]] [/R[X]:folder]
      [/E:command]
```

The brackets identify optional switches, and the italics highlight information that you need to supply — for example, path names and filenames. You don't type the brackets when you enter the WINNT command.

Table 4-1 explains the WINNT setup switches. You need to memorize this information for the exam.

Table 4-1	WINNT.EXE Setup Parameters
Parameter	*What It Does*
/S:sourcepath	Specifies the source location of the setup files. The sourcepath must be a full network path.
/T:tempdrive	Tells Setup where to place temporary files on a specified drive.

Parameter	What It Does
/I:*inffile*	Specifies the filename of the Setup information file. The default name is DOSNET.INF.
/X	Skips the creation of the Setup boot floppy disks.
/C	Skips the free disk space verification of the Setup boot floppy disks.
/U:*answer_file*	Performs unattended setup using an answer file. This parameter requires /S.
/R:*folder*	Specifies an optional folder to be installed.
/RX[:*folder*]	Specifies an optional folder to be copied.
/E:*command*	Specifies a command to be run at the end of the GUI-mode portion of Setup.

You also need to know the WINNT32 setup switches for the exam. Here's the syntax for WINNT32.EXE:

```
WINNT32 [/S:sourcepath] [/tempdrive:drive_letter] [/unattend
        [num] [:answer_file]] [/copydir:folder_name]
        [/copysource:folder_name] [/cmd:command_line]
        [/debug [level] [: filename]] [/udf: id [,
        UDF_file]] [/syspart:drive_letter]
        [/checkupgradeonly] [/cmdcons] [/m:folder_name]
        [/makelocalsource] [/noreboot]
```

Table 4-2 explains the WINNT32 setup switches.

Table 4-2	WINNT32.EXE Setup Parameters
Parameter	What It Does
/S:*sourcepath*	Specifies the location of the Windows 2000 files.
/tempdrive:*drive_letter*	Tells Setup to place temporary files on a specified drive and to install Windows 2000 on that drive.
/unattend[*num*][:*answer_file*]	Installs Windows 2000 in unattended mode using the answer file.
/copydir:*folder_name*	Creates an additional folder within the folder that contains the Windows 2000 files.
/copysource:*folder_name*	Creates a temporary folder in the folder that contains the Windows 2000 files.

(continued)

Table 4-2 *(continued)*

Parameter	What It Does
/cmd:*command_line*	Tells Setup to carry out a specific command before setup is complete.
/debug*[level][:filename]*	Creates a debug log at the level specified.
/udf:*id[,UDF_file]*	Indicates an identifier (id) that Setup uses to specify how a Uniqueness Database File (UDF) modifies an answer file.
/syspart:*drive_letter*	Enables you to copy Setup startup files to a hard drive, mark the drive as active, and then install the drive in another computer. You must use the /tempdrive parameter with /syspart.
/checkupgradeonly	Checks your computer for upgrade compatibility with Windows 2000. For Windows 95 or Windows 98 upgrades, Setup creates a report named UPGRADE.TXT in the Windows installation folder. For Windows NT 3.51 or 4.0 upgrades, it saves the report to the WINNT32.LOG file in the installation folder.
/cmdcons	Adds to the operating system selection screen a Recovery Console option for repairing a failed installation. It is only used post-Setup.
/m:*folder_name*	Specifies that Setup copies replacement files from an alternate location. Instructs Setup to look in the alternate location first and if files are present, use them instead of the files from the default location.
/makelocalsource	Instructs Setup to copy all installation source files to your local hard disk. Use /makelocalsource when installing from a CD to provide installation files when the CD is not available later in the installation.
/noreboot	Specifies that Setup should not restart the computer after the file-copy phase of WINNT32 is completed, so you can execute another command.

Creating an Answer File

During an attended installation, you interact with the Setup program by manually entering answers to the questions that Setup asks about your installation. In this way, you tailor the installation to meet your needs. For an unattended installation, however, you supply an *answer file* that Setup uses to get the answers to its questions.

To prepare for an unattended installation, you first create a distribution folder and review the command-line syntax for WINNT.EXE and WINNT32.EXE. (See the preceding section in this chapter.) Then, you create an answer file. The default name for the answer file is UNATTENDED.TXT, but you can use any desired name, as long as you point to the correct name when you enter the command to start the setup process. This feature enables you to create multiple answer files for different Windows 2000 installations.

You can create an answer file in either of two ways: manually or by using Setup Manager, which you find on the Windows 2000 CD-ROM. Because using Setup Manager is the preferred method (and the one you need to know for the exam), this section focuses only on Setup Manager.

You use Setup Manager to start the Windows 2000 installation and create an answer file for an unattended installation. Launch SETUPMGR.EXE on the installation CD-ROM or from the Windows 2000 Resource Kit.

Setup Manager provides a wizard that helps you create an answer file or edit an existing one. Lab 4-1 walks you through the steps for using Setup Manager. You need to know the options presented for the exam, so use this lab to practice creating answer files on your server.

Lab 4-1	Creating an Answer File

1. **Launch Setup Manager from the Windows 2000 CD-ROM or from the Resource Kit.**

2. **Click Next on the Welcome screen.**

3. **Click the Create a New Answer File radio button and then click Next.**

4. **In the Product to Install dialog box, select Windows 2000 Server and click Next.**

5. **In the User Interaction Level dialog box, shown in Figure 4-1, select the level of user interaction desired. For a complete unattended setup, select Fully Automated. Click Next.**

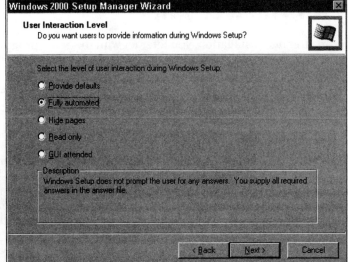

Figure 4-1:
Select the
Level of
User
Interaction
from this
dialog box.

6. **Accept the license agreement by clicking the check box and clicking Next.**

7. **Type your name and organization and click Next.**

8. **Enter the CD Key for the computers you want to set up and then click Next.**

   You need a separate license for each copy of Windows that you install.

9. **Select either Per Server or Per Seat for the licensing mode and then click Next.**

   Per-server licensing requires a separate CAL for each concurrent connection to the server, and per-seat licensing requires a separate CAL for each client computer that accesses a Windows 2000 Server.

10. **Enter the desired names of the destination computer(s) and click Next.**

    You can also choose to automatically generate computer names based on your organization's name by selecting the check box at the bottom of the dialog box.

11. **Enter and confirm the administrator password and then click Next.**

    You can also specify for the system to automatically log on with the administrator password when the system first boots.

12. **In the Display settings dialog box, use the drop-down lists to select colors, screen area, and refresh frequency, or click Custom to select additional display setting options. Click Next.**

13. **In the Network Settings dialog box, select either Typical Settings (which installs TCP/IP, enables DHCP, and installs Client for Microsoft Networks) or Custom. If you choose Custom, select the desired networking components to install. Click Next.**

14. **In the Join a Domain dialog box, enter the domain or workgroup that the server should join. To join a domain, enter the name of the domain and provide a user account that has permission to join a computer to a domain (such as an administrator's user name and password). Click Next.**

15. **Select the appropriate time zone and click Next.**

16. **If necessary, configure additional settings. Click Next.**

    Additional settings include such information as telephony and regional settings.

    In the Distribution Folder dialog box, you specify whether Setup should create or modify a distribution folder if the unattended installation will be performed from a CD-ROM.

17. **Make your selection and click Next.**

18. **Enter a name and path for your answer file (the default name is UNATTENDED.TXT) and click Next.**

19. **Click Finish.**

After you create the answer file, you can view it and even manually edit the file by using Notepad, as shown in Figure 4-2.

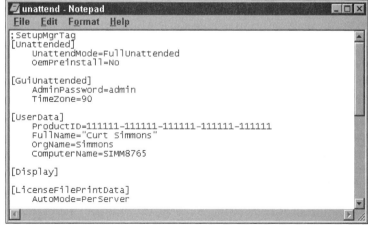

Figure 4-2:
You can
view
and edit
UNAT-
TENDED.TXT
using
Notepad.

```
;SetupMgrTag
[Unattended]
    UnattendMode=FullUnattended
    OemPreinstall=No

[GuiUnattended]
    AdminPassword=admin
    TimeZone=90

[UserData]
    ProductID=111111-111111-111111-111111-111111
    FullName="Curt Simmons"
    OrgName=Simmons
    ComputerName=SIMM8765

[Display]

[LicenseFilePrintData]
    AutoMode=PerServer
```

After you create the answer file, you can run Setup so that it uses the answer file. Review the list of parameters to determine how you want to run Setup. Typically, you provide the WINNT parameters that point to the location of the setup files and the answer file. The following example shows how to run Setup from a CD-ROM and point to a desired answer file:

```
Winnt /S:drive_letter\I386 /U:drive_letter\unattended.txt
```

Using Other Setup Methods

In addition to attended and unattended installation of Windows 2000 Server (see Chapter 3 and previous sections in this chapter), the exam also expects you to understand two other major setup options. The following sections explore what you need to know about these additional setup methods.

Using Sysprep

You can use the Sysprep utility to duplicate a disk and install the image on another computer. For example, you can install a Windows 2000 Server, configure it as desired, and install additional software. Then, you use Sysprep to create an image of the server's hard disk that you can copy to another server. You use the Sysprep utility along with a SYSPREP.INF file that serves as the answer file for cloning. You find Sysprep in the DEPLOYMENT.CAB file on your installation CD-ROM.

You don't need to know a lot about Sysprep for the exam, but you might run across a question that asks how you use Sysprep to install images on a computer without using a Security Identifier (SID). You can perform this action by using the *nosidgen* switch with Sysprep.

Using Syspart

Syspart is like Sysprep, but you use it when the master computer on which you create the image has different hardware from the computer to which you are copying the image. Essentially, this method greatly speeds up installation by removing the file-copy portion of Setup (because it is already contained on the image). Like Sysprep, Syspart is available in the DEPLOYMENT.CAB file on your installation CD-ROM.

Prep Test

1 You want to use WINNT.EXE so that a temporary drive is used. Which parameter do you use?

A ○ /T

B ○ /C

C ○ /E

D ○ /D

2 You want to use WINNT to run an unattended setup, but you also want Setup to copy a folder named Temp that will be deleted after installation is complete. Which command switch do you use?

A ○ /R :temp

B ○ /X :temp

C ○ /RX :temp

D ○ /Ex :temp

3 You have an answer file named UNATTENDED4.TXT. You want to use this file to run an unattended setup on a computer using the installation CD-ROM. The CD-ROM letter is D. Which command-line syntax is correct for this installation?

A ○ Winnt /C:D\I386 /X:D\unattended4.txt

B ○ Winnt /UDF:D\I386 /UDF:D\unattended4.txt

C ○ Winnt /CMD:D\I386 /S:D\unattended4.txt

D ○ Winnt /S:D\I386 /U:D\unattended4.txt

4 Which tool provides a wizard that helps you create and edit an answer file?

A ○ WINNT

B ○ WINNT32

C ○ Setup

D ○ Setup Manager

5 During the creation of an answer file using Setup Manager, you have the option to install Typical network settings or create custom settings. If you select Typical network settings, which components are installed? (Choose all that apply.)

A ❏ TCP/IP

B ❏ DHCP (enabled)

C ❏ Client for Microsoft Networks

D ❏ Client for Novell Networks

6 You want to create an image of a particular drive that can be copied to other Windows 2000 Servers. However, the other servers have differing hardware. Which tool do you need to use?

A ○ UDF:id

B ○ Sysprep

C ○ Syspart

D ○ Winnt32

7 You configure a Windows 2000 server and install several custom applications. You want to create an image that you can copy to several other computers that have the exact same hardware. Which tool do you need to use?

A ○ UDF:id

B ○ Sysprep

C ○ Syspart

D ○ Winnt32

Answers

1 *A. /T.* To specify a drive where Setup can place temporary files, use the /T:*tempdrive* switch. *Review "Preparing for Unattended Installations."*

2 *C. /RX :temp.* The RX command specifies that an optional folder should be copied during setup. In this example, you want the Temp folder to be copied. *Read "Preparing for Unattended Installations."*

3 *D. Winnt /S:D\I386 /U:D\unattended4.txt.* This command syntax provides a sourcepath to the installation files (/S:D), and it provides the unattended (/U) portion of setup by pointing to the UNATTENDED4.TXT file. *Study "Creating an Answer File."*

4 *D. Setup Manager.* Setup Manager, available on the Windows 2000 installation CD-ROM, provides a wizard to help you create answer files or edit existing answer files. You can also create and edit answer files with any text editor, such as Notepad. *See "Creating an Answer File."*

5 *A, B, C. TCP/IP, DHCP(enabled), Client for Microsoft Networks.* These three settings are the default (typical) settings installed by Windows 2000 if the Typical selection is made using Setup Manager. *Study "Creating an Answer File."*

6 *C. Syspart.* You can use Syspart to copy drive images to computers that do not have the same hardware. *Study "Using Other Setup Methods."*

7 *B. Sysprep.* You can use Sysprep to copy drive images to other computers that have the exact same hardware. *Study "Using Other Setup Methods."*

Part III

Installing, Configuring, and Troubleshooting Access to Resources

The 5th Wave   By Rich Tennant

"I don't care how well he did on the MCSE exam, he still lacks people skills."

In this part . . .

When you boil it all down, a server exists to provide services to network clients. Windows 2000 offers a wealth of services and functions that help your network clients function properly.

In Chapters 5, 6, and 7, you review DHCP, WINS, and DNS. Chapter 8 examines the new printing features in Windows 2000. In Chapters 9 and 10, you study the file and folder options for both local and Web access. And in Chapter 11, you examine Windows 2000's new Distributed File System (Dfs).

Chapter 5

Installing and Configuring DHCP

● ●

Exam Objectives

▶ Installing and configuring network services

▶ Installing and configuring network services for interoperability

● ●

*I*f you have worked with Windows NT at all, you are probably familiar with Dynamic Host Configuration Protocol (DHCP) — a server service that enables the server to dynamically assign IP addresses to network clients. Because Windows 2000 networking has TCP/IP as its foundation, DHCP also plays an important role in Windows 2000 networks.

For the exam, you need to know how to install and configure DHCP on a Windows 2000 server, as well as how to manage its operations. To help you prepare for the DHCP-related questions on the Windows 2000 Server exam, this chapter focuses on the following topics:

✔ Installing DHCP

✔ Creating scopes

✔ Authorizing the DHCP server

✔ Managing the DHCP server

✔ Enabling DHCP clients

Quick Assessment

Installing and configuring network services

1 A DHCP _____ is the full range of IP addresses that can be leased on a subnet.

2 The client broadcast message sent to find a DHCP server is called _____.

3 A multicast scope must have an IP address range within TCP/IP class _____.

4 The amount of time a DHCP client may use an IP address is called a(n) _____.

5 Windows 2000 DHCP servers are authorized by the _____.

Installing and configuring network services for interoper-ability

6 DHCP can _____ update DNS.

7 A "rogue" DHCP server is one that has not been _____.

8 A superscope contains at least one _____.

9 MADCAP leases IP addresses for _____.

10 Windows 2000 and _____ clients can autoconfigure an IP address if a DHCP server is not available.

Answers

1 *Scope.* Review "What Is DHCP, Anyway?".

2 *DHCPDISCOVER.* Study "What Is DHCP, Anyway?".

3 *D.* See "What Is DHCP, Anyway?".

4 *Lease.* Examine "What Is DHCP, Anyway?".

5 *Active Directory.* Review "Authorizing the DHCP Server."

6 *Dynamically.* See "Managing Servers and Scopes."

7 *Authorized.* Read "Authorizing the DHCP Server."

8 *Scope.* Study "Creating DHCP Scopes."

9 *Multicasting.* See "Creating DHCP Scopes."

10 *Windows 98.* See "Enabling DHCP Clients."

What Is DHCP, Anyway?

DHCP (Dynamic Host Configuration Protocol) is a server service that dynamically assigns, or *leases,* IP addresses and related IP information to network clients. At first glance, this may not seem like an important task. However, you have to remember that, on a TCP/IP network, each network client must have a unique IP address and an appropriate subnet mask. Without these items, a client cannot communicate on the network. For example, if two clients have the same IP address, neither will be able to communicate on the network.

Back in its early days, TCP/IP gained the reputation of being a *high-overhead protocol* — it required more configuration than other networking protocols. The prospect of having to visit each client machine and manually enter a correct IP address and subnet mask without making a duplication error was enough to give network administrators severe panic attacks.

DHCP handles all this work automatically. Each client gets a unique IP address, subnet mask, and other IP information such as default gateways and the IP addresses of WINS (Windows Internet Name Service) and DNS (Domain Name System) servers. DHCP makes certain that no clients have duplicate addresses, and this entire process is invisible to network administrators and network users. As you can see, DHCP is very important, and the exam expects you to know how to install and configure it.

How does DHCP work?

DHCP works by leasing IP addresses and IP information to network clients for a period of time. For the lease to happen, the following *negotiation* process occurs:

1. During the boot process, a client computer that is configured as a DHCP client sends out a broadcast packet called DHCPDISCOVER. This Discover packet contains the client's computer name and Media Access Control (MAC) address so the DHCP servers can respond to it. Basically, the Discover packet says, "I'm looking for a DHCP server who can lease an IP address."

2. DHCP servers on the network respond to the broadcast with a DHCPOFFER. In essence, the DHCPOFFER says, "I am a DHCP server and I have a lease for you." If several DHCP servers respond to the request, the client accepts the first offer that it receives.

3. The client responds via a broadcast message called a DHCPREQUEST. This message basically says, "I accept your lease offer and would like an IP address." If other DHCP servers made offers, they also see their lease offers were not accepted by the broadcast message, so they rescind their offers. (They must not like getting snubbed by a client computer.)

4. The DHCP server whose offer was accepted responds with a DHCPACK message, which acknowledges the lease acceptance and contains the client's IP address lease as well as other IP addressing information that you configure the server to provide. The client is now a TCP/IP client and can participate on the network.

Keep in mind that a lease is for a period of time. Typically, a client can keep its IP address for several days (or whatever you configure). When half the lease time expires, the client attempts to renew its lease for the IP address. After a client obtains the lease for an IP address, it attempts to keep the lease by renewing it over and over. If unsuccessful, the client simply must get a new IP address lease.

Reviewing important DHCP terms

You should memorize the DHCP terms listed in Table 5-1, because you need to know them for the exam. You will work with these terms throughout the chapter and during any hands-on configuration of DHCP.

Table 5-1	Important DHCP Terms
DHCP Term	*What It Means*
Scope	A full range of IP addresses that can be leased from a particular DHCP server.
Superscope	A grouping of scopes used to support logical IP subnets that exist on one physical IP subnet (called a *multinet*).
Multicast Scope	A scope that contains multicast IP addresses, which treat multicast clients as a group. Multicast is an extension of DHCP and uses a multicast address range of 224.0.0.0 to 239.255.255.255.
Address Pool	The IP addresses in a scope that are available for lease.
Exclusion Range	A group of IP address in the scope that are excluded from leasing. Excluded addresses are normally used to give hardware devices, such as routers, a static IP address.

(continued)

Table 5-1 *(continued)*

DHCP Term	What It Means
Reservation	A means for assigning a permanent IP address to a particular client, server, or hardware device. Reservations are typically made for servers or hardware devices that need a static IP address.
Lease	The amount of time that a client may use an IP address before the client must re-lease the IP address or request another one.

Installing DHCP

As with other networking components in Windows 2000 Server, you can install DHCP in either of two ways:

- ✔ Using Add/Remove Programs in the Control Panel
- ✔ Using the Configure Your Server tool

You can review the installation process for server services in Chapter 2.

Like most other Windows 2000 components, DHCP functions as a Microsoft Management Console (MMC) snap-in. After you install DHCP, you must configure the service for operation.

To open the DHCP Manager, click Start⇨Programs⇨Administrative Tools⇨ DHCP. The right pane within the snap-in tells you that you must configure the service.

DHCP does not begin leasing IP addresses and it is not functional until an administrator configures it. You can review how to configure DHCP for operation in the following sections of this chapter.

Creating DHCP Scopes

A *scope* is the full range of IP addresses that clients can lease from a particular DHCP server. Each DHCP server has its own scope of IP addresses that are appropriate for the subnet on which the DHCP server leases addresses.

DHCP servers do not share scopes, and their scopes must not overlap. Otherwise, the same IP addresses would be leased to different network clients, and the clients would not be able to communicate on the network.

Before the DHCP server can lease IP addresses to clients, you must configure a scope, and the Active Directory must authorize the server. In the following sections, you review the steps for creating various scopes. For all the details about authorization, see the section "Authorizing the DHCP Server," later in this chapter.

Creating a standard scope

Lab 5-1 details the steps for creating a standard DHCP scope. The exam expects you to know how to create scopes, so study this lab carefully.

Lab 5-1   Creating a Standard Scope

1. **Click Start➪Programs➪Administrative Tools➪DHCP.**

2. **Select the server in the console tree and then choose Action➪ New Scope.**

   The New Scope wizard displays its welcome screen.

3. **Click Next.**

4. **In the Scope Name dialog box, enter a name for the scope and a description, if desired, and then click Next.**

5. **In the IP Address Range dialog box, enter the starting and ending IP addresses of the full scope for this server, as shown in Figure 5-1. Enter the subnet mask for the IP subnet and then click Next.**

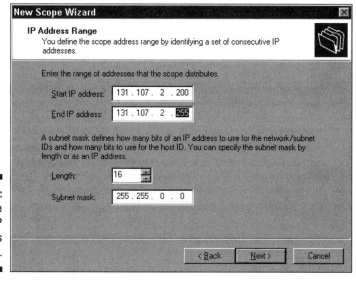

Figure 5-1: Defining the scope's IP address range.

6. **In the Add Exclusions dialog box, enter any exclusion ranges desired by entering the starting and ending IP addresses of the range(s). Click Add to add the exclusion range to the list and then repeat this step to define more exclusion ranges. Click Next.**

7. **In the Lease Duration dialog box, enter the desired lease duration in the provided boxes and then click Next.**

   The default lease time is 8 days. If you have primarily mobile computers, you may want to reduce the lease times to free up more IP addresses when those computers are not connected. For stable, desktop networks, longer leases are fine. In most cases, the default setting is best.

   After you click Next in the Lease Duration dialog box, the Configure DHCP Options dialog box appears. DHCP options enable you to specify additional IP addressing information that is returned to clients with an IP lease, such as the address of the default gateway, WINS, and DNS servers.

8. **Click Yes and then click Next.**

9. **In the Router (Default Gateway) dialog box, shown in Figure 5-2, enter the IP address(es) of the routers for your subnet and then click Next.**

   The default gateway enables IP traffic to flow between different subnets. If you do not enter this information, client computers can still find the default gateway through broadcast packets, but you can reduce network broadcast traffic by providing the IP address.

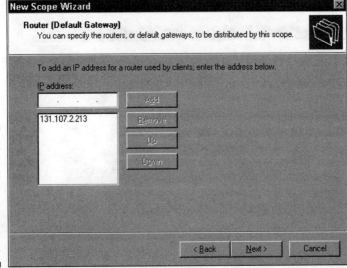

Figure 5-2:
The router default gateway allows traffic to move between subnets.

10. **In the Domain Name and DNS Servers dialog box, shown in Figure 5-3, enter the name of the parent domain and the names and IP addresses of any DNS servers and then click Next.**

    The parent domain provides the name of the domain that clients use for DNS resolution, and the server names and IP addresses point the clients to appropriate servers. Click Add to enter the addresses you provide and then click Next.

11. **In the WINS Servers dialog box, enter the server name(s) and IP address(es) of WINS servers on your network that you want sent to your client computers. Click Add to add the WINS servers to the list and then click Next when you are done.**

    The Activate Scope dialog box appears.

12. **Click Yes and then click Next.**

13. **Click Finish to complete the wizard.**

The New Scope wizard helps you configure the scope you need, and you can easily make changes to the scope by using the DHCP Manager, as I explain in the section "Managing Servers and Scopes," later in this chapter.

After you complete the New Scope wizard, the scope is activated, but it still cannot lease IP addresses to clients until the server is authorized by the Active Directory. Watch out for tricky exam questions concerning this issue. I explain how to authorize the server in the section "Authorizing the DHCP Server," later in this chapter.

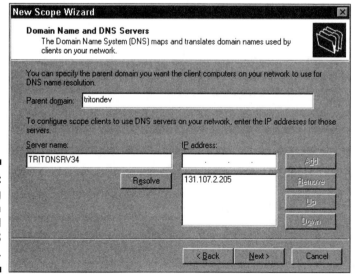

Figure 5-3:
Identifying
the domain
name and
DNS
servers.

Configuring a superscope

A network subnet has one scope in which IP addresses are leased to clients on that subnet from the scope. Because of network growth, however, you may need to extend the scope to provide additional IP addresses. Instead of creating additional subnets with additional scopes, you can use a concept called *multinets.*

A multinet enables you to combine several scopes so they appear as one scope on an IP subnet. This scope combination is called a *superscope.*

The multinet enables you to create logical IP subnets where only one physical subnet exists. This administrative solution extends a subnet's IP address range without creating a new subnet.

You can easily configure a superscope in the DHCP Manager, but as with all aspects of networking, careful planning must take place first to ensure that your multinet will meet your administrative needs and ensure client connectivity. To create a superscope, follow the steps in Lab 5-2.

Lab 5-2   Creating a Superscope

1. **In the DHCP Manager console, select the server for which you want to create a superscope and then choose _A_ction⇨New S_u_perscope.**

   The New Superscope wizard displays its welcome screen.

2. **Click Next.**

3. **In the Superscope Name dialog box, enter the name of the superscope and then click Next.**

4. **From the list of available scopes shown in the Select Scopes dialog box, select one or more scopes to add to the superscope and then click Next.**

5. **Click Finish to complete the wizard.**

Configuring a multicast scope

Multicasting is the process of sending multiple messages to network clients. In much the same way as you can send an e-mail message to a group of people, multicasting enables a group of clients to appear as one client.

You can use multicasting for various purposes. For example, you can configure a multicast group so that you can send a video conference over the network to all members of the group. By using the multicast features in DHCP, the server can automatically assign the multicast IP address.

Multicasting is accomplished using a Class D IP address range that is reserved for multicasting purposes. The address range, which you should remember for the exam, is 224.0.0.0 to 239.255.255.255. The class D address enables you to use multicasting on your network without interfering with typical IP communication. In other words, multicast clients have a typical IP address appropriate for their subnet and they also have a multicast IP address.

Multicast Address Dynamic Client Allocation Protocol (MADCAP) is an extension of the typical DHCP service, but they are still separate protocols. DHCP and MADCAP work together to dynamically assign multicast IP addresses to multicast clients. Each multicast client must have both a standard DHCP IP lease and a multicast IP address lease.

As with a typical DHCP scope or superscope, you can also configure a multicast scope if multicasting is in use on your network. Lab 5-3 shows you how to configure a multicast scope.

Lab 5-3   Creating a Multicast Scope

1. **In the DHCP Manager, select the server on which you want to create a multicast scope and then choose Action⇨New Multicast Scope.**

   The New Multicast Scope wizard displays its welcome screen.

2. **Click Next.**

3. **Enter a name for the multicast scope and a description if desired, and then click Next.**

4. **Enter a valid IP address range for the multicast, which must fall in the range from 224.0.0.0 to 239.255.255.255. You can also enter a Time to Live (TTL), which specifies the number of routers that multicast traffic passes through on your network. The default is 32. Make your selections and then click Next.**

5. **In the Add Exclusion dialog box, enter an exclusion range, if desired, by entering the starting and ending IP addresses of the exclusion range. Click Add to add the exclusion range to the list and then click Next.**

6. **In the Lease Duration dialog box, enter the desired multicast lease duration and then click Next.**

   The default is 30 days. Configure the lease duration depending on your multicast needs, based on the amount of time a multicast group may need to exist.

7. **In the Activate Multicast Scope dialog box, click Yes to activate the multicast scope and then click Next.**

8. **Click Finish to complete the wizard.**

Authorizing the DHCP Server

After you configure the desired scopes for your subnet (see the previous sections in this chapter), you authorize the DHCP server in the Active Directory. DHCP servers cannot lease IP addresses in Windows 2000 networks without being authorized. Keep this in mind for the exam!

In most cases, the Active Directory automatically authorizes domain controllers that function as DHCP servers, but you must manually authorize member servers. Watch out for tricky test questions on this issue — you must manually authorize member servers.

Authorization is a security precaution to ensure that only authorized DHCP servers operate on the network. In this way, you prevent unauthorized, or "rogue" DHCP servers from coming online and issuing IP addresses. This security feature prevents DHCP servers from accidentally or intentionally coming online and leasing incorrect or inappropriate IP addresses to network clients. When the Active Directory authorizes a DHCP server, it adds the server's IP address to a list of authorized servers. If an unauthorized server comes online, the Active Directory can detect that the server is not on the authorized list and shut it down. So, in order for a DHCP server to lease IP addresses, it must be authorized by the Active Directory.

To authorize a DHCP server, select the DHCP server you want to authorize in the DHCP Manager console and then choose Action⇨Authorize. The authorization process may take a few moments. To refresh your server so you can verify that the authorization has taken place, choose Action⇨Refresh (or simply click F5). An authorized server object in the console appears with a green icon. The server can now lease IP addresses to clients.

Managing Servers and Scopes

After you configure your desired scopes and authorize the member server with the Active Directory (see the previous sections in this chapter), you can further configure the server or scope(s) in various ways. You can also use this information to manage the server and scopes as necessary. In general, DHCP does not need lots of maintenance from network administrators, but the exam does expect you to know about the configuration issues that I describe in the following sections.

Managing the DHCP server

You can manage the DHCP server by selecting it in the console and then using the options in the Action menu. You have two major options. First, you can click Display Server Statistics. As shown in Figure 5-4, this option gives you statistical information about the server, including leases, releases, and the percentage of the scope that is in use. By using the Display Server Statistics option, you can quickly gain information about the server's DHCP functions.

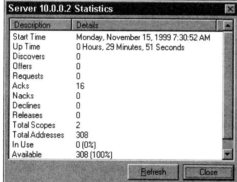

Figure 5-4:
Checking
DHCP
server
statistics.

The Action menu also has an option that enables you to access and manage the server's properties. Select the desired server in the console and then choose Action⇨Properties. The Properties dialog box for a server has three tabs: General, DNS, and Advanced.

On the General tab, you have three check boxes:

✔ **Automatically Update Statistics:** You can change the statistics update time, if desired. The default is every 10 minutes.

✔ **Enable DHCP Logging:** This option, which is selected by default, writes a daily file that you can use to troubleshoot and monitor the DHCP service.

✔ **Show the BOOTP Table Folder:** You can enable this option so you can see the BOOTP table folder if your network uses BOOTP clients. BOOTP clients are diskless workstations that obtain their IP addresses and boot program from the server. BOOTP is an older technology solution that is supported in Windows 2000 for backward compatibility.

As shown in Figure 5-5, the DNS tab gives you options to specify how the DHCP server interoperates with DNS. DNS and DHCP are integrated in Windows 2000, and due to the dynamic nature of Dynamic DNS (DDNS — see Chapter 7), DHCP can automatically update DNS when a client's IP address changes.

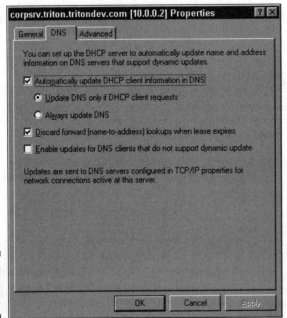

Figure 5-5:
The DNS
tab.

You can expect the exam to ask you some questions about the settings that you can configure on the DNS tab. You should memorize and understand the importance of each of these settings:

- **Automatically update DHCP client information in DNS:** This option is selected by default, and you should leave it selected so DHCP can automatically update DNS. You have two additional options here: updating DNS only if the DHCP client requests it (only Windows 2000 Professional clients can do this), or always update DNS. The Update DNS Only If DHCP Client Requests option is selected by default.

- **Discard forward (name-to-address) lookups when lease expires:** This option, which is selected by default, enables the DHCP server to discard name-to-IP address lookups by the DNS server when the leases expire. This feature helps make certain that incorrect name-to-IP address information is not returned to DNS.

✔ **Enable updates for DNS clients that do not support dynamic update:**
This option is also selected by default. Previous, or down-level, versions
of Windows (such as NT and 9*x*) do not support dynamic updates, so
the DHCP server can handle the updates with the DNS server when this
option is selected. In pure Windows 2000 networks, this option is not
needed.

On the Advanced tab, you have a few configuration options. First, you can set
conflict detection, if desired. Conflict detection enables the DHCP server to
attempt to detect IP lease conflicts before leasing an IP address to a network
client. Under normal circumstances, this option is not needed, and if you
choose to use conflict detection, the leasing negotiation between the server
and client will operate more slowly.

You can also use the Advanced tab to change the audit log file and database
paths if desired. The default is C:\WINNT\System32\dhcp. You can also click
the Bindings button to change the server network connection that communi-
cates with network clients. This feature is useful for servers that have multiple network interface cards (NICs).

Managing scopes

Just as you can manage the DHCP server, you have several options that
enable you to manage the scope.

You don't need to worry about these features for the exam, so this section
gives you a quick look at the management features for scopes.

First, you can access the Properties dialog box for the scope just as you can
for the server. Select the scope in the console and then choose
Action⇨Properties.

The General tab in the scope's Properties dialog box contains the scope
name, the starting and ending IP address, and the lease time. All this information was configured when you created the scope, but you can easily change it
as needed on the General tab.

The DNS tab gives you the same settings as seen in the server properties, so
refer to the previous section in this chapter for more information.

The Advanced tab contains three radio buttons. You can choose to assign IP
addresses to DHCP clients only, to BOOTP clients only, or to both. If you
choose to lease IP addresses to BOOTP clients, you can set the lease duration
for them on this tab as well.

You can also use the Action menu to delete or deactivate a scope. If you deactivate a scope, you can use the Action menu to reactivate it, but the scope will not be able to lease IP addresses to clients as long as it remains deactivated.

If you expand the scope in the console tree, you see several subcontainers, as shown in Figure 5-6.

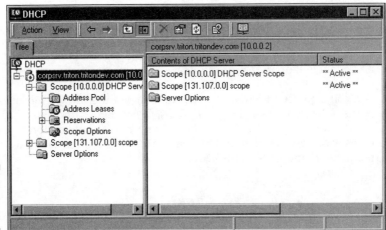

Figure 5-6:
Scope subcontainers.

Here's what you can do with each of those subcontainers:

- **Address Pool:** If you click Address Pool, the details pane displays your current address pool. By clicking the Action menu, you can add a new exclusion range, if desired.

- **Address Leases:** If you click Address Leases, the details pane displays a list of leased IP address and the clients who hold the leases, as well as the lease expiration dates.

- **Reservations:** If you click Reservations, the details pane displays a list of your current reservations. You can add a new reservation by choosing Action⇨New Reservation.

- **Scope Options:** If you click Scope options, you can configure additional IP options for the scope. See the next section in this chapter for more information.

Configuring scope options

Scope options are additional IP configuration information you can have returned to clients when they lease an IP address. Just as you can have the IP addresses of the default gateways, WINS servers, and DNS servers returned to clients, you can also have several other server types and options returned. These options enable you to tailor DHCP to the needs of your network.

To configure scope options, expand the desired scope in the console tree, select Scope Options, and then choose Action➪Configure Options.

As shown in Figure 5-7, the Scope Options dialog box has a General tab and an Advanced tab. On the General tab, you can browse through the list of available options, click the ones you want, and then enter the IP configuration information for those options. For example, in Figure 5-7, a Cookie server is in use on my network, and I want that information returned to DHCP clients. I select the Cookie Servers check box and then enter the server name and IP address in the bottom of the dialog box. Now, when clients receive an IP address lease, the IP address of the Cookie Server will be returned to them as well.

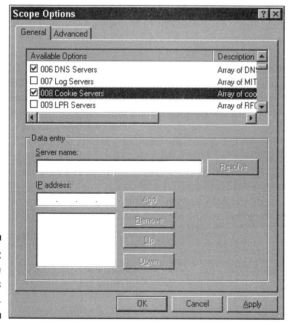

Figure 5-7:
Scope
Options
General tab.

The Advanced tab works in a similar fashion, except on the Advanced tab, you can configure options for vendor and user classes. By default, standard DHCP options are selected for the vendor class, but you can click the drop-down menu and select Microsoft options, Windows 2000 options, or Windows 98 options.

When you select a desired vendor class, a list of options appears which you can select to use. The same is true for the user class. A default user class is selected, but you can use the drop-down menu and select the BOOTP class or Routing and Remote Access Class. When you select a different class, a list of options appears that you can select for that class.

In most cases, the default setting are all you need for an effective DHCP implementation; however, you can configure different vendor and user classes to tailor your DHCP implementation to your network needs.

Enabling DHCP Clients

In Windows 2000, both Windows 2000 Professional and down-level Windows clients (NT, 9x) can be DHCP clients. To configure a client computer to act as a DHCP client, simply access the client's TCP/IP properties and then select the Obtain an IP Address Automatically radio button. This option tells the client to contact a DHCP server for TCP/IP configuration at boot-up.

Windows 2000 Professional and Windows 98 client computers can autoconfigure themselves with a TCP/IP address if a DHCP server is not available. If this occurs, the client continues to attempt to contact the DHCP server so it can gain a leased IP address instead of using the one it has temporarily assigned itself. If autoconfiguration occurs, the clients use a reserved B-class address in the 169.254.0.0 range with a subnet mask of 255.255.0.0. The client tests its autoconfigured IP address using a *gratuitous ARP*, which is broadcast using Address Resolution Protocol, to see if another client is using the address. If not, the client uses the address until it can reach the DHCP server. This entire process is transparent to end-users, who are not aware of the client computer's DHCP configuration or autoconfiguration.

Prep Test

1 Which computers can function as DHCP servers? (Choose all that apply.)

A ❑ Windows 2000 Domain Controller

B ❑ Windows 2000 Professional

C ❑ Windows 2000 Member Server

D ❑ Windows NT 4.0 Server

2 You want your DHCP clients to contact a particular DNS server for host-name-to-IP address resolution. During the creation of the scope, how do you use this dialog box to configure the scope to return the DNS server information to the clients?

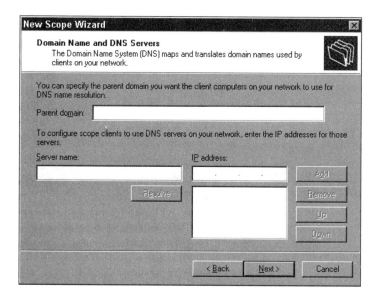

3 How do you create a new scope for a DHCP server?

A ○ Select the server in the DHCP console and click the Scope link in the details pane.

B ○ Select the server in the DHCP console and then choose Action⇨Properties.

C ○ Select the server in the DHCP console and then choose Action⇨New Scope.

D ○ You cannot create a new scope.

4 An administrator configures only a multicast scope on a newly installed DHCP server and then authorizes the server in the Active Directory. The server, however, does not issue MADCAP IP addresses. What did the administrator do wrong?

A ○ The multicast scope is not configured accurately.

B ○ The administrator did not configure a standard DHCP scope.

C ○ There are no multicast clients on the network

D ○ DHCP does not support multicasting on IP subnets.

5 On a newly installed DHCP server, you configure a scope and then authorize the DHCP server in the Active Directory. You wait for a period of time, but the server's icon remains red. What do you need to do?

A ○ Reinstall Windows 2000.

B ○ Reinstall DHCP.

C ○ Reauthorize the server.

D ○ Refresh the server.

6 You want your DHCP server to dynamically update DNS when clients' IP addresses change. You want Windows 2000 computers to request the DNS update, but you also want the DHCP server to perform the updates for down-level clients who cannot make the request. What do you need to do on the DNS tab?

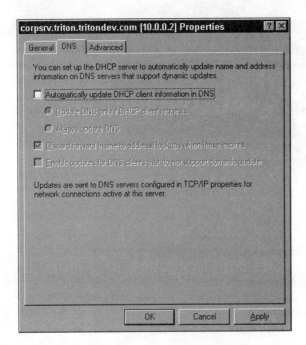

7 You want your DHCP server to attempt to detect conflicts before it leases IP addresses to clients. Where can you configure this setting?

A ○ Scope Properties, General tab.

B ○ Server Properties, General tab.

C ○ Server Properties, Advanced tab.

D ○ Conflict Detection is not supported in Windows 2000.

8 You want a particular scope to provide the IP address of an SMTP server to DHCP clients. Where can you configure this setting?

A ○ Scope Properties, General tab.

B ○ Server Properties, Advanced tab.

C ○ Scope Options, General tab.

D ○ Scope Options, Advanced tab.

9 You want to define a particular router for clients using remote access. What do you need to do on the Scope Options Advanced tab to configure this setting?

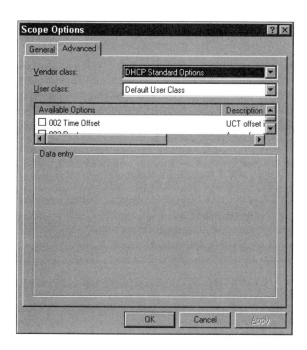

10 When a Windows 2000 client autoconfigures its own IP address because a DHCP server is not available, what method does the client use to ensure that no other network client is using the IP address?

A ○ PING

B ○ SNIF

C ○ NBSTAT

D ○ ARP

Answers

1 *A, C, D.* Windows 2000 Domain Controllers and Member Servers, as well as Windows NT 4.0 Servers, can function as DHCP servers on a Windows 2000 network. Windows 2000 Professional, or any other client operating system, cannot. *Review "Installing DHCP."*

2 *Enter the parent domain name, enter the server name and IP address, and then click Add.* You can configure scopes to return a particular DNS server or servers to client computers by simply entering the parent domain, DNS name, and IP address for the DNS server during scope creation. *Read "Creating DHCP Scopes."*

3 *C. Select the Server in the console and then choose Action⇨New Scope.* You create new scopes by selecting the desired server in the console and then launching the New Scope wizard from the Action menu. You can also right-click the server and then choose New Scope to launch the wizard. *Review "Creating DHCP Scopes."*

4 *B. The administrator did not configure a standard DHCP scope.* DHCP and MADCAP work together, but DHCP servers must be configured to lease IP addresses to network clients. Clients cannot obtain a multicast IP address without a typical IP address appropriate for the subnet. *See "Creating DHCP Scopes."*

5 *D. Refresh the server.* After authorizing the server with the Active Directory, you should wait a few moments and then refresh the server to see if it has been authorized. You can use the Action menu to refresh the server, or simply press F5. *Study "Authorizing the DHCP Server."*

6 *Click the Automatically Update DHCP Client Information in DNS check box and then click the Update DNS Only if DHCP Client Requests radio button. Then, click the Enable Updates for DNS Clients That Do not Support Dynamic Update check box. Apply the changes.* DHCP can automatically update Dynamic DNS when client IP addresses change due to lease expiration. To support down-level clients, the DHCP server can also perform the update for those clients. *Study "Managing Servers and Scopes."*

7 *C. Server Properties, Advanced tab.* DHCP can perform conflict detection before leasing an IP address to clients. You configure this option by accessing the Server's properties in the DHCP console and then entering an attempt number on the Advanced tab. *Study "Managing Servers and Scopes."*

8 *C. Scope Options, General tab.* You can enable a DHCP scope to provide a variety of information to DHCP clients. To have the scope return the IP address of an SMTP server, access the General tab in the Scope Options, select SMTP Server from the option list, and then enter the name and IP address for the server(s). *Study "Managing Servers and Scopes."*

9 *Click the User Class drop-down menu, select Default Routing and Remote Access Class, select 003 Router in the Available Options window, and then define the router's IP address.* DHCP enables you to define certain options for different user classes, such as Windows 2000, Windows 98, and RAS. When you select a class, you can make your option selection in the list and then configure it as needed. *Study "Managing Servers and Scopes."*

10 *D. ARP.* Windows 2000 and Windows 98 clients can autoconfigure an IP address when a DHCP server is not available. To ensure that the IP address autoconfigured is unique on the network, the client performs a gratuitous ARP to check other IP addresses. *Study "Enabling DHCP Clients."*

Chapter 6

Installing and Configuring WINS

● ●

Exam Objectives

▶ Installing and configuring network services

▶ Installing and configuring network services for interoperability

● ●

*W*indows Internet Name Service (WINS) is a server service that resolves NetBIOS names to IP addresses. WINS functionality enables you to assign a friendly name to a computer — for example, Computer12 — instead of an IP address, such as 131.107.2.200.

You do not need WINS in a pure Windows 2000 environment, because Windows 2000 computers use DNS for name resolution. For down-level compatibility in mixed environments, however, Windows 2000 provides WINS.

The exam expects you to know how to install and configure WINS on a Windows 2000 server, as well as how to manage its operations. However, because Windows 2000 provides WINS strictly for backward compatibility, you will not see many exam questions about WINS. This chapter reviews the following WINS issues, which you can expect to see on the exam:

✔ Installing WINS

✔ Configuring the WINS server

✔ Managing the WINS database

✔ Managing active registrations

✔ Managing replication partners

Quick Assessment

Installing and configuring network services

1 WINS resolves _____ names to IP addresses.

2 Windows 2000 computers use _____ for name resolution.

3 You do not need WINS in pure _____ networks.

4 By default, Windows 2000 updates WINS server statistics every _____ minutes.

5 The _____ is the amount of time that passes between marking a record as released and marking it as extinct.

Installing and configuring network services for interoperability

6 The _____ is the amount of time that passes between marking a WINS record as extinct and actually deleting that record from the database.

7 WINS servers use _____ to manage heavy loads of name registrations and renewal traffic.

8 The removal of old records from the WINS database is called _____.

9 WINS enables you to import _____ files.

10 A(n) _____ replication occurs when a WINS server informs other WINS servers of changes that have taken place in the database.

Answers

1 *NetBIOS.* Review "What Is WINS?"

2 *DNS.* Study "What Is WINS?"

3 *Windows 2000.* See "What Is WINS?"

4 *5.* Examine "Configuring the WINS Server."

5 *Extinction Interval.* Review "Configuring the WINS Server."

6 *Timeout.* See "Configuring the WINS Server."

7 *Burst Handling.* Read "Configuring the WINS Server."

8 *Scavenging.* Study "Managing the WINS Database."

9 *LMHOSTS.* See "Managing Active Registrations."

10 *Push.* See "Managing Replication."

What Is WINS?

Windows Internet Name Service (WINS) is a server service that resolves NetBIOS names to IP addresses. NetBIOS enables computers to have friendly names, such as Computer5 or Wkst45. In a TCP/IP network, however, communication occurs between network clients via IP address — not by NetBIOS name. In order for a client computer to contact another client computer, the network must have some means for resolving NetBIOS names to IP addresses and thus enable communication to occur. A WINS server provides this service by maintaining a database with NetBIOS-to-IP-address mappings. Client computers can query a WINS server for name resolution so they can discover the IP address of another network computer. This entire process is invisible to network users, who simply establish communication with a computer by its NetBIOS name.

Windows 2000 provides WINS for backward compatibility. In a pure Windows 2000 network where all servers and clients run Windows 2000 operating systems, you do not need WINS because Windows 2000 computers use DNS for name resolution. However, most environments contain a mix of Windows 2000 computers and down-level Windows computers (NT and 9*x*). In those mixed environments, you need WINS. For the exam, you need to know how to install and configure WINS on a Windows 2000 member server.

Who can be WINS clients?

Computers running any of the following systems can function as WINS clients:

- Windows 2000
- Windows 95 or 98
- Windows NT 3.5 or later
- Windows for Workgroups 3.11 running TCP/IP-32
- Microsoft Network Client 3.0 for MS-DOS with real-mode TCP/IP driver
- LAN Manager 2.2c for MS-DOS

How does WINS work?

WINS servers maintain a database of name-to-IP-address mappings. When a WINS client starts, it registers its name and IP address with the WINS server, which adds the client to the database. If this information changes, such as in the case of a new DHCP IP lease, the client updates its information with the WINS server. If a client needs to communicate with another WINS client, it queries the WINS server for the name-to-IP-address resolution. The WINS server checks its database and returns this information to the client.

Like DHCP, WINS records are temporary, so the WINS client must renew its registration with the WINS server when the registration expires. Whenever a WINS client shuts down, it sends a name-release request to the WINS server so the WINS server always has the latest browse list.

Installing WINS

As with other networking components in Windows 2000 Server, you can install WINS in either of two ways:

- ✔ Using Add/Remove Programs in Control Panel.
- ✔ Using the Configure Your Server tool, which you access by clicking Start⇨Programs⇨Administrative Tools⇨Configure Your Server.

In the Configure Your Server tool, expand the Networking link and then click WINS to start the installation. See Chapter 2 for step-by-step instructions to install server services.

Both Windows 2000 domain controllers and Windows 2000 member servers can be WINS servers. You can also use Windows NT 4.0 servers.

Configuring the WINS Server

After you install WINS, you can access the WINS Manager, which is an MMC snap-in, by clicking Start⇨Programs⇨Administrative Tools⇨WINS. As you can see in Figure 6-1, the tree pane in the WINS Manager console presents you with a WINS icon, a server status icon, and an icon for your WINS server. The tree pane in Figure 6-1 includes an icon for a WINS server named CORPSRV.

To add other WINS servers to the console, click the WINS icon in the tree pane and then choose Action⇨Add Server. This feature is very useful to WINS administrators because you can load all WINS servers into one console and manage them all from one location without having to physically visit each machine.

By clicking the Server Status icon, you can find out whether the server is running and when the last update occurred. By default, the server's status is updated every 5 minutes.

You perform most of your WINS configuration work with the server icon in the tree pane. If you click the server icon in the console's tree pane, it expands to show you containers for Active Registrations and Replication Partners.

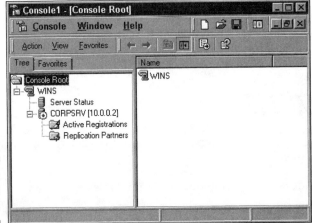

If you select your server and then click the Action menu, you see several actions that you can perform concerning the WINS database. I explain these actions in the section "Managing the WINS Database," later in this chapter. In this section, I give you a look at the server properties and what you can configure.

Select the icon for your WINS server in the console's tree pane and then choose Action⇨Properties. The WINS Manager displays a Properties dialog box with four tabs — General, Intervals, Database Verification, and Advanced.

On the General tab, you can adjust the statistical update in terms of hours, minutes, and seconds. The default is every 5 minutes, and in most cases, the default interval is all you need.

If you decrease the default interval, you increase the number of server refreshes that must take place, and an interval that is too short may cause performance problems with your server. If the interval is too long, your statistical data will be outdated. Unless you have a specific reason for changing the refresh time, the 5-minute default is the best setting.

You can also use the General tab to browse for a default backup path, and you can choose to back up your server database during shutdown.

Although it's a good practice, backing up your database every time the server shuts down does increase the amount of shutdown time required.

On the Intervals tab, you can set the rate at which records are renewed, deleted, and verified. Each of these options has a default setting, and the WINS server does a good job of managing its default settings. Figure 6-2 shows the Intervals tab.

![Screenshot of XPROD23 [10.0.0.1] Properties dialog, Intervals tab. "Set the rate at which records are renewed, deleted, and verified." Columns: Days, Hours, Minutes. Renew interval: 6, 0, 0. Extinction interval: 4, 0, 0. Extinction timeout: 6, 0, 0. Verification interval: 24, 0, 0. Restore Defaults button. OK, Cancel, Apply.]

Figure 6-2:
Intervals settings for a WINS server.

For the exam, you need to know what each interval means and the default rate setting. To make this easy for you, I put this information in Table 6-1 so you can quickly memorize it.

Table 6-1	Default Record Intervals	
Interval	*What It Means*	*Default Setting*
Renewal	How often a client renews its name registrations	6 days
Extinction	For replication, the amount of time between marking a record as released and marking it as extinct	4 days
Timeout	The amount of time between marking a record as extinct and actually deleting it from the database	6 days
Verification	The time after which the server verifies active records	24 days

On the Database Verification tab, you can set an interval to control when the WINS server performs database verification. This setting coincides with the Verification setting on the Intervals tab. By default, the WINS server verifies the database every 24 hours. You can use this tab to set the verification time, if desired, and the maximum number of records that the server verifies after each period. Verification can be performed against owner servers, which are the servers that own particular records, or against randomly selected partners.

The Advanced tab enables you to set two major configuration options. First, you can choose to log WINS events to the Windows event log.

This option is not selected by default, and you should only use this option when you need to troubleshoot WINS problems. The detailed logging of events can seriously degrade the WINS server's performance.

Also on the Advanced tab, you can enable *burst handling*. Burst handling is a method to manage high loads of WINS registration and renewal traffic — in other words, the WINS server must manage a sudden burst of activity. If you enable burst handling, the WINS server uses a burst queue size as a threshold value. When the burst exceeds the threshold, burst handling goes into effect. The server begins answering requests with an immediate positive response, but assigns a 5-minute TTL (Time to Live). This buys the server time so it can catch up before the TTLs expire, and registration and renewal traffic continues. You have four options for configuring the size of the burst queue:

- ✔ **Low:** 300 name refresh and registration requests for the burst threshold
- ✔ **Medium:** 500 name refresh and registration requests for the burst threshold
- ✔ **High:** 1,000 name refresh and registration requests for the burst threshold
- ✔ **Custom:** Enables you to assign the value for the burst threshold

By default, burst handling is in effect and set to Medium. If you have a slower server, you may want to change the setting to Low, and if you change the server setting to High or Custom, make certain your server has the processing power to handle the job.

You may see a question or two about burst handling on the exam, and you should remember the default setting of medium (500 burst queue threshold) as the optimal selection.

Managing the WINS Database

A WINS server stores WINS name-to-IP-address records in the WINS database. When a client computer queries the WINS server for a name-to-IP-address resolution, the WINS server queries the database to service the request. WINS maintains its database automatically in Windows 2000, but you can perform several actions to ensure that the WINS database operates at peak efficiency.

The test questions you can expect concerning management of the WINS database involve actions that you perform by selecting the WINS server in the console and then clicking options in the Action menu. You should know these actions for the exam:

- ✔ **Scavenge Database:** As with all databases, information in the WINS database can become outdated over time. To remove outdated information, a process called *scavenging* occurs. The WINS database automatically performs scavenging on a periodic basis, but if you believe the WINS database to be outdated due to an excessive number of failed queries, you can manually scavenge the database by choosing Action⇨Scavenge Database.

- ✔ **Verify Database Consistency:** The Action menu includes an option that enables you to verify database consistency. This check makes certain that the WINS server is consistent with other WINS server databases. By default, the WINS server checks database consistency every 24 hours (which you can change on the Database Verification tab of the server's Properties dialog box), but you can run verification at any time by choosing Action⇨Verify Database Consistency. However, Database Consistency verification is a CPU- and network-intensive task, and you should run it only during nonpeak hours. Running the consistency check during peak hours may degrade WINS server performance and increases network traffic.

- ✔ **Verify Version ID Consistency:** Choosing Action⇨Verify Version ID Consistency retrieves owner-version maps from WINS servers on your network and then checks the database consistency by ensuring that the WINS server has the highest version number among network servers for records it owns. This test ensures that all WINS servers have the latest information by running the ID check. The operation can take some time and is best run during off-peak hours.

- ✔ **Back Up Database:** You can manually back up the WINS database by choosing Action⇨Back Up Database. When you select this action, you are prompted for a location to store the database. You can also configure a default backup path on the General tab of the server's Properties dialog box.

Managing Active Registrations

If you expand the WINS server in the tree pane of the WINS Manager console, you see containers for Active Registrations and Replication Partners. The Active Registrations container holds the current WINS name-to-IP-address registrations. If you select the container and then click the Action menu, you can choose commands that enable you to find records either by name or by owner.

You can also create a *static mapping*. A static mapping is a *static* name-to-IP-address registration. In other words, it does not change, and the mapping remains constant in the WINS database. You use static mappings for clients that cannot dynamically update their WINS records. Static mappings replicate throughout the WINS environment, overwriting any conflicting dynamic WINS records. If you choose Action⊃New Static Mapping, the WINS Manager displays a dialog box in which you can enter the computer name, the type of NetBIOS name, and the IP address.

Typically, you should leave the box for entering a NetBIOS scope blank. You use this optional setting if you have NetBIOS scopes configured for your environment.

The Action menu also has a command that enables you to import an LMHOSTS file. An LMHOSTS file is a static file used to map names to IP addresses. The use of LMHOSTS files has been widely replaced by WINS, but if you have an LMHOSTS file, you can use this feature to import it into the database by choosing Action⊃Import LMHOSTS File.

Finally, the Action menu includes a command for verifying name records. By choosing Action⊃Verify Name Records, you can verify name records on a file-by-file basis or a server-by-server basis. When you choose this command, WINS Manager displays a dialog box in which you can enter the desired verification information and check the database or servers for those records.

Managing Replication

WINS servers share their database information with other WINS servers on your network through *replication*. The replication process updates each WINS server so they all hold current, accurate name-to-IP-address information for network clients.

You configure replication by using the Replication Partners container under the desired server in the tree pane of the WINS Manager console. To create a new replication partner for the server, select Replication Partners and then choose Action⊃New Replication Partner.

Typically, WINS replication occurs through partnering with other WINS servers. This feature ensures that all servers are linked together and that replication between them takes place. After you choose Action⊃New Replication Partner, you can select the replication partner by entering either the name or the IP address of the WINS server.

You can also access the replication properties for the server by choosing Action➪Properties. The Properties dialog box has four tabs, and the exam expects you to know what you can configure on each tab. To prepare for the exam, spend some time on your server configuring the settings on these tabs:

✔ **General:** On the General tab, you have two check boxes: Replicate Only With Partners and Overwrite Unique Static Mappings At This Server. By default, the Replicate Only With Partners check box is selected.

✔ **Push Replication:** The Push Replication tab enables you to configure push replications to occur when the service starts or when an address changes in the database. *Push replication* enables the server to push the changes by informing replication partners that changes have occurred. When partners receive a push from the server, they can then pull the replication data from the server.

✔ **Pull Replication:** This tab enables you to set the schedule for pull replications to occur. The default time is every 30 minutes.

✔ **Advanced:** The Advanced tab enables you to configure two items. First, you can create a list of servers where records are blocked from replicating to your server. This, in effect, stops replication from occurring to your server from the servers you select. This feature is often used to block records from decommissioned servers that are still being replicated (and are outdated). You can also use the Advanced tab to enable automatic partner configuration. This feature enables WINS servers to automatically configure their own partners through multicasting. This technology is designed for small networks and should not be used in enterprise environments.

Rather than use the Replication Partners container, you can select the server in the console tree and then use commands in the Action menu to manually start push or pull replication. Typically, however, you do not need to do this because WINS handles replication by its scheduled replication time.

Prep Test

1 In a pure Windows 2000 network, a system administrator implements WINS on several member servers. What mistake has the administrator made?

A ○ Windows 2000 computers cannot be WINS clients.

B ○ DNS does not allow WINS to interoperate.

C ○ At least one domain controller must be a WINS server.

D ○ WINS is not necessary in a pure Windows 2000 network.

2 You are having problems with a particular WINS server. It seems that extinct records are not being deleted from the database in a timely manner. You check the Intervals tab on the Server's properties. Which setting is incorrect?

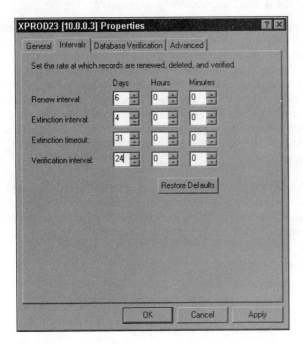

3 Where can you set up automatic database consistency verification?

A ○ Server Properties, Intervals tab
B ○ Server Properties, Database Verification tab
C ○ Replication Properties, Database Verification tab
D ○ Registration Properties, Database Verification tab

4 You want to check owner-version maps on a WINS server in your network to ensure that it has the highest version number among WINS servers in your network. How can you manually perform this action?

A ○ Select the desired server in the console and then choose Action⇨Verify Version ID Consistency.
B ○ Select the desired server in the console and then choose Action⇨Verify Database Consistency.
C ○ Select the desired server in the console, select Replication Partners, and then choose Action⇨Verify Version ID Consistency.
D ○ Select the desired server in the console, select Replication Partners, and then choose Action⇨Verify Database Consistency.

5 A particular WINS server cannot seem to keep up with the number of name registration requests. The server's processing power is optimal for the operation. What should you do?

A ○ Add more RAM.
B ○ Enable push replication.
C ○ Enable burst handling.
D ○ Run a database consistency check.

6 You want to manually remove old records from the WINS database on a particular server. After selecting the server in the WINS Manager, what do you need to do next?

A ○ Choose Action⇨Scavenge Database.
B ○ Choose Action⇨Verify Database Consistency.
C ○ Choose Action⇨Verify Version ID Consistency.
D ○ This operation cannot be performed manually.

7 On a particular WINS server, you want burst handling to go into effect at a threshold of 300 name registrations and renewal requests. How can you configure this setting on the Advanced tab?

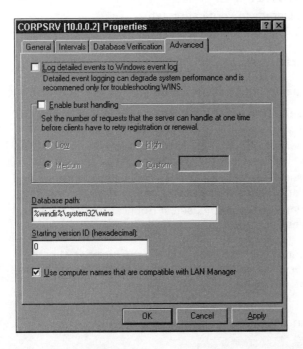

8 You want to create a static mapping in the WINS database. Which setting is optional in the New Static Mapping dialog box?

A ○ Computer Name

B ○ NetBIOS Scope

C ○ Type

D ○ IP Address

9 Replication between a particular WINS server and its partner does not seem to be occurring in a timely manner. You believe the problem is in the Pull Replication settings for the server. You access the Pull Replication tab to check the settings. What do you need to change?

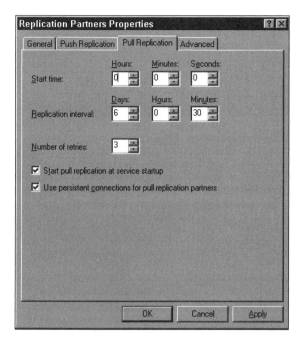

10 You have a small network with only four WINS servers. How can you enable the WINS servers to automatically configure partner replication among themselves?

A ○ Enable Automatic Partner Configuration on the General Replication Partners Properties tab.

B ○ Enable Automatic Partner Configuration on the General Server Properties tab.

C ○ Enable Automatic Partner Configuration on the Advanced Server tab.

D ○ Enable Automatic Partner Configuration on the Advanced Replication Partners Properties tab.

Answers

1 D. WINS is not necessary in a pure Windows 2000 network. Although Windows 2000 clients can be WINS clients in mixed networks, WINS is not necessary in pure Windows 2000 networks because Windows 2000 computers use DNS for name resolution. *Review "What Is WINS?"*

2 *The Extinction Timeout value is too high.* Extinction timeout is the amount of time between marking a WINS record as extinct and actually deleting it from the database. A value of 31 days leaves the records in the database for too long — the default setting is 6. *Read "Configuring the WINS Server."*

3 B. Server Properties, Database Verification tab. You can enable automatic database verification by clicking the check box on the Database Verification tab and entering a time value (the default is every 24 hours). *Review "Configuring the WINS Server."*

4 A. Select the desired server in the console and then choose Action⇨Verify Version ID Consistency. Use the Verify Version ID Consistency check on the server you want to verify for correct version ID. *See "Configuring the WINS Server."*

5 C. Enable Burst Handling. Burst handling enables the WINS server to handle sudden bursts of name registration and renewal requests. The Burst Queue sets a threshold of requests that must be met before burst handling takes effect. *Study "Configuring the WINS Server."*

6 A. Choose Action⇨Scavenge Database. Database scavenging removes old WINS records and is performed automatically by the server. However, you can manually perform this action by choosing the appropriate command in the Action menu. *Study "Configuring the WINS Server."*

7 *Enable Burst Handling, and then click the Low radio button.* You can set levels for burst handling that define the threshold of name registration and renewal requests that occur before burst handling takes effect. The Low setting equals 300; Medium equals 500; High equals 1,000; and you can set a custom value. *Study "Configuring the WINS Server."*

8 B. NetBIOS Scope. The NetBIOS Scope setting is provided for environments that use scopes to define NetBIOS groupings. This setting is optional and normally should be left blank. *Study "Managing Active Registrations."*

9 *The replication interval is too high. The default setting is every 30 minutes.* Pull Replication occurs by default every 30 minutes. A setting of 6 days is too long to keep WINS database records accurate. *Study "Managing Replication."*

10 D. Enable Automatic Partner Configuration on the Advanced Replication Partners Properties tab. In small networks, WINS server can automatically configure partner replication through multicasting. Use the Advanced Replication Partners Properties tab to enable it. *Study "Managing Replication."*

Chapter 7

Installing and Configuring DNS

● ●

Exam Objectives

▶ Installing and configuring network services

▶ Installing and configuring network services for interoperability

● ●

*D*omain Name System (DNS) resolves host names, such as
www.microsoft.com, to IP addresses. By resolving host names to IP
addresses, DNS enables communication between computers on a TCP/IP network. DNS is the most widely used name-resolution method. Every time you
use the Internet, you use DNS. Windows 2000 networks are fully integrated
with DNS, and Windows 2000 computers use DNS for name-to-IP-address resolution instead of WINS.

Because Windows 2000 is integrated with DNS, you can expect to see some
exam questions about using a member server as a DNS server. To help you
prepare for those questions, this chapter reviews the following DNS-related
topics:

    ✔ Installing and configuring DNS

    ✔ Managing the DNS server

    ✔ Managing zones

Quick Assessment

Installing and configuring network services

1   Windows 2000 supports _____ so that DNS records can be dynamically updated.

2   Zone database replication occurs between the primary and secondary zone servers through a process called _____.

3   A discrete and contiguous area of a DNS namespace is called a(n) _____.

4   The three zone types available are _____, primary, and secondary.

5   To configure a DNS server to send unresolved queries to another DNS server, you use the _____ tab in the DNS server's Properties dialog box.

Installing and configuring network services for interoperability

6   _____ name checking strictly enforces RFC-compliant rules for all DNS names.

7   DNS logging is written to the _____ file.

8   The process of removing old DNS records from the database is called _____.

9   A(n) _____ resource record enables a host to have an alias name.

10 You can use _____ to resolve host names to IP addresses that do not appear in the DNS database.

Answers

1 *DDNS.* Read "Reviewing DNS Concepts."

2 *Zone Transfer.* Study "Reviewing DNS Concepts."

3 *Zone.* See "Reviewing DNS Concepts."

4 *Active Directory Integrated.* Examine "Setting Up DNS."

5 *Forwarders.* Review "Managing the DNS Server."

6 *Strict RFC.* See "Managing the DNS Server."

7 *DNS.LOG.* Read "Managing the DNS Server."

8 *Scavenging.* Study "Managing the server's database."

9 *CNAME.* See "Managing Zone Resource Records."

10 *WINS.* See "Managing Zone Properties."

Reviewing DNS Concepts

Windows 2000 offers complete integration with the Domain Name System (DNS) — the industry standard for resolving host names to IP addresses. DNS is very *extensible*. In other words, as your organization grows, your network's DNS-based naming structure, or *namespace,* can grow accordingly — with virtually no limits.

Because DNS is fully integrated with Windows 2000, a domain, such as www.microsoft.com, can also be the name of a local network. For example, KarenS@tritondev.com is an e-mail address, and it can be a user name in a Windows 2000 network. Windows 2000 networking with the Active Directory is based on DNS, and all Active Directory names are DNS names. This approach provides a global naming system so that the local network has the same naming structure as the Internet. In short, you can't separate Windows 2000 and DNS.

The exam expects you to understand basic DNS concepts and the use of a Windows 2000 member server as a DNS server. The following sections offer a quick review of DNS concepts. If your DNS knowledge is up to par, you can skip these sections. Subsequent sections in this chapter cover the installation, configuration, and management of a DNS server.

Understanding the DNS namespace

In order to understand DNS, you need to understand the DNS namespace. A *namespace* is an area that can be resolved. A postal address on a letter uses a namespace that contains a ZIP code, state, city, street address, and name. Because all letters follow this namespace, your mail reaches only you, out of the millions of possible addressees. (Well, most of your mail reaches you.)

To resolve the namespace used on a piece of mail, you start by examining the ZIP code, then the state, and then the city. This process narrows the resolution to one geographical area. Next, you resolve the address by narrowing it to one street and one street number. The final portion of the resolution process is your name.

This system works because all mail follows this namespace. If letter writers put whatever information they wanted on the envelope, your mail would probably never reach you. A namespace, then, is an area that can be resolved.

DNS functions in the same manner. Because host names follow a namespace, they can be resolved to IP addresses. For example, www.microsoft.com is a host name that represents an IP address. Because computers must have an IP address to communicate, the host name must be resolved to an IP address.

To resolve a host name to an IP address, DNS starts by considering the root domain, which is represented by a period (.). Next, the address is read, beginning with the top-level domain, such as com, edu, mil, gov, org, or net. For example, microsoft.com is a part of the com first-level domain, so at this point in the resolution process, all other first-level domains are excluded.

Next, the second-level domain is usually a "friendly" name of a company, organization, or person. Microsoft is an original, unique, friendly, name, so it is resolved next. At this point, a particular server or group of servers, called *third-level domains,* can be resolved. For example, sales.microsoft.com may point to a particular server.

Using this method, any DNS name can be resolved to the host computer so its IP address can be retrieved. The name-resolution process on the Internet usually requires numerous domain servers. For example, com servers would be used to resolve Microsoft, and so on. Figure 7-1 shows a graphical example of the resolution process for servera.sales.tritondev.com.

Understanding DNS zones

The DNS name-resolution process uses DNS database files. Different servers in a network hold portions of the DNS database file so that name resolution can occur. In small networks, a DNS server may even hold the entire name-to-IP-address database file. When a DNS server is queried for name resolution, it checks its database file to determine whether it has an entry for the query. If not, the DNS server can forward the request to another DNS server.

To subdivide DNS duties and administrative control, DNS zones are often used in DNS networks. A *zone* is a discrete, contiguous portion of the DNS namespace. For example, sales.tritondev.com and acct.tritondev.com could be DNS zones. Servers in the sales zone hold all DNS records for that zone, while DNS servers in the acct zone hold all records for the acct zone. This feature enables different administrators to manage DNS servers in different portions of the namespace. By using the zone feature, you can partition the DNS namespace to make it more manageable.

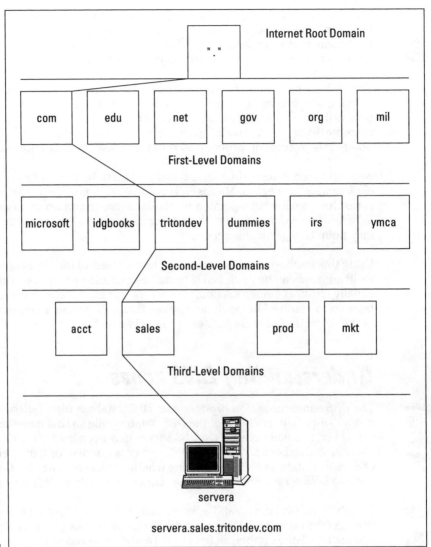

Figure 7-1:
The DNS namespace resolution process.

Within a zone, you have two kinds of DNS database files: primary and secondary. As shown in Figure 7-2, one server in the zone contains the *primary zone database file*, and all other DNS servers in the zone contain copies of that primary database file called *secondary zone database files.*

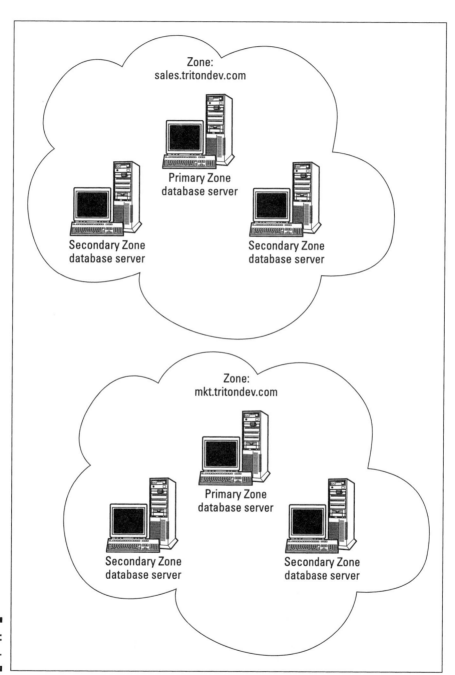

Figure 7-2:
DNS zones.

Only the primary zone database file can have updates or changes made to it. A process called *zone transfer* replicates any changes made to the primary zone database file to the secondary zone database files. The server that holds the primary zone database file is called an *authoritative server* because it has authority over the other DNS servers in the zone. Secondary database file servers in the zone are used to reduce the traffic and query load on the primary zone database server.

Windows 2000 DNS is Dynamic DNS (DDNS). In previous versions of Windows, DNS database files were *static* — an administrator had to change them manually. In Windows 2000, DNS can dynamically update its database when host-name-to-IP-address changes occur.

Installing DNS

You install DNS just as you would any other Windows 2000 server service. You can install DNS by using either the Configure Your Server tool in Administrative Tools or Add/Remove Programs in Control Panel. Chapter 2 describes the steps for installing services on a Windows 2000 server.

DNS is automatically installed on domain controllers because DNS must be present for the Active Directory. It is not automatically installed on member servers, however. Keep this point in mind for tricky exam questions.

Setting Up DNS

After you install DNS, it is not operational until you set up the service. Fortunately, Windows 2000 Server provides a handy wizard to help you configure your DNS server for the role you want it to play in your DNS network.

Lab 7-1 walks you through the steps for using the Configure DNS Server wizard. For the exam, you need to know the options that the wizard presents, so make certain you practice configuring DNS using Lab 7-1.

Lab 7-1	Setting Up DNS

1. **Click Start⇨Programs⇨Administrative Tools⇨DNS.**

2. **In the console's tree pane, select your DNS server and then choose Action⇨Configure the Server.**

   The Configure DNS Server wizard displays its welcome screen.

3. **Click Next.**

   The system collects setup information.

   The wizard displays the Root Server dialog box. In a DNS network, you must have a root server.

4. **If this is the first DNS server on your network, click the Create a Root Server radio button. If you already have other DNS servers running, click the Additional Server radio button and enter an IP address.**

   If you choose to create a root server, the wizard prompts you to create a forward lookup zone. A *forward lookup zone* is a name-to-IP-address database that helps computers resolve names to IP addresses. It also contains information about network services.

5. **Specify whether you want to create the forward lookup zone now by clicking either Yes or No.**

   As shown in Figure 7-3, the Zone Type dialog box gives you options for creating either an Active Directory-integrated zone, a standard primary zone, or a standard secondary zone. In pure Active Directory environments, you should select the Active Directory-Integrated option so that all zone and database data is stored in the Active Directory. Selecting the Standard Primary option creates a new zone where the database is stored locally, and selecting the Standard Secondary option enables your server to become a secondary server in an existing zone.

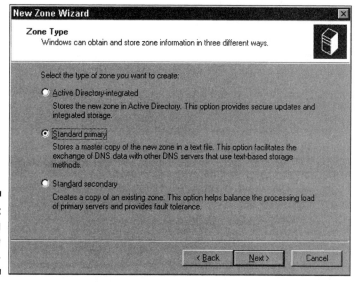

Figure 7-3:
Selecting
the zone
type.

6. **Select the type of zone you want to create and then click Next.**

7. **In the Zone Name dialog box, enter the name of the zone and click Next.**

   In the resulting Zone File dialog box, you can choose to create a new zone database file or use one that you have copied from another computer.

8. **Make your selection by clicking the appropriate radio button and then click Next.**

   The wizard prompts you to create a reverse lookup zone. A *reverse lookup zone* enables a computer to resolve IP addresses to DNS names. (Normally, DNS names are resolved to IP addresses.) You can choose to provide this capability now, or you can create a reverse lookup zone later.

9. **Indicate whether you want to create a reverse lookup zone and click Next.**

   If you choose to create a reverse lookup zone, the wizard displays the Zone Type dialog box. Otherwise, the wizard displays a summary dialog box.

10. **Review your selections and click Finish.**

Managing the DNS Server

After you install and configure DNS (see the previous sections in this chapter), you must manage the server so it performs in the desired manner. The exam expects you to know how to perform several DNS server-management tasks, so this section points out those issues and shows you how to manage the DNS server.

Configuring server properties

To access the Properties dialog box that you use for configuring your DNS server, select your DNS server in the DNS Manager console's tree pane and then choose Action⇨Properties. You have numerous configuration options on the seven tabs in the Properties dialog box, and you need to know about several of these for the exam.

On the Interfaces tab, you can specify the IP addresses for which your DNS server answers DNS queries. With the default setting, your server listens to all IP addresses. However, you can select the Only The Following IP Addresses radio button and then enter the desired IP addresses. This feature is useful if you want your DNS server to service only a select group of computers.

On the Forwarders tab, you can click the check box to enable forwarders. Forwarders enable your DNS server to forward unresolved queries to other DNS servers that you specify on this tab. If your server is the root server, this option is not available because your server is already at the top of the hierarchy.

The Advanced tab, shown in Figure 7-4, offers several server options, which you can select by clicking the appropriate check boxes.

By default, the BIND Secondaries, Enable Round Robin, and Enable Netmask Ordering options are selected. You can also disable recursion, which prevents a DNS server from carrying the full responsibility for name-to-IP-address resolution (allows forwarding). You can choose to fail if the DNS server detects bad zone data when attempting to load, and you can use a cache method that prevents pollution from occurring.

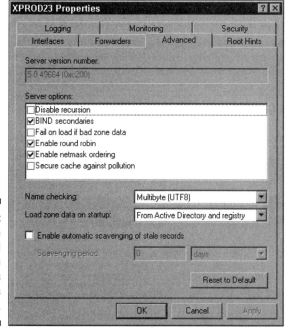

Figure 7-4:
The Advanced tab of the server's Properties dialog box.

For the Name Checking option on the Advanced tab, you can select the following methods, which you should remember for the exam:

- ✔ **Strict RFC:** Strictly enforces the use of RFC-compliant rules for all DNS names. Non-RFC names are treated as errors.

- ✔ **Non RFC:** Any names can be used, including names that are not RFC-compliant.

- ✔ **Multibyte:** Uses the Unicode 8-bit translation encoding scheme.

- ✔ **All Names:** Allows all names to be used with the DNS server.

You also can specify how you want the DNS server to load zone data at startup. Depending on your network configuration, you can make the appropriate selection from the following options:

- ✔ From the Active Directory and the registry

- ✔ From the registry

- ✔ From the file \WINNT\System32\BOOT.DNS.

You can also use the Advanced tab to enable automatic scavenging of stale records. This feature enables the server to automatically clean old records out of the database at an interval you select on the Advanced tab. The default automatic scavenge interval is every seven days.

The Root Hints tab specifies other DNS servers and IP addresses that your DNS server can use for query resolution. On the Root Hints tab, you can enter the names and IP addresses of other DNS servers that your server can contact for name resolution, or you can edit and remove them, as necessary. This feature helps an authoritative zone server to find servers above it in the hierarchy.

As shown in Figure 7-5, the Logging tab gives you the option to log various events, such as query, notify, and update.

You use the logging feature to specify the kind of DNS activity you want written to DNS.LOG, which the system stores in %SystemRoot%\System32\DNS. This feature is useful for troubleshooting purposes.

However, you should only enable logging for monitoring particular problems or events. This feature consumes lots of disk space, and you may see performance problems on the server, so use logging of DNS events for troubleshooting only.

Finally, you have Monitoring and Security tabs. On the Monitoring tab, you can perform simple DNS tests against your server so you can verify its configuration. Like all other Security tabs in Windows 2000 Server, this one has options that enable you to configure who can access and configure the DNS service on this server.

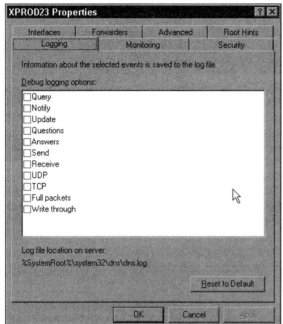

Managing the server's database

In addition to configuring the server's properties (see the preceding section of this chapter), you can manually manage the server's DNS database and perform a few other actions by selecting the server in the DNS Manager console's tree pane and then clicking options in the console's Action menu.

For the exam, you need to know the following options, which you find on the DNS Manager console's Action menu:

✔ **New Zone:** This action launches the New Zone wizard, which you also see during the initial server configuration. You can use this feature to configure new zones as needed.

✔ **Set Aging/Scavenging For All Zones:** This command displays the Server Aging/Scavenging Properties dialog box, shown in Figure 7-6, where you configure the scavenging of stale resource records. *Scavenging* is a server task that cleans old records out of the DNS database. You can configure the no-refresh and refresh intervals (both of which are 7 days by default). The no-refresh interval is the time between the most recent refresh of a record timestamp and the moment when the timestamp may be refreshed again. The refresh interval is the time between the earliest moment when a record timestamp can be refreshed and when it can be scavenged.

✔ **Scavenge Stale Resource Records:** This action enables you to manually scavenge the database. You do not need to perform this action because the database scavenges itself every 7 days by default, but you can use it if you believe the database has old records that need to be cleaned.

✔ **Update Server Data Files:** Normally, a DNS server updates data files at predefined intervals and when the server shuts down. You can manually force the action by choosing Action⇨Update Server Data Files, which causes the DNS server to write all changes to the zone data files immediately.

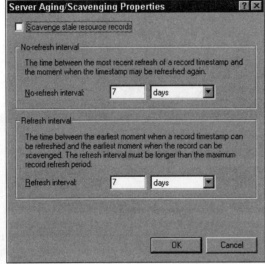

Figure 7-6:
Use this
Server
Aging/
Scavenging
Properties
to configure
scavenging.

Managing Zone Resource Records

Each zone database file may contain any number of resource records. A *resource record* is simply an entry in the database — a record that helps the DNS server resolve queries.

When a new zone is created, two default resource records are automatically created. The first is the Start of Authority (SOA), which defines the authoritative server for the zone. The second is the Name Server (NS) record, which lists all DNS servers operating in the zone. Keep these in mind for the exam.

In addition to the SOA and NS records, you can create several other records. To create these records, simply expand the DNS server in the tree pane, select the appropriate zone, click the Action menu, and choose the kind of record you want to create from the list that appears.

Table 7-1 explains the major resource records that you can create. You need to memorize them for the exam.

Table 7-1	Zone Resource Records
Resource Record	*What It Does*
Host (A)	Provides a host-to-IP-address mapping for a forward lookup zone.
Pointer (PTR)	Created with an A record, it points to another portion of the namespace where you can map an IP address to a host name.
Alias (CNAME)	Enables a host to have a different name. CNAME records are often used for load-balancing purposes, and each CNAME record contains a host's alias as well as the fully qualified domain name. CNAME records can be used to group DNS servers so they appear as one server.
Mail Exchanger (MX)	Identifies a mail server with a particular host or domain.

In addition to these standard resource records, you can also create specific records for your environment by choosing Action⇨Other New Records. When you choose this command, the console displays a list of possible records that you can create, and you can even create custom records.

You do not need to know all about these other records for the exam, but you should remember that the option exists.

Managing Zone Properties

To access the Properties dialog box for a zone, expand the zone in the DNS Manager's tree pane, select the desired zone, and then choose Action⇨Properties. You need to know the configuration options available on each tab in the Properties dialog box, so study this section carefully.

The General tab lists the status of the zone (such as running or paused) and the type of zone (primary, secondary, and so on) If you click Change, you see the Zone Type dialog box, which you also use in the Create New Zone wizard. You can change the zone type to either Active Directory-integrated, primary, or secondary, as necessary.

The General tab also includes a drop-down list that enables you to specify whether you want to allow dynamic updates. An important feature in Windows 2000 is dynamic DNS (DDNS), which allows the server to dynamically update records within a zone when they change (such as DHCP IP address lease changes). You should enable this feature so dynamic updates can occur.

The SOA and NS tabs provide the resource records for the start of authority and name server records. These are configured automatically when you create a new zone, but you can make changes as needed using these two tabs.

The WINS tab enables you to use WINS to resolve name-to-IP-address mappings that DNS cannot resolve. This feature is useful in networks that contain down-level clients and servers (such as Windows NT and 9x). Typically, you do not need this feature if you have a pure Windows 2000 network.

On the Zone Transfers tab, you can enable zone transfer to occur (it's enabled by default). You can specify that zone transfers can be sent to any server in the zone or only to servers you specify.

Prep Test

1 You have a mixed DNS zone of Windows 2000 computers, NT Workstations, and Windows 98 computers. What DNS feature should you implement for the zone for name-to-IP-address lookup?

A ○ WINS lookup

B ○ DHCP lookup

C ○ DDNS

D ○ NS Records

2 You want to create a resource record for a zone that contains a mail-server-to-IP-address mapping. What kind of resource record do you need to create?

A ○ NS

B ○ A

C ○ MX

D ○ CNAME

3 You want a primary zone server to become a secondary zone server so that a new server can become the primary server for the zone. How can you configure this on the tab shown here?

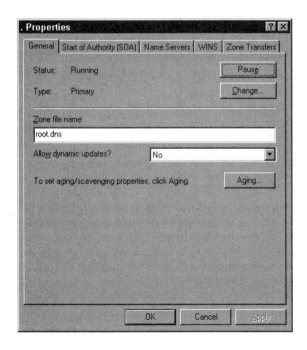

4 You believe that a particular DNS server's database file may have outdated records. How can you manually clean the file?

A ○ Select the desired server in the console and then choose <u>A</u>ction⇨Set Aging/Sca<u>v</u>enging.

B ○ Select the desired server in the console and then choose <u>A</u>ction⇨Scav<u>e</u>nge Stale Resource Records.

C ○ Select the desired server in the console and then choose <u>A</u>ction⇨<u>U</u>pdate Server Database Files.

D ○ You cannot perform this action manually.

5 Your server is experiencing performance problems due to excessive logging. What do you need to do on the Logging tab to alleviate this problem?

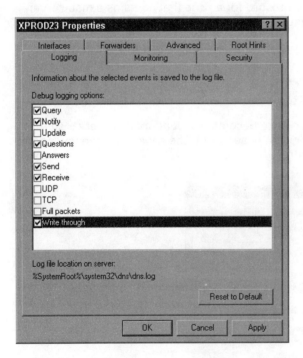

6 You are having a discussion with another administrator who believes that DNS is automatically installed on all Windows 2000 servers. Which response to this assumption is correct?

A ○ DNS is installed automatically on domain controllers only.

B ○ DNS is installed automatically on member servers only.

C ○ DNS is installed automatically on both domain controllers and member servers.

D ○ DNS is not automatically installed on any Windows 2000 server.

7 A particular DNS server should only listen for query requests on certain IP addresses. On which tab of the server's Properties dialog box can you configure this setting?

A ○ Interfaces

B ○ Forwarders

C ○ Advanced

D ○ Root Hints

8 A particular DNS server's record aging and scavenging seems to have a problem. You access the Aging/Scavenging Properties dialog box, shown in the accompanying figure. What should you change so you are using the server's default settings?

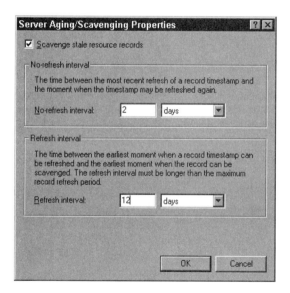

9 You want to disable recursion on a particular DNS server. On which tab in the server's Properties dialog box do you configure this option?

A ○ Interfaces

B ○ Forwarders

C ○ Advanced

D ○ Root Hints

10 For a particular zone, you need to create a resource record that maps a DNS domain name to an ISDN telephone number. How can you create this record?

A ○ Select the zone in the console and then choose Action⇨New Mail Exchanger.

B ○ Select the zone in the console and then choose Action⇨New Host.

C ○ Select the zone in the console and then choose Action⇨Other New Records.

D ○ You cannot create this kind of record.

Answers

1 *A. WINS lookup.* You can use the WINS tab in a zone's Properties dialog box to enable WINS lookup queries so that DNS servers can find the name-to-IP-address mappings not found in the DNS database. *Review "Managing Zone Properties."*

2 *C. MX.* An MX (Mail Exchanger) record identifies a mail server's IP address. *Read "Managing Zone Resource Records."*

3 *Click Change and then select Standard Secondary in the resulting dialog box.* You have one primary zone server in a zone, and all other DNS servers function as secondaries. To change the role that a server plays, access the server's zone properties and then click the Change button on the General tab. *Review "Managing Zone Properties."*

4 *B. Select the desired server in the console and then choose A̱ction⇨Sca̱venge Stale Resource Records.* Scavenging occurs automatically on DNS servers, but you can manually force it to occur by choosing A̱ction⇨Sca̱venge Stale Resource Records. *See "Managing the DNS Server."*

5 *Clear all the check boxes.* The Logging tab allows the server to record DNS events in the DNS.LOG file. You should use logging for troubleshooting purposes. If you are not troubleshooting, turn off all the debug logging options. *Study "Managing the DNS Server."*

6 *A. DNS is installed automatically on Windows 2000 domain controllers only.* Because domain controllers run the Active Directory, DNS is installed automatically when you promote a server to domain controller status. DNS is installed as a part of the Active Directory installation. *Study "Installing DNS."*

7 *A. Interfaces.* On the Interfaces tab, you can specify that a DNS server should listen for queries on all IP addresses or only on ones that you specify. *Study "Managing the DNS Server."*

8 *Change both the no-refresh and refresh intervals to 7 days.* The default setting for the no-refresh and refresh intervals is 7 days. Incorrect changes to these intervals can cause refresh and scavenging problems in the DNS database. *Study "Managing the DNS Server."*

9 *C. Advanced.* On the Advanced tab, you can enable several server options, such as disable recursion, by selecting the desired check box. *Study "Managing the DNS Server."*

10 *C. Select the zone in the console and then choose A̱ction⇨Other New Records.* Choosing A̱ction⇨Other New Re̱cords opens an extensive list of other resource records, including an ISDN record. *Study "Managing Zone Resource Records."*

Chapter 8

Managing Printing

● ●

▶ Monitoring, configuring, troubleshooting, and controlling access to printers

▶ Installing and configuring network services for interoperability

● ●

*A*s a system administrator, you have to manage network printing, printer availability, and printer security — ongoing processes that caused plenty of headaches for administrators working with previous versions of Windows. Fortunately, Windows 2000 offers much easier printing, a wider range of printer support, and easier configuration. Windows 2000 member servers are often used as print servers so that one administrator can manage network printers and security issues.

The exam expects you to know how to set up and manage print shares, as well as how to use the new print technology available in Windows 2000. In this chapter, you can review the following topics:

  ✔ Setting up printers

  ✔ Configuring printers and security

  ✔ Monitoring and troubleshooting printers

Quick Assessment

Monitoring, configuring, trouble-shooting, and controlling access to printers

1   Windows 2000 can print to directly connected network printers using _____.

2   Windows 2000 computers can automatically publish shared printers to the _____.

3   In Windows 2000, you can use _____ Print Queue counters to monitor printers.

4   Windows 2000 is _____ compliant, which means the operating system can automatically detect and install the printer.

5   A group of identical print devices configured as one device is called a(n) _____.

Installing and configuring network services for interoper-ability

6   Windows 2000 networks can automatically download printer _____ to clients.

7   A print _____ writes the print job to the hard disk for background printing.

8   An advanced print permission entry that should be assigned cautiously is _____.

9   If a document does not print, or it prints in garbled text, the problem probably involves the _____.

10   If documents do not print, the print server may not have enough _____ for the spooler.

Answers

1 *TCP/IP.* Review "Examining Windows 2000 Print Features."

2 *Active Directory.* Study "Examining Windows 2000 Print Features."

3 *Performance Monitor.* See "Examining Windows 2000 Print Features."

4 *Plug-and-Play.* Examine "Installing Printers."

5 *Printer Pool.* Review "Configuring Printers."

6 *Drivers.* See "Configuring Printers."

7 *Spool.* Read "Configuring Printers."

8 *Take Ownership.* Study "Configuring Printers."

9 *Driver.* See "Monitoring and Troubleshooting Printers."

10 *Disk Space.* See "Monitoring and Troubleshooting Printers."

Examining Windows 2000 Print Features

For the most part, the printing process in Windows 2000 works the same as in down-level versions of Windows. However, Windows 2000 does have several new printing features that give your network print environment greater flexibility and more possibilities.

You should know these new features for the exam:

- **Standard port monitor:** Windows 2000 supports a standard port monitor that enables Windows 2000 computers to print to network interface printers using TCP/IP. This feature replaces LPRMON for TCP/IP printers connected directly to the network with a network adapter card and is 50 percent faster than LPRMON.

- **Remote port support:** Windows 2000 supports remote port configurations that enable a print administrator to manage any remote network printer without physically visiting the printer or the computer to which it is connected.

- **Active Directory integration:** Windows 2000 computers can automatically store network printers in the Active Directory so network users can easily find the printers and use them.

- **Internet printing:** Windows 2000 allows client computers (running Windows 2000) to print to a print server using a URL. This feature further integrates the Internet or intranet with the local network.

- **Performance monitoring:** Performance Monitor in Windows 2000 contains a new Print Queue object so you can set up counters in Performance Monitor to troubleshoot printing problems.

- **Macintosh and UNIX support:** Windows 2000 supports printing to Macintosh and UNIX printers.

Installing Printers

All printer installation and configuration takes place in the Printers folder on a Windows 2000 member server. You access the Printers folder by clicking Start➪Settings➪Printers, or through Control Panel.

The Printers folder contains icons for any installed printers and an Add Printer wizard that takes you through the steps for installing a new printer. For the most part, installing a new printer is rather easy, but you do need to understand some new print features that Windows 2000 offers. Lab 8-1 describes the steps for installing a new printer with the Add Printer wizard.

Lab 8-1   Installing a New Printer

1. **Open the Printers folder by clicking Start⇨Settings⇨Printers.**

2. **Double-click the Add Printer icon.**

   The Add Printer wizard displays its welcome screen.

3. **Click Next.**

4. **Indicate whether you want to install a local printer or a network printer. (You can install the printer software for a printer connected locally to your server or to another computer on the network.)**

   If you are installing a plug-and-play-compatible local printer, select the check box so that Windows can automatically detect your plug-and-play printer. Windows 2000 is plug-and-play compliant, which can make the process of setting up printers much easier than it was in Windows NT.

5. **Click Next.**

   If you do not allow Windows 2000 to detect and install your printer, the wizard prompts you to select the printer port that is in use, or you can even create a new port (local port, standard TCP/IP port, AppleTalk Printing Device, and so on), as shown in Figure 8-1.

6. **Select the port you want to use, or select the type of port you want to create, and then click Next.**

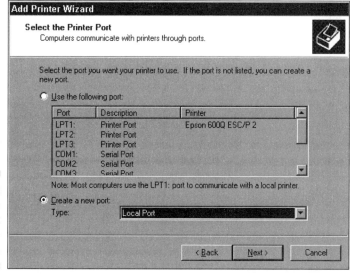

Figure 8-1: Select the printer port you want to use.

7. **If you chose to create a new TCP/IP port, enter the TCP/IP addressing information for the printer in the resulting dialog box and then click Next.**

   In most cases, printers use LPT1 when connected to the local computer.

   If Windows 2000 did not detect your printer, the wizard prompts you for the manufacturer and model type and then asks if you want to share the printer. If you do not want to share the printer at this time, you can always share it later.

8. **Enter the requested information about your printer and click Finish.**

   After the wizard gathers all the information it needs, the new printer is installed.

Configuring Printers

After you install a printer (see the preceding section), you can configure the printer as desired by accessing the printer's properties. In the Printers folder, select the printer and then choose File⇨Properties. The resulting Properties dialog box has numerous configuration options available for your printer, and the exam expects you to know what options you have and where you configure them.

The following sections examine each tab in a printer's Properties dialog box and point out only the information you need to know for the test.

Understanding the general properties

The General tab in your printer's Properties dialog box gives you basic information about the printer, including the printer's name and location, and your comments, which you can add to or change if desired. Also, the second half of the General tab lists the printer's features, such as color printing, double-sided printing, and stapling capabilities.

By clicking the Printing Preferences button at the bottom of the General tab, you open a dialog box in which you can adjust such qualities as page layout and paper quality. Also, depending on your printer, clicking this button may enable you to use various utilities. The options available vary depending on the printer you have installed.

At first glance, the General tab may not seem very important, but you can store the information listed on the General tab in the Active Directory. Then, users can search for printers that offer the capabilities they need — color, stapling, and so on — and find the desired printer. To ensure that the Active Directory has accurate information about each printer, you must have the correct information on the General tab in each printer's Properties dialog box.

Using the Sharing tab

The Sharing tab in your printer's Properties dialog box enables you to share the printer so other users can access it and print to it. To share the printer, you simply click Shared As and then give the printer a share name.

Only Windows 2000 computers can automatically publish printers to the Active Directory. As shown in Figure 8-2, the Sharing tab includes a List in the Directory check box, which is automatically selected. With this setting, Windows 2000 computers can automatically publish shared printers to the Active Directory. Printers connected to down-level computers (such as NT and 9x) can also be published in the Active Directory, but an Active Directory administrator must manually add those printer objects to the directory. Watch out for tricky exam questions on this issue.

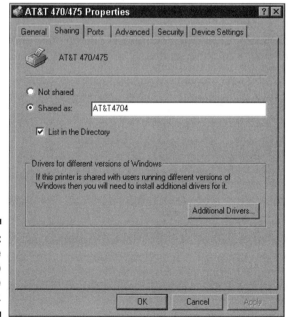

Figure 8-2:
Use the Sharing tab to share the printer.

The Sharing tab also has an Additional Drivers button. Windows 2000 computers can connect to Windows 2000 print shares and automatically download the printer drivers. This process is invisible to users, who simply determine which printer they want to use and then connect to it. Because the print drivers are needed for network printers, the Active Directory downloads the drivers to the client. If you have other clients — for example, NT and 9x — on your network, you need to click the Additional Drivers button and make drivers for those operating systems available for downloading to down-level clients. In the dialog box that's displayed after you click Additional Drivers, click the check box corresponding to each operating system to which you want to provide drivers. You may be prompted for an installation CD or disk.

Pulling in to the Ports tab

On the Ports tab in your printer's Properties dialog box, you select ports the printer can use. If you configure several ports, documents will print to the first free port. You can also add new ports and delete ports. By clicking the Configure Port button, you open the Port Settings dialog box, where you can change settings for a selected port. Typically, however, you don't need to change port settings.

You also use the Ports tab to enable *printer pooling*. Printer pooling enables printing to two or more identical print devices that users see as one printer. For example, you could have three identical print devices and configure them so they appear as one device. Users simply print to the one printer, yet three print devices are available to accommodate the printing tasks. This management option may help you reduce confusion for end-users. To enable printer pooling, click the check box and then select all ports that are in use by the print devices.

Configuring the Advanced tab

On the Advanced tab in your printer's Properties dialog box, you can configure various options that determine how the print device behaves. First, if desired, you can determine a time period each day when the printer is available, and you can set the printer's priority.

The printer device priority range is 1 to 99, with 1 being the lowest and 99 being the highest. For example, if you have multiple print devices connected to the same port, a print device with a priority of 2 will always print before a print device with a priority of 1. You can use this feature to send critical documents to a printer that has the highest priority so those documents always print first. For the exam, just remember that a higher number means a higher print priority.

You have several other check box and radio button options on the Advanced tab. You need to be familiar with these options for the exam:

- ✔ **Spool Print Documents So Programs Finish Printing Faster:** With this option, a print job can be held in a spool so users can get control of their programs and move on to other tasks. To start printing immediately, users can choose to begin printing as soon as the last page is spooled.

- ✔ **Print Directly to the Printer:** This option skips the spooling process and prints directly to the printer. Only use this option if you cannot print using the spooling options.

- ✔ **Hold Mismatched Documents:** This option tells the spooler to check the printer setup and match it with the document setup before the document goes to the printer. If the information does not match, the spooler holds the print job in the print queue. This action does not stop other properly matched documents from printing.

- ✔ **Print Spooled Documents First:** If several print jobs are being spooled, this option tells the spooler to print the jobs as spooling is complete. This action can override priority settings, so you may not want to use it if your priority settings are very important.

- ✔ **Keep Printed Documents:** This option tells the spooler to keep print documents after they are printed instead of deleting them. Then, documents can be reprinted directly from the print queue instead of the program from which the user originally printed.

- ✔ **Enable Advanced Printing Features:** This option turns on metafile spooling so that advanced options, such as page order, booklet printing, and pages per sheet are available. This option is normally enabled by default.

Configuring the Security tab

You can determine who can print to a particular printer and what additional rights users or administrators may have by using the Security tab in a printer's Properties dialog box. Figure 8-3 shows the Security tab.

By default, the available permissions are Print, Manage Printers, and Manage Documents. And by default, administrators, print operators, and server operators have rights to all these permissions. Also by default, all users in the Everyone group have Print permissions.

You can, of course, change these default permissions as needed. Use the Add and Remove buttons to make changes to the list as desired.

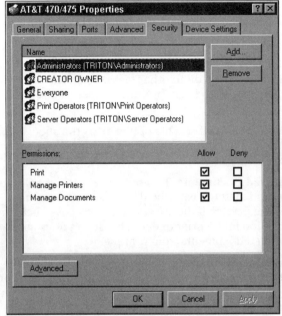

Figure 8-3:
Configure
permissions
using the
Security tab.

You can also configure advanced permissions by clicking the Advanced button. This feature opens the Access Control Settings dialog box for the printer, as shown in Figure 8-4. Select a user or group in the list and then click View/Edit to make additional permission changes, or click Add to add new users or groups to the list.

When you click View/Edit, the Permission Entry dialog box opens, giving you the additional permission options of Read, Change, and Take Ownership.

By assigning the Take Ownership permission, you allow another user to take ownership of the printer, which essentially gives that person full control permissions to the printer. By default, administrators have Take Ownership permission, and you should plan carefully before giving this permission to any other user.

Using the Device Settings tab

In a printer's Properties dialog box, the Device Settings tab shows you a tree structure of different device settings, such as paper tray configuration. Expand the list and click the drop-down menus to make changes as desired.

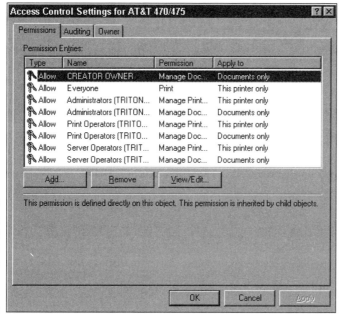

Figure 8-4:
Set
advanced
permissions
by clicking
View/Edit.

In addition to the tabs that I describe in the preceding sections of this chapter, a printer's Properties dialog box may include other tabs, such as Color Management and Utilities, depending on the printer you have installed. You won't see any questions about these printer-specific tabs on the exam.

Managing Printers

You manage printers by configuring the printer's properties (see the preceding sections in this chapter), or by simply selecting the printer icon in the Printers folder and choosing options from the File menu. The options presented to you are rather simple, but you need to know them for the exam.

Table 8-1 explains the options you can choose from the Printers folder's File menu. You should memorize these options for the exam.

Table 8-1	File Menu Options in the Printers Folder
Option	*What It Does*
Open	Opens the print queue, which shows a list of documents waiting to be printed. From this interface, you can cancel documents or pause the printing of certain documents as needed.
Set as Default Printer	Sets the selected printer as the default printer. All print jobs from your server will automatically default to this printer.
Printing Preferences	Opens the Preferences dialog box, which is also available from the General tab in the printer's Properties dialog box.
Pause Printing	Holds all documents in the queue.
Cancel all Documents	Deletes all documents from the print queue.
Sharing	Opens the Sharing tab in the printer's Properties dialog box, so you can make changes.
Use Printer Offline	Takes the printer offline so you can troubleshoot problems or configure the printer before you use it.

Monitoring and Troubleshooting Printers

You can monitor printers in Windows 2000 using Performance Monitor, which now contains print queue objects. This is an effective tool for troubleshooting printer problems. To access Performance Monitor, click Start⇨Programs⇨ Administrative Tools⇨Performance.

Figure 8-5 shows the Performance Monitor console. To add a counter, select System Monitor in the console's tree pane and then click the Add icon (+ sign) on the toolbar in the right-hand pane.

In the resulting Add Counters dialog box, select the appropriate server and then select Print Queue from the Performance Object drop-down list. You can then choose to use all counters or select the desired counters from the list.

You can then use the chart to examine the performance of the different counters. Consistently high counters (75 to 100) may indicate bottlenecks or problems with those particular components.

In addition to knowing how to use Performance Monitor to monitor and troubleshoot print problems, the exam expects you to understand some of the more common printing problems and solutions. In particular, you should memorize these common problems and solutions:

✔ **A printer connected to a computer does not print:** The failure usually involves a physical problem with the printer, an incorrect printer driver, a problem with the print server, or the application from which you want to print. Systematically examine each of these possibilities.

✔ **A printer connected directly to the network does not print:** The problem may be the physical printer or NIC, the logical printer setting on the client computer, or the application from which you are printing. Systematically examine each of these possibilities.

✔ **The printer does not automatically appear in the Active Directory:** The printer is connected to a down-level server or client. Only Windows 2000 computers can automatically publish printers to the directory.

✔ **Windows 9x computers cannot connect to a printer:** The printer does not have the drivers for Windows 9x installed. Use the Sharing tab on the printer's Properties dialog box to install the 9x drivers.

✔ **A document does not print or prints garbled text:** The driver is incorrect or corrupt. Update the driver using the New Driver button on the Advanced tab in the printer's Properties dialog box.

✔ **Documents do not print and cannot be deleted from the print queue:** The server may not have enough disk space for the print spooler, or the spooler may be stalled. Check for necessary disk space, and stop and restart the spooler.

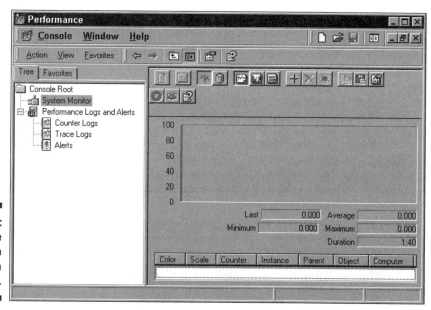

Figure 8-5:
Click the
Add sign to
add a
counter.

Prep Test

1 What Windows 2000 print feature enables administrators to manage network printers without physically visiting the print server?

  A ○ Port Monitor

  B ○ Remote Port

  C ○ TCP/IP Port

  D ○ AppleTalk Port

2 You need to install drivers for a printer so that Windows NT 4.0 Workstation clients can have the drivers automatically downloaded to them. Where can you configure this capability?

  A ○ Printer Properties, General tab

  B ○ Printer Properties, Sharing tab

  C ○ Printer Properties, Ports tab

  D ○ Printer Properties, Advanced tab

3 You want only a select group to be able to print to a particular printer. You do not want any other network users, except administrators, to use the printer. How can you configure this?

  A ○ On the Advanced tab in the Server Properties dialog box, select the desired group and assign Print permission.

  B ○ On the Advanced tab in the Printer Properties dialog box, select the desired group and assign Print permission.

  C ○ On the Security tab in the Printer Properties dialog box, add the desired group and assign Print permissions.

  D ○ On the Security tab in the Printer Properties dialog box, remove all undesired groups and then add the desired group and assign Print permissions.

4 An administrator installs a printer on a server. The administrator wants to share the printer and have it listed in the Active Directory automatically. However, the printer is never published in the directory. Which of the following are possible solutions to the problem? (Choose all that apply.)

  A ○ The physical printer is not working.

  B ○ The server is not a Windows 2000 Server.

  C ○ The administrator never actually shared the printer.

  D ○ There is not enough disk space for the print spooler.

5 You have three identical printers. You want the printers to appear as one printer to network users. What do you need to do on the Ports tab to configure this?

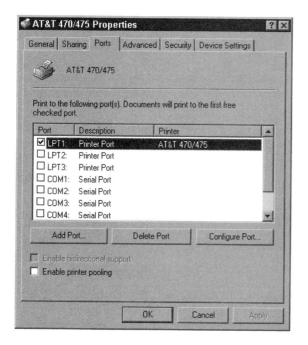

6 You want to make certain that high-priority documents always print to a certain printer. On the printer's Advanced tab, what do you need to do to configure this?

A ○ Set the priority for the printer to 99.

B ○ Set the priority for the printer to 1.

C ○ Update the driver.

D ○ Enable the Keep Printed Documents feature.

7 You want to set a schedule so that a particular printer is only available from 2:00 p.m. to 4:00 p.m. How can you do this?

A ○ On the General tab in the printer's Properties dialog box, adjust the schedule boxes.

B ○ On the Sharing tab in the printer's Properties dialog box, adjust the schedule boxes.

C ○ On the Ports tab in the printer's Properties dialog box, adjust the schedule boxes.

D ○ On the Advanced tab in the printer's Properties dialog box, adjust the schedule boxes.

8 You want to make certain that spooled documents always print first, even if they are of a lower priority than other documents. What do you need to do on the Advanced tab to enable this feature?

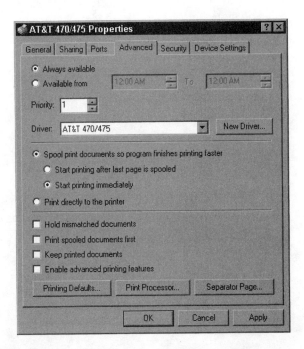

9 You have a shared printer connected to a Windows 98 computer on your network. What do you need to do to have the printer published in the Active Directory?

A ○ Nothing. Publication occurs automatically.

B ○ An Active Directory administrator must install the printer on the Windows 2000 server.

C ○ An Active Directory administrator must manually add the printer object to the directory.

D ○ Printers connected to down-level servers or clients cannot be published in the Active Directory.

10 A particular print device has started printing garbled text. What is most likely the problem?

A ○ The Active Directory configuration is incorrect.

B ○ The driver is corrupt.

C ○ Down-level clients are attempting to print to the device.

D ○ The spooler is not working.

Answers

1 *B. Remote Port.* Windows 2000 contains a *remote port,* which enables print administrators to manager printers without physically visiting the print server. *Review "Examining Windows 2000 Print Features."*

2 *B. Printer Properties, Sharing tab.* You can enable Windows 2000 to download drivers for down-level print clients. Click the Additional Drivers button on the Sharing tab in the printer's Properties dialog box and then select the desired operating system(s) from the list. *Read "Configuring Printers."*

3 *D. On the Security tab in the Printer Properties dialog box, remove all undesired groups and then add the desired group and assign Print permissions.* By default, the Everyone group has Print permissions. You can change this setting by removing the group (and any other groups) and adding the desired group or users. Then, assign the group the desired permissions. *Review "Configuring Printers."*

4 *B and C.* To be published automatically to the Active Directory, the printer must be shared on a Windows 2000 computer. Hardware or spooler problems would not affect Active Directory publication. *See "Monitoring and Troubleshooting Printers."*

5 *Click the Enable Printer Pooling check box and then select the ports for the printers.* By using printer pooling, you can configure identical print devices to appear as one printer. You configure this setting on the Ports tab by selecting the Enable Printer Pooling check box and then selecting the ports to which the printers are connected. *Study "Configuring Printers."*

6 *A. Set the printer priority to 99.* Priority settings affect which documents are printed first. High-priority documents print before low-priority documents, and a printer with higher priority settings will print high-priority documents. The priority range is 1 to 99, with 99 being the highest priority. *Study "Configuring Printers."*

7 *D. On the Advanced tab in the printer's Properties dialog box, adjust the schedule boxes.* You can set a schedule so that a printer is available only at particular time periods. Access the Advanced tab in the printer's Properties dialog box and enter the desired start and end times in the appropriate boxes. *Study "Configuring Printers."*

8 *Select the Print Spooled Documents First check box.* The Print Spooled Documents First option makes certain that completely spooled documents print before those currently being spooled, even if they have a lower priority. *Study "Configuring Printers."*

9 *C. An Active Directory administrator must manually add the printer object to the directory.* Printers shared on down-level computers must be manually added to the Active Directory by an Active Directory (Enterprise) administrator. The administrator manually adds the printer object and network path so users can find the printer in the directory. *Study "Configuring Printers."*

10 *B. The driver is corrupt.* If a printer prints pages, but the text is garbled, you probably have a corrupt print driver and you need to reinstall the driver. You can reinstall the driver by accessing the Advanced tab in the printer's Properties dialog box. *Study "Monitoring and Troubleshooting Printers."*

Chapter 9

Managing Shared Files and Folders

● ●

Exam Objectives

▶ Monitoring, configuring, troubleshooting, and controlling security on files and folders

▶ Monitoring, configuring, troubleshooting, and controlling access to files and folders in a shared folder

● ●

*S*etting up and managing a network presents lots of potential problems — also known as job security — for network administrators. Despite those headaches, however, your well-managed network offers an important benefit to its users: access to shared resources. By sharing documents, applications, databases, and other resources, you give network users the tools they need to perform their jobs without having to provide local copies of those resources. In a Windows 2000 network using Windows 2000 member servers, one of a server's fundamental jobs is to provide shared files and folders containing needed resources.

The exam expects you to know how to set up and manage shares — a rather easy task. In this chapter, you can review the information you need to know for the exam questions that relate to managing shared files and folders. Specifically, this chapter focuses on the following tasks:

   ✔ Setting up shared files and folders

   ✔ Managing security for shared files and folders

   ✔ Monitoring files and folders

Quick Assessment

Monitoring,
configuring,
trouble-
shooting,
and
controlling
security on
files and
folders

1   The ability to download shared files to the client's computer is called _____.

2   You cannot use NTFS permissions on _____ or _____ volumes.

3   _____ permission gives a user all the permission rights of Read and Read & Execute as well as permission to modify or delete the file.

4   Users with the _____ permission can see the names and subfolders in a shared folder.

5   The _____ permission overrides all other permissions.

6   By default, files and subfolders within a shared folder _____ permissions from the parent.

Monitoring,
configuring,
trouble-
shooting,
and
controlling
access to
files and
folders in a
shared
folder

7   If you move a folder within the same NTFS volume, the folder _____ its permissions.

8   To prevent a file from inheriting the permissions of the shared folder, you can change a setting on the _____ tab in the file's Properties dialog box.

9   If a user is a member of two different groups with different permissions for a shared folder, the user's combined permissions are called _____ permissions.

10   You can monitor shared folder connections by using the _____ snap-in.

Answers

1 *Caching.* Review "Creating Shares."

2 *FAT; FAT32.* Study "Managing Share Permissions and Security."

3 *Modify.* See "Managing Share Permissions and Security."

4 *List Folder Contents.* Examine "Managing Share Permissions and Security."

5 *Deny.* Review "Managing Share Permissions and Security."

6 *Inherit.* See "Managing Share Permissions and Security."

7 *Retains.* Read "Managing Share Permissions and Security."

8 *Security.* Study "Managing Share Permissions and Security."

9 *Effective.* See "Managing Share Permissions and Security."

10 *Shared Folder.* See "Monitoring Shared Folders."

Creating Shares

In Windows 2000, you can easily share files and folders — even files and folders within folders. Typically, you manage shares by grouping files into appropriate folders and then sharing those folders with appropriate permissions. This method of organization simplifies your work as an administrator and reduces the number of shares you have to manage.

To share a folder, locate the folder on your computer by either browsing or using Windows Explorer, right-click the folder, and choose Sharing from the pop-up menu.

If an exam question indicates that the Sharing option is not available when you right-click a folder, look for an answer that involves enabling File and Printer Sharing. To share folders or printers, you must enable File and Printer Sharing. This feature is enabled by default, but if necessary, you can enable it by right-clicking My Network Places, then right-clicking the Local Area Connection icon and choosing Properties. Click the Install button and select File and Printer Sharing for Microsoft Networks.

After you right-click a folder and choose Sharing from the pop-up menu, Windows 2000 displays the Sharing tab in the Properties dialog box for the folder you selected, as shown in Figure 9-1. On the Sharing tab, click Share This Folder and then enter a name for the share.

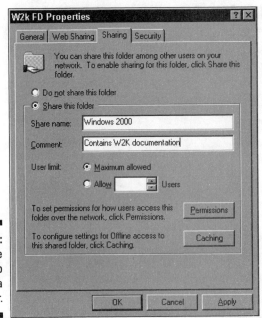

Figure 9-1:
Use the Sharing tab to share a folder.

If you want to create a hidden share, add $ to the end of the share name (such as share$). Network users cannot browse and find the hidden share, but they can map to it.

You can also enter a comment about the share, if desired.

To limit the number of users who can connect to the folder at one time, click the Allow radio button and then use the up- and down-arrow buttons to select the maximum number allowed.

The Sharing tab also has a Permissions button. I discuss the Permissions button and the Security tab in the section "Managing Share Permissions and Security," later in this chapter.

Finally, the Sharing tab has a Caching button. Caching is a new feature of Windows 2000 that enables users to cache network documents on their computers so they can work with the documents when not connected to the network. By clicking the Caching button when you share a folder, you enable users to cache the folder or documents within the folder.

If you click the Caching button, Windows 2000 displays the Caching Settings dialog box, as shown in Figure 9-2.

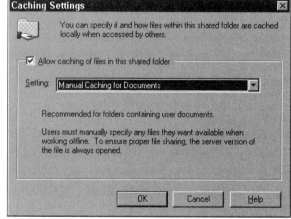

Figure 9-2:
Use the
Caching
Settings
dialog box
to configure
offline
caching.

To allow caching for the shared folder, select the Allow Caching of Files in This Shared Folder check box and then select a setting from the drop-down list.

You can expect the exam to ask you a question about the options in the Settings drop-down list. You should memorize the three Settings options:

- **Automatic Caching For Documents:** This setting is recommended for folders containing user documents. Opened files are automatically downloaded and cached on the user's computer so they will be available when the user works offline. Older versions of the file are automatically deleted from the cache and updated with the newest version.

- **Automatic Caching For Programs:** This setting is recommended for folders with read-only data as well as for run-from-network applications.

- **Manual Caching For Documents:** This setting is also recommended for folders containing user documents. Users must manually specify any files they want available when working offline.

Managing Share Permissions and Security

NTFS is the recommended file system for Windows 2000 computers. NTFS is available in both Windows 2000 Server and Windows 2000 Professional. Although Windows 2000 supports FAT and FAT32 file systems, NTFS gives you exceptional security features in all aspects of networking, including file and folder security.

Reviewing NTFS permissions

With NTFS permissions, you can control the security of a shared folder as well as each file within the folder. In this way, you can allow a user to access a folder, but not necessarily all the files within the folder. Or, a user may have full control over one file in a folder but only read permission on another file in the same folder. In other words, NTFS gives you complete control over which shares you make available to users and groups and what permissions those users and groups have with the shared file or folder.

NTFS permissions are available only on Windows 2000 hard disk volumes formatted with NTFS. You cannot use NTFS permissions on volumes formatted with FAT or FAT32.

NTFS permissions function the same in Windows 2000 as they do in Windows NT. For the exam, you need to have a firm understanding of the different file permissions that can you assign. Table 9-1 reviews these permissions.

Table 9-1	NTFS Permissions for Files
With This Permission . . .	*A User Can . . .*
Read	Read the file and view its attributes, permissions, and owner.
Write	Perform any Read function and edit the file and change its attributes.
Read & Execute	Perform all the Read actions and run applications.
Modify	Perform all actions of Read and Read & Execute, as well as modify or delete the file.
Full Control	Perform any action permitted by other permissions and change the permissions and take ownership.

You also need to understand the different folder permissions that you can assign. Table 9-2 describes these permissions.

Table 9-2	NTFS Permissions for Folders
With This Permission . . .	*A User Can . . .*
Read	View the files and subfolders within the folder and view the folder ownership, attributes, and permissions.
Write	Create new files and subfolders within the folder, make changes to the folder attributes, and view folder ownership and permissions.
List Folder Contents	See the names of files and subfolders in the folder.
Read & Execute	Perform all actions of Read and List Folder Contents and move through the folders to other files and folders without permission for each folder.
Modify	Perform all actions of Write and Read & Execute and delete the folder.
Full Control	Perform all actions provided by other permissions and change the folder permissions, take ownership, and delete files and subfolders.

For each permission, both for files and folders, you can either grant the permission or deny the permission. If you deny all permissions for a user or group, the user or group has no access rights to the file or folder. For each file and folder, NTFS maintains an access control list (ACL) that lists the users and groups that have been granted access to a file or folder. If a user tries to access a file or folder, NTFS checks the ACL to see if the user has any permissions for the file or folder.

Understanding effective permissions

At first glance, assigning permissions may seem like any easy task, but you must be careful. You can assign users and groups permissions for a file or folder, but users may be members of several groups, each with different permissions. In such cases, a user who belongs to different groups with differing permissions will have *effective permissions*.

Effective permissions are combined NTFS permissions. For example, assume that a user is a member of two groups. One group has Read permission for a folder, and the other group has Modify permission for the same folder. In that case, the user's effective permission is Read and Modify. As you can see, effective permissions may give some users more permissions than you would like them to have. Planning is of key importance.

The exception to the effective-permissions rule is Deny. If a user has Read permission for a folder in one group, but is denied permission in another group, the user has no access. Deny overrides all other effective permissions.

Understanding inheritance

You need to understand the relationship between sharing folders and inheritance. By default, all files and folders within a folder inherit the permissions of the parent folder. You can prevent inheritance by assigning different permissions to a subfolder. When you perform this action, the subfolder becomes the new parent folder for all the files and folders that it contains. You can find more details about this action — called *blocking inheritance* — in the section "Setting up permissions," later in this chapter.

Moving and copying shared files and folders

For the exam, you need to know how moving and copying files and folders affect permissions. These permission rules are not difficult, but they can be confusing.

You should memorize these rules for the exam:

- ✔ If you copy a file or folder to a new folder on the same NTFS volume or a different NTFS volume, the file or folder inherits the permissions of the destination folder.

- ✔ If you copy a file or folder to a FAT or FAT32 volume, you lose all NTFS permissions.

- ✔ If you move a file or folder within the same NTFS volume, the file or folder retains its permissions.

- ✔ If you move a file or folder to a different NTFS volume, the file or folder inherits the permissions of the destination folder.

- ✔ If you move a file or folder to a FAT or FAT32 volume, you lose all NTFS permissions.

Setting up permissions

After you establish a shared folder (see the previous sections in this chapter), you need to assign permissions for that shared folder. You have two kinds of permission: NTFS and folder permissions. On the Sharing tab in the share's Properties dialog box, click the Permissions button to view the share permissions.

By default, the Everyone group has Full Control permissions (which you would want to change). Your other options are Change and Read. The share permissions apply on NTFS and FAT or FAT32 volumes. Of course, you have problems controlling shared folders on FAT or FAT32 volumes. If users have Full Control permissions, they have full control for all files and folders within the folder. Clearly, NTFS volumes are your best choice because of the security features.

To assign NTFS permissions for a folder, you use the options on the Security tab in the folder's Properties dialog box. On the Security tab, you see the list of available permissions and the default groups and users who have permission. You can make changes to the permissions as desired, and you can use the Add and Remove buttons to establish or remove permissions from users and groups.

By clicking the Advanced button on the Security tab, you open the Access Control Settings for the shared folder, where you can fine-tune the permissions for a user or group. Select the desired user or group and click View/Edit to open the Permission Entry dialog box for that user or group. As shown in Figure 9-3, the Permission Entry dialog box gives you an extended list of permissions that you can manipulate.

You don't need to memorize all the Permission Entry settings for the exam, but you do need to know that this advanced configuration option is available. In short, NTFS gives you precise control of permissions for shared folders and files on NTFS volumes using the Advanced ACL features.

In addition to setting up folder permission, you can block inheritance for files and folders within a folder. With this feature, the permission settings from the parent do not apply to a file or subfolder within the parent. To set the desired permissions and block inheritance, right-click the desired file or subfolder and choose Properties from the pop-up menu. In the resulting Properties dialog box, click the Security tab and then clear the check mark from the check box with the lengthy label Allow Inheritable Permissions From Parent to Propagate to This Object, as shown in Figure 9-4.

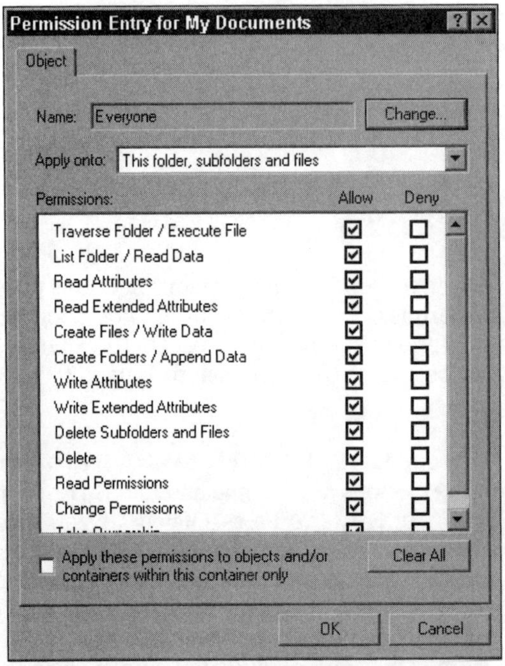

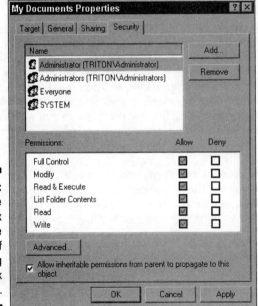

Figure 9-3:
Use the
Permission
Entry dialog
box to
fine-tune
permissions.

Figure 9-4:
Clear the
check box
at the
bottom of
the dialog
box to block
inheritance.

When you clear the check box, a Security dialog box appears, as shown in Figure 9-5. You can choose to copy the permissions from the parent and then change them as desired, or you can remove them all and then establish new permissions as desired.

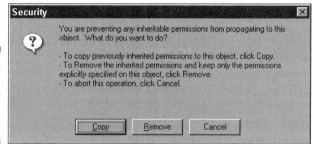

Figure 9-5:
Choose to
copy or
remove
permissions.

Monitoring Shared Folders

In many cases, you may need to monitor user access to shared folders and files. You can easily perform this action using Windows 2000 Server's Shared Folder MMC snap-in.

To open the Shared Folder snap-in, follow the steps in Lab 9-1.

Lab 9-1   Opening the Shared Folder Snap-in

1. **Click Start⇨Run.**

2. **In the Run dialog box, type** MMC **and click OK.**

3. **Choose Console⇨Add/Remove Snap-in.**

4. **Click Add.**

5. **In the snap-in list, select Shared Folders, and then click Add.**

6. **In the resulting Shared Folders dialog box, select Local Computer, choose to View All Sessions, and then click Finish.**

7. **Click Close.**

8. **Click OK.**

The snap-in now appears in the console. If you expand Shared Folders in the console, you can see containers for Shares, Sessions, and Open Files, as shown in Figure 9-6.

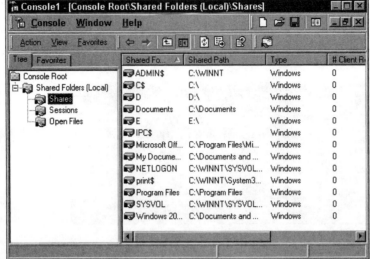

Figure 9-6:
Expand
Shared
Folders and
click the
desired
container to
view its
contents.

With the Shared Folders console, you can view the shares on your computer, the sessions currently in progress, and the open files. Click each container to see the sessions and open files (or shares). Click Sessions, and you see the user connected to the share along with the number of open files, the amount of time connected, and the idle time. To disconnect a specific user, right-click the user in the right window and then choose Close Session from the pop-up menu. To disconnect everyone, choose Action⇨Disconnect All Sessions.

The Open Files container displays the shared files that are open, which users have the files open, and the user's permissions for the file. You can right-click any file in the window and choose Close Open File to force the user to close the file, or you can choose Action⇨Disconnect All Open Files.

Prep Test

1 You share a folder that contains company documents. All users have Read access to the documents, but you want one group to have full control to one of the documents. What can you do to stop the folder permissions from affecting this document?

A ○ Block inheritance on the General tab in the file's Properties dialog box.

B ○ Block inheritance on the Sharing tab in the file's Properties dialog box.

C ○ Block inheritance on the Security tab in the file's Properties dialog box.

D ○ You cannot perform this action.

2 You want to allow users to cache documents in a shared folder, but you want the users to select which documents they want to cache. How can you configure this on the Caching Settings tab?

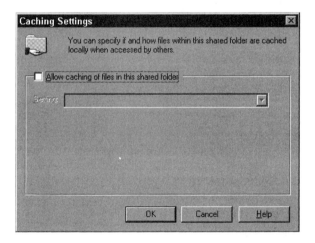

3 A user is a member of two groups. For a particular shared folder, one group has Modify permission while another group has all permissions denied. What effective permission does the user have for the shared folder?

A ○ Modify

B ○ Read

C ○ Write

D ○ None

4 For a particular share, you want the Everyone group to have Read permissions. How can you configure this on the Security tab?

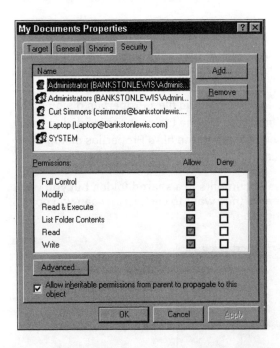

5 You need to assign a particular user the permission to Write Attributes for a shared folder. This permission does not appear in the list on the Security tab. How can you configure this?

A ○ Configure the permission for individual files.

B ○ Place the user in a group and assign the permission.

C ○ Click the Advanced button and then assign the permission.

D ○ You cannot assign this permission.

6 Which NTFS folder permission allows the user to delete the folder?

A ○ Write

B ○ List Folder Contents

C ○ Read & Execute

D ○ Modify

7 When a user attempts to access a shared folder, what does the system check to see if the user has permission?

A ○ NTFS

B ○ FAT32

C ○ ACL

D ○ User Properties

8 You move a folder to a new folder on a different NTFS volume. What happens to the permissions of the folder?

A ○ They remain the same.

B ○ The permissions of the target folder are inherited.

C ○ The permissions are modified to Read Only.

D ○ You cannot move a shared folder to a different NTFS volume.

9 You move a shared folder from an NTFS volume to a FAT32 volume. What happens to the permissions of the shared folder?

A ○ They remain the same.

B ○ The permissions of the target folder are inherited.

C ○ The NTFS permissions are lost.

D ○ You cannot move a shared folder to a FAT32 volume.

10 You want to disconnect a particular user from a shared folder. How can you perform this action?

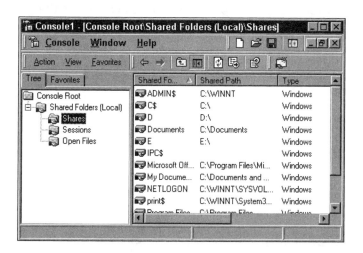

Answers

1 *C. Block inheritance on the Security tab in the file's Properties dialog box.* By default, all files and subfolders inherit permissions from the parent folder. You can block this inheritance process by clearing the check box at the bottom of the Security tab. *Review "Managing Share Permissions and Security."*

2 *Click the Allow Caching check box and then select Manual Caching for Documents from the drop-down list.* You can enable caching on any shared folder so users can download files for offline use. To force users to select which documents to download, use the Manual Caching option. *Read "Creating Shares."*

3 *D. None.* Effective permissions are cumulative, with the exception of Deny or No Access. In this case, the user has no access to the folder. *Review "Managing Share Permissions and Security."*

4 *Click Add, select Everyone, click OK, and then click the Read check box.* You can manage permissions for a share by using the Add and Remove buttons on the Security tab and assigning desired permissions. *See "Managing Share Permissions and Security."*

5 *C. Click the Advanced button and then assign the permission.* NTFS enables you to fine-tune permissions by using the Advanced button to access the Permission Entries for a user or group. The permission list enables you to assign the Write Attributes permission. *Study "Managing Share Permissions and Security."*

6 *D. Modify.* The Modify permission gives the user all permissions of Write sand Read & Execute, as well as the permission to delete the folder. *Study "Managing Share Permissions and Security."*

7 *C. ACL.* The ACL (Access Control List) identifies which permissions users and groups have for a shared folder. *Study "Managing Share Permissions and Security."*

8 *B. The permissions of the target folder are inherited.* When you move a folder to a different NTFS volume, the system sees it as a new folder, and it inherits the permissions of the target folder. *Study "Managing Share Permissions and Security."*

9 *C. The NTFS permissions are lost.* FAT and FAT32 volumes do not support NTFS permissions, so when you move a shared folder from an NTFS volume to a FAT32 volume, the NTFS permissions are lost. *Study "Managing Share Permissions and Security."*

10 *Select the Sessions container, right-click the user you want to disconnect, and then choose Close Session.* The Shared Folders snap-in enables you to monitor sessions and open files for shared folders as well as disconnect users from those resources. *Study "Monitoring Shared Folders."*

Chapter 10

Managing Web Folders and Web Access

• •

Exam Objectives

▶ Monitoring, configuring, troubleshooting, and controlling access to files and folders via Web services

▶ Monitoring, configuring, troubleshooting, and controlling access to Web sites

• •

*W*indows 2000 includes fully integrated Web technologies with which you can easily create and manage Internet or intranet sites. Many environments now use intranet sites to disseminate corporate information and even share folders, files, and documents. In such environments, Windows 2000 member servers make excellent server choices for Web technology implementations.

This chapter reviews the information you need to know for the exam questions that relate to managing Web folders and controlling access to Web sites. For the exam, you need to know how to set up and manage Web shares and control access to them on a Windows 2000 member server. You can review the following topics in this chapter:

✔ Creating Web folders

✔ Configuring Web folders and Web folder access

✔ Managing Web permissions

Quick Assessment

Monitoring, configuring, trouble-shooting, and controlling access to files and folders via Web services

1 When you share a Web folder, you can also assign a(n) _____ for the folder name.

2 You can configure access to a Web folder on your computer, another computer, or even a(n) _____.

3 If you move a Web folder on your drive to a different place on your drive, you need to update the path on the _____ tab in the folder's Properties dialog box.

4 To keep a record of the visitors who access a Web folder, you can choose to _____ on the Virtual Directory tab in the folder's Properties dialog box.

5 You can allow anonymous access to a Web folder, which does not require a(n) _____.

6 If you want a user's username and password sent in clear text when accessing a Web folder, you should choose _____ authentication.

7 On the _____ tab in a Web folder's Properties dialog box, you can configure the folder so an expiration date applies to the folder's content.

Monitoring, configuring, trouble-shooting, and controlling access to Web sites

8 Internet Information Server (IIS) 5.0 in Windows 2000 provides the _____ to help you configure access permissions and security.

Answers

1   *Alias.* Review "Sharing Web Folders."

2   *URL.* Study "Configuring Web Folder Properties."

3   *Virtual Directory.* See "Configuring Web Folder Properties."

4   *Log Visits.* Examine "Configuring Web Folder Properties."

5   *Username and Password.* Review "Configuring Web Folder Properties."

6   *Basic.* See "Configuring Web Folder Properties."

7   *HTTP Headers.* Read "Configuring Web Folder Properties."

8   *Permissions Wizard.* Study "Using the Permissions Wizard."

Sharing Web Folders

In Windows 2000, you can share any folder as a shared Web folder on a Web site that you specify. The shared folder appears on your Internet or intranet site, where users can access the contents of the shared folder.

You share a Web folder in the same way you share any other folder on your system. Lab 10-1 describes the steps for sharing a Web folder.

Lab 10-1   Sharing a Web Folder

1. **Right-click the folder you want to share and choose Sharing from the pop-up menu.**

2. **In the resulting Properties dialog box, click the Web Sharing tab.**

3. **Using the drop-down list, select the Web site on which you want to share the folder.**

4. **Click the Share This Folder radio button, as shown in Figure 10-1.**

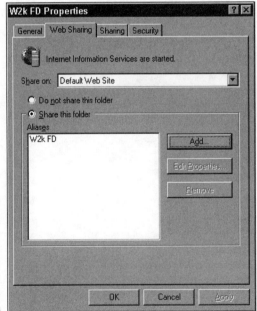

Figure 10-1:
Use the Web Sharing tab to share a Web folder.

5. **In the Edit Alias dialog box that's displayed, give the Web folder an alias name, if desired.**

   As shown in Figure 10-2, the Edit Alias dialog box also gives you options for assigning access permissions and application permissions. Under Access Permissions, you can select Read, Write, Script Source Access, or Directory Browsing. Under Application Permissions, you can select None, Scripts, or Execute (Includes Scripts).

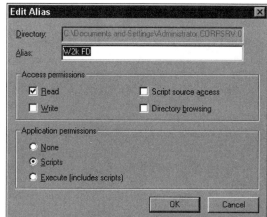

Figure 10-2:
Set share properties on the Edit Alias tab.

6. **Select the desired permissions and then click OK to make the share active.**

Configuring Web Folder Properties

After you share a Web folder (see the preceding section in this chapter), you can access its properties from within Internet Services Manager. Click Start⇨Programs⇨Administrative Tools⇨Internet Services Manager. Expand your server in the tree pane and then expand the desired Web site. You now see the shared folder within the Web site. Select the shared folder and choose Action⇨Properties. On the five tabs in the resulting Properties dialog box, you can further configure the shared Web folder.

For the exam, you need to know what you can do on each of the five tabs in the Properties dialog box for a shared Web folder. The following sections explore what you need to know for the exam.

Configuring the Virtual Directory tab settings

You use the Virtual Directory tab in a Web folder's Properties dialog box to configure the location and the way in which users access a Web folder. Figure 10-3 shows the Virtual Directory tab.

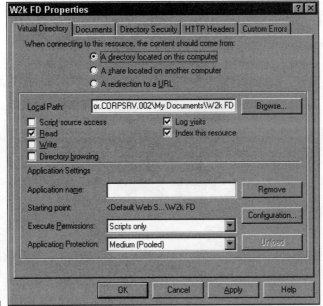

Figure 10-3:
Use the Virtual Directory tab to set the directory location and access rights.

First, you need to specify the location of the content for the shared Web folder. Depending on the setting you choose in the top part of the Virtual Directory tab, the content of the shared Web folder may come from a directory on your local machine, a share on another computer, or a redirection to another URL. Your selection in the top part of this tab also determines what options you see in the lower part of the dialog box. For example, if you select another computer, you provide the path to that computer. If you share a Web folder on your local machine, you need to specify the path to that directory. If you specify that the content comes from a URL redirect, you enter information about the URL.

The middle part of the Virtual Directory tab contains the local path to the Web folder, which you can change by clicking Browse and then browsing to the desired folder.

If you subsequently move the shared Web folder to a different location on your computer, you need to change the local path setting accordingly, or Web users will not be able to access the directory.

The Virtual Directory tab also has several check boxes that you can select to determine what users can do with the shared folder and how it is configured on the Web server.

You need to know these options for the exam:

- **Script Source Access:** Allows users to access the source of any scripts that run with the directory.
- **Read:** Allows users to read the directory information.
- **Write:** Allows users to write directory information.
- **Directory Browsing:** Allows users to browse the directory.
- **Log Visits:** Creates a log file of all visitors.
- **Index This Resource:** Enables the index server to include this directory when the Web site is indexed.

Also, if you are sharing applications in the Web folder, you can configure an application name, determine execution permissions, and configure application protection. The execution permissions enable users to execute either scripts, executable files, or both. The Application Protection feature enables you to select low, medium, or high protection.

Configuring the Documents tab

On the Documents tab in a Web folder's Properties dialog box, you can select a default document that launches when a user accesses the shared folder. For example, you can create a DEFAULT.HTM document that contains links to the contents of the shared folder. This feature is optional, but you may want to use it, depending on the structure of your Web site.

Managing the Directory Security tab

The settings on the Directory Security tab in a Web folder's Properties dialog box enable you to configure different kinds of security for the shared folder. You have three options:

- Anonymous access and authentication control
- IP address and domain name restrictions
- Secure communications

For anonymous access and authentication control, you can click Edit and then select the desired authentication methods, as shown in Figure 10-4.

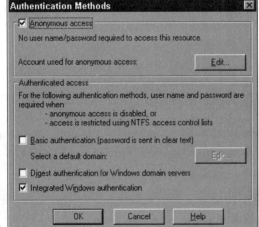

Figure 10-4:
Configuring
the desired
access
methods.

In the Authentication Methods dialog box, you can allow anonymous access to the directory by clicking the Anonymous Access check box. With this setting, users can access the directory without a username and password. Instead, they use a default username and password, such as IUSR_*servername*. You can change this default account as desired by clicking Edit.

In the Authenticated Access section, you can configure the kind of authentication that's required when anonymous access is disabled or when access is restricted due to NTFS ACLs. You have three options, which you should remember for the exam:

- **Basic Authentication:** Users access the directory with a username and password that the system sends in clear text. You can also specify a default domain by clicking Edit.

- **Digest Authentication for Windows Domain Servers:** This feature allows IIS to manage authentication using usernames and passwords from Windows domain controllers.

- **Integrated Windows Authentication:** This feature integrates the authentication process with Windows 2000 domain controllers.

On the Directory Security tab in a Web folder's Properties dialog box, you can determine directory security based on IP address and domain name restrictions. If you select this option and then click Edit, you can create an IP address and domain name acceptance or restriction list, as shown in Figure 10-5.

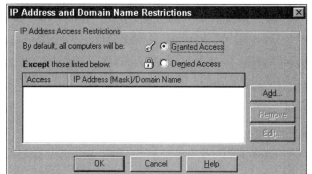

Figure 10-5:
Managing
access by
IP address.

You have two options in the IP Address and Domain Name Restrictions dialog box. First, you can click the Granted Access radio button so that all IP addresses are granted access except the ones that you add to the list. Alternatively, you can click the Denied Access radio button, in which case all IP addresses are denied access except the ones that you provide in the list. Click Add to enter the desired IP addresses.

Finally, if you use certificates in your network, you can use secure communications through certificate services. If you use certificate services, users must have a valid digital certificate in order to log on to the network or access the Web directory. You don't have to worry about this option for the exam, so I don't go into any more detail here.

Enabling HTTP headers

With the options on the HTTP Headers tab in a shared Web folder's Properties dialog box, you can configure HTTP headers that Windows 2000 sends to a user's browser when the user accesses the directory. You can configure content expiration, content ratings, and additional MIME types.

For the exam, you only need to know about the content expiration option. You can click the Enable Content Expiration check box and then enter a day and time at which the Web folder content expires. This feature is very useful for time-sensitive documents or files.

Understanding the settings on the Custom Errors tab

On the Custom Errors tab in the Properties dialog box for a shared Web folder, you can create custom error messages for the directory. This feature is useful for particular kinds of directory files or applications. You can create a custom error message that Windows 2000 sends to the user for a particular error that may be encountered.

For the exam, you only need to know what this option does. You will not see detailed questions about creating custom error messages.

Using the Permissions Wizard

IIS 5 includes a handy wizard that gives you great control over Web directory access. Through the Permissions wizard, you can control how users access the entire Web site or particular Web folders.

You need to know what options the wizard offers, so practice Lab 10-2 to get familiar with the Permissions wizard.

Lab 10-2   Using the Permissions Wizard

1. **To start the wizard, look in the console's tree pane and click either the Web site itself or a particular folder and then choose Action⇨ All Tasks⇨Permissions Wizard.**

2. **On the welcome screen, click Next.**

3. **In the Security Settings dialog box, specify whether you want to inherit all security settings or select security settings from a template and then click Next.**

4. **If you specified that you want to use a template, select one from the list that's displayed.**

   The wizard displays its Windows Directory and File Permissions dialog box. As shown in Figure 10-6, this dialog box shows the basic rights provided and allows you to replace all directory and file permissions with this one, leave the current directory and file permissions intact and add the new ones, or leave the directory and file permissions as they are.

5. **Select the desired security setting and click Next.**

   The Security Summary dialog box lists the permissions that Windows 2000 will apply to your setting.

6. **Click Next to accept them, or click Back and then make any needed changes.**

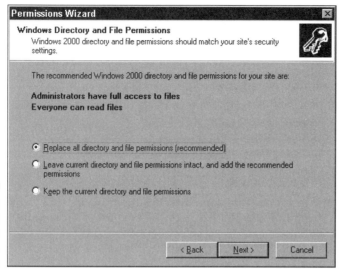

Figure 10-6:
Determining
permission
settings.

7. Click Finish to complete the wizard.

In addition to using the Permissions wizard, you can control access to individual Web folders by configuring the desired access settings on the Directory Security tab in a folder's Properties dialog box. For more information, see "Configuring Web Folder Properties," earlier in this chapter.

And when you create Web sites with the Web Site Creation wizard, you can set standard user permissions. To create a new Web site, select the server name in the left console pane and then choose Action➪New➪Web Site. When you run the Web Site Creation wizard, you can select the default Web-site permissions you want to use. The default permissions provided in the wizard are:

- ✔ **Read:** Enables Web users to read file information on the Web site.

- ✔ **Run Scripts:** Enables a user to run a Web script, such as an Active Server Page (ASP) script.

- ✔ **Execute:** Enables a user to execute an application you have available on the site, such as a Common Gateway Interface (CGI) application. If you enable this permission, the Run Scripts permission is also enabled.

- ✔ **Write:** Enables users to upload files to the Web server or enter information on a Web page and submit it.

- ✔ **Browse:** Enables a user to browse the folder and directory structure of your Web site.

Of course, you can always make permissions changes later or configure different permissions for any folder within the site.

Prep Test

1 You want to make certain that a shared folder is indexed on the Web site. Where can you configure this option?

A ○ Folder properties, Documents tab

B ○ Folder properties, Virtual Directory tab

C ○ Folder properties, Directory Security tab

D ○ Folder properties, HTTP Headers tab

2 A particular Web folder has time-sensitive documents. You want to have the folder's content expire on a particular date. Where can you configure expiration for the content?

A ○ Folder properties, Documents tab

B ○ Folder properties, Virtual Directory tab

C ○ Folder properties, Directory Security tab

D ○ Folder properties, HTTP Headers tab

3 You decide to implement IP address and domain name security on a particular Web folder. You want to deny access to all IP addresses except a certain list that you specify. How do you configure this security setting in the IP Address and Domain Name Restrictions dialog box?

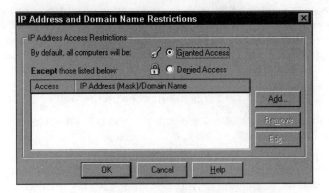

4 For a particular Web folder, you want to allow anonymous access, but you want to specify an anonymous access password. How can you configure this security setting in the Authentication Methods dialog box?

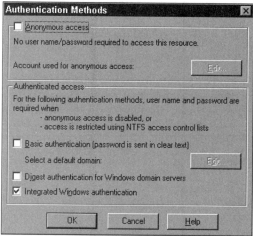

5 You have a shared folder that users access via URL redirection. This folder is managed by another administrator on another Web site. Suddenly, users begin getting a `404 Not Found` error. What has happened? (Choose all possible answers.)

A ❑ The URL has changed and has not been updated on your Web site.

B ❑ The shared folder has been removed.

C ❑ Higher security has been set on the folder.

D ❑ The Web site that hosts the folder is down.

6 Web folders shared on IIS 5.0 can be accessed from _____ with appropriate permissions.

A ○ The network

B ○ The intranet

C ○ The Internet

D ○ All of the above

7 The Permissions wizard enables you to use a _____ approach to configuring Web folder permissions.

A ○ Site

B ○ Template

C ○ Build

D ○ Manual

Answers

1 **B. Folder properties, Virtual Directory tab.** If you want to have a Web folder indexed, click the Index This Resource check box on the Virtual Directory tab in the Web folder's Properties dialog box. *Review "Configuring Web Folder Properties."*

2 **D. Folder properties, HTTP Headers tab.** The HTTP Headers tab in the folder's Properties dialog box includes a setting that enables you to set a content expiration date. Click the Enable Content Expiration option and then enter the desired expiration date. *Read "Configuring Web Folder Properties."*

3 *Select the Denied Access radio button, click Add, and then enter the IP addresses that can have access.* You can use the IP address security feature to grant access to all and then create an exception list of IP addresses that are denied. Alternatively, you can deny all and then create an exception list of IP addresses that are granted access. *Review "Configuring Web Folder Properties."*

4 *Click the Anonymous Access check box, click Edit, clear the Allow IIS to Control Password check box, and then enter the desired password.* You can use anonymous access so that IIS manages the anonymous password, or you can create an anonymous password, if desired. *See "Configuring Web Folder Properties."*

5 *A, B, and D.* Either the URL has changed and has not been updated on your Web site, the shared folder has been removed, or the Web site that hosts the folder is down. A 404 error message occurs when a resource cannot be found. Any of these could be the problem. Security would not be the problem because users would receive a different error message if they did not have access rights. *Study "Configuring Web Folder Properties."*

6 *D. All of the above.* Web folders, depending on permissions and configuration, can be accessed from the local network, the intranet, or the Internet. *Study "Sharing Web Folders."*

7 **B. Template.** The Permissions wizard enables you to use a template to configure permissions for shared Web folders. This approach streamlines permission configuration and makes your administrative job easier. *Study "Using the Permissions Wizard."*

Chapter 11

Using Distributed File Systems (Dfs)

Exam Objectives

▶ Configuring, managing, and troubleshooting a standalone Distributed file system (Dfs)

▶ Configuring, managing, and troubleshooting a domain-based Dfs

*1*n enterprise environments, the number of shared folders can overwhelm administrators, and network users can have difficulty locating the shared folders they need. With Windows 2000's Distributed file system (Dfs), however, you can create a tree-like structure for the shared folders on your network. Dfs organizes network folders so that users can easily find what they need without having to know which server holds each shared folder.

For the exam you are expected to know how to set up and manage Dfs. This chapter explores what you need to know about Dfs for the exam, focusing on the following topics:

- ✔ Understanding Dfs
- ✔ Managing a standalone Dfs
- ✔ Managing a domain-based Dfs

Quick Assessment

Configuring, managing, and trouble-shooting a standalone Dfs

1 A standalone Dfs does not provide any inherent _____.

2 Clients running Windows 2000, Windows NT, and _____ have built-in Dfs support.

3 You begin the Dfs configuration process by creating the Dfs _____.

4 Dfs is best used on a(n) _____ volume.

5 Shared folders configured in the Dfs root are called Dfs _____.

6 You have no Dfs _____ limit when using a domain-based Dfs.

Configuring, managing, and trouble-shooting a domain-based Dfs

7 _____ are used to store multiple copies of roots and links that are synchronized when changes occur.

8 Automatic replication between Dfs folder replicas occurs using _____.

9 Replication can be performed either _____ or _____ for Dfs folders.

10 You should not mix automatic and manual replication within a replica _____.

Answers

1 *Fault Tolerance.* Review "Managing a Standalone Dfs."

2 *Windows 98.* Study "Understanding Dfs."

3 *Root.* See "Managing a Standalone Dfs."

4 *NTFS.* Examine "Managing a Standalone Dfs."

5 *Links.* Review "Managing a Standalone Dfs."

6 *Hierarchy.* See "Managing a Domain-based Dfs."

7 *Replicas.* Read "Managing a Domain-based Dfs."

8 *FRS.* Study "Managing a Domain-based Dfs."

9 *Automatically; Manually.* See "Managing a Domain-based Dfs."

10 *Set.* See "Managing a Domain-based Dfs."

Understanding Dfs

In previous versions of Windows, users have to browse through different servers to find the shared folders they need to use. In large networks, this process can be time-consuming and frustrating. With Windows 2000's Dfs, you can organize shared folders in a network environment so they appear as one, structured location to users.

Dfs and the Active Directory free end-users from worrying about the network structure. In other words, users do not need to know where resources on the network physically reside. They can easily access and use those resources.

Dfs organizes resources on the network in a tree-like structure that users can simply browse to find the shared folder they need. To end-users, all the folders appear as though they are located in one place. Users do not see where the folders actually reside on the network. As you can see in Figure 11-1, various servers may hold the shared resources, but in Dfs, they appear as though they reside in one location. This feature makes the network architecture transparent to users, and ultimately makes finding resources quicker and easier.

Windows 2000 supports two kinds of Dfs: standalone and domain-based (or fault-tolerant). You store a standalone Dfs on a single server that network users access. The Dfs server holds the folder information for all other servers and presents that information to users in a tree-like structure. However, a standalone Dfs has no fault tolerance. If the server fails, Dfs will not be available to users. A domain-based Dfs stores the folder structure in the Active Directory. If one server fails, a domain-based Dfs is still available on other servers within the Active Directory environment. Domain-based Dfs roots must be stored on volumes formatted as NTFS 5.0.

Only clients that support Dfs can use the Dfs features. Clients running Windows 2000, Windows NT, and Windows 98 have built-in support for a standalone Dfs. Windows 2000 and NT clients also have built-in support for a domain-based Dfs. Windows 98 clients can download the 5.0-compliant client, and clients running Windows 95 can download the Dfs client from www.microsoft.com.

For the exam you are expected to know about both standalone and domain-based Dfs. The following sections explore both types of Dfs and what you need to know for the exam.

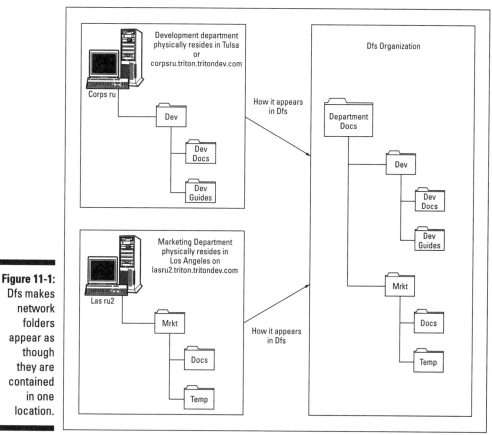

Figure 11-1: Dfs makes network folders appear as though they are contained in one location.

Managing a Standalone Dfs

Dfs is available on your Windows 2000 server after an initial server installation. Dfs functions as an MMC snap-in, but it does not appear in your Administrative Tools folder. Instead, you manually add the snap-in to an MMC and then save the console for future use.

Lab 11-1 lists the steps for adding the Dfs snap-in.

Lab 11-1 Adding the Dfs Snap-in

1. **Choose Start⇨Run.**

2. **In the Run dialog box, type** MMC.

3. **Choose Console⇨Add/Remove Snap-in.**

4. Select Distributed File System from the snap-in list and then click OK.

5. Save the console after you have the Dfs snap-in loaded.

Setting up the Dfs root

You set up Dfs by establishing a Dfs root. A Dfs root is simply a container for files and Dfs links.

You can create a Dfs root on FAT or NTFS partitions, but FAT does not provide the security features of NTFS. If possible, you should always create the root on an NTFS partition.

A standalone Dfs root has some limitations. First, the standalone Dfs root does not use the Active Directory, so it has no fault tolerance. Second, a standalone Dfs root cannot have root-level Dfs shared folders. In other words, you can have only one root, and all shared folders must fall under the hierarchy of the root. Also, you have a limited hierarchy available. A standalone Dfs root can have only a single level of Dfs links.

Lab 11-2 explains the steps for creating a new standalone Dfs root. For the exam, you should know what options the New Dfs Root wizard offers.

Lab 11-2	Creating a Standalone Dfs Root

1. **Choose Action➪New Dfs Root.**

   Windows 2000 displays the welcome screen for the New Dfs Root wizard.

2. **Click Next.**

3. **In the New Dfs Root Type dialog box, select the Create a Standalone Dfs Root radio button and then click Next.**

4. **In the Host Server dialog box, enter the name of the host server for the Dfs root and click Next.**

5. **In the Specify Dfs Root Share dialog box, choose to use an existing share, or create a new one by entering the desired share name and path. Click Next.**

   The Dfs share holds the Dfs information, so you can simply use a share already available on your server, or you may want to create a new one strictly for the Dfs root.

6. **In the Name the Dfs Root dialog box, enter a name for the Dfs root and enter a comment, if desired. Click Next.**

7. **Click Finish to complete the wizard.**

Creating a Dfs link

Dfs links provide a folder name to the users. When a user accesses the folder, the system transparently redirects the user to the server that actually holds the shared folder.

Lab 11-3 describes the steps for creating a Dfs link.

Lab 11-3   Creating a Dfs Link

1. **Select the Dfs root in the console and then choose Action⇨ New Dfs Link.**

   The Create a New Dfs Link dialog box appears, as shown in Figure 11-2.

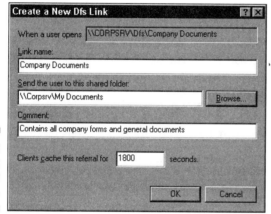

Figure 11-2: Creating a new Dfs link.

2. **Enter the desired name for the Dfs link and the network path to the shared folder.**

3. **If desired, enter a comment. The comment box is provided for administrative notes you may want to make.**

4. **If necessary, change the amount of time that clients cache the link information on their systems and then click OK.**

   The default time is 1,800 seconds. If the link seldom changes, you can extend the cache timeout value if desired.

   After you establish the Dfs link, it appears in the Dfs tree, as shown in Figure 11-3.

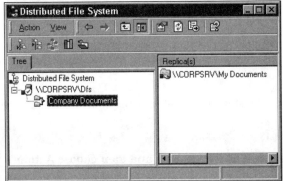

Figure 11-3:
A new Dfs
link appears
in the
Dfs tree.

Creating replicas

After you establish a Dfs link (see the preceding section), you can create additional replicas for the link. A *replica* is an alternate location of a shared folder. For example, the Dfs link Company Documents may reside in several locations.

By definition, a replica participates in replication, so you may have two or more shared folders that hold the same information and replicate with each other as that information changes. The replica set keeps track of the possible locations that Dfs can use to service clients. The alternate must be stored on a Windows 2000 server running NTFS and the Dfs service.

To create a replica, select the desired Dfs link in the console and then choose Action⇨New Replica. In the dialog box that's displayed, enter the alternate for the shared folder and then click OK. Keep in mind that the standalone Dfs offers no replication or backup. You can create a replica, but file replication does not work.

Understanding Dfs security

Dfs basically provides a link interface to users. When a user opens a Dfs link, Dfs redirects the user to the server that holds the shared folder. Dfs itself does not provide any inherent security because it only provides an interface for users to access shares. You set security for the shared folders on each folder on the server where the folder actually resides. Likewise, if you delete a Dfs link, you are not deleting any shared information in the folder; you are simply removing the link to the shared folder in the Dfs tree. See Chapter 9 for more information about setting up and configuring security on shared folders.

Managing a Domain-based Dfs

The domain-based Dfs is your best choice for implementing Dfs on a network. When you implement a domain-based DFS, you provide fault tolerance for the Dfs. Also, you can have root-level shared folders and you have no Dfs hierarchy limit — that is, you can have multiple levels of Dfs links.

When you implement a domain-based Dfs root, you must use a domain member server as the host, and you must store the Dfs *topology* — that is, the structure of the Dfs (such as roots and links) — in the Active Directory.

Setting up the Dfs root

Although you can create a Dfs root on either a FAT or an NTFS partition, FAT does not provide the security features of NTFS. Consequently, you should always create the root on an NTFS partition.

You create a domain-based Dfs root using the New Dfs Root wizard. Lab 11-4 shows you how to use the wizard to configure a domain-based Dfs root. You need to know these steps for the exam.

Lab 11-4   Creating a Domain-based Dfs Root

1. To start the New Dfs Root wizard, open the Dfs console and then choose Action⇨New Dfs Root.

2. Click Next on the wizard's welcome screen.

3. In the wizard's Select Dfs Root Type dialog box, click the Create a Domain Dfs Root radio button and then click Next.

4. Select the host domain for the Dfs root and click Next.

5. Enter the name of the server in the host domain that will host the Dfs root and click Next.

6. In the Specify Dfs Root Share dialog box, choose to use an existing share, or create a new one by entering the desired share name and path. Click Next.

   The DFS share holds the DFS information, so you can simply use a share already available on your server, or you may want to create a new one strictly for the Dfs root.

7. Enter a new name for the Dfs root and a comment, if desired. Click Next.

8. Click Finish.

Configuring the domain-based Dfs root

To configure a domain-based Dfs root, you use the same process as you use for a standalone Dfs. Refer to the section "Managing a Standalone Dfs," earlier in this chapter, for information on creating Dfs links and replicas.

For a domain-based Dfs, you can also create a new root replica by using the Action menu. This feature enables you to create a root replica on another domain member server.

Understanding domain-based Dfs replication

Because one of the major purposes of a domain-based Dfs is to provide fault tolerance, replication must occur between Dfs roots and shared folders to ensure that replicas hold an exact copy. In a standalone Dfs root, you can create folder replicas, but you have to perform replication manually. In a domain-based Dfs, replication can occur automatically.

You cannot use automatic replication on FAT volumes on Windows 2000 servers. By using only NTFS volumes for domain-based Dfs, you ensure that replication can occur automatically.

When you create a root replica in the Dfs console, a wizard appears that enables you to specify the server where the replica will reside. Dfs shared folders can also be replicated automatically on a domain-based Dfs. When you create a new replica for a shared folder, click the Automatic Replication radio button, as shown in Figure 11-4, so that replication can occur automatically.

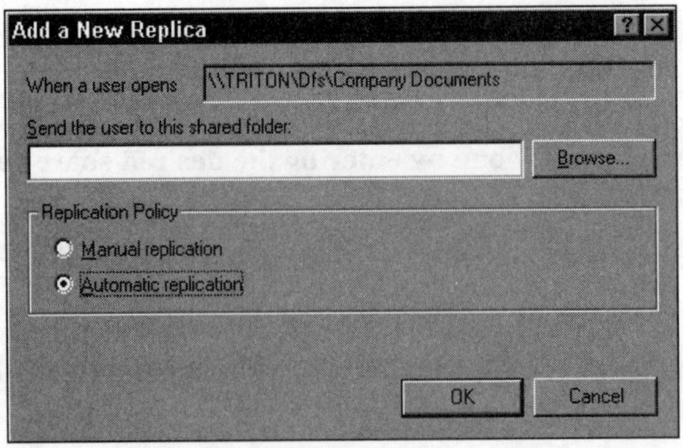

Figure 11-4:
Click the
Automatic
Replication
radio button
to use
automatic
folder
replication.

Add a New Replica

When a user opens   \\TRITON\Dfs\Company Documents

Send the user to this shared folder:

[   ]   Browse...

Replication Policy
○ Manual replication
● Automatic replication

OK   Cancel

Dfs uses the File Replication Service (FRS) to perform replication automatically. FRS manages updates across shared folders configured for replication. By default, FRS synchronizes the folder contents at 15-minute intervals.

When you set up the automatic replication, the Dfs console displays a dialog box in which you configure the replication policy. You can specify one share as the primary (or initial master). The primary replicates its contents to the other Dfs shared folder in the set.

Of course, you can choose to perform *manual replication,* in which you manually update the folder contents if a change occurs. For replica sets that seldom change, this may be a wise choice to reduce unnecessary synchronization traffic.

Within a set of Dfs shared folders, do not mix automatic and manual replication. Use one or the other to ensure that replication occurs properly.

Prep Test

1 On a domain-based Dfs, automatic replication does not seem to be occurring. You make certain that the Dfs is domain-based, and all other components appear to be configured correctly. What is the most likely cause of the problem?

A ○ The Dfs root is not configured for automatic replication.

B ○ The Dfs links are not configured correctly.

C ○ The Dfs is installed on a FAT volume.

D ○ Dfs does not support automatic replication.

2 You need to install a new Dfs link on the Dfs root. What do you need to do from this interface?

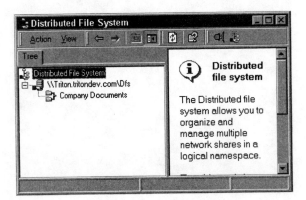

3 What is the Dfs client default timeout cache value?

A ○ 800 seconds

B ○ 1,200 seconds

C ○ 1,600 seconds

D ○ 1,800 seconds

4 On which file system(s) can you implement a Dfs?

A ○ NTFS, FAT, FAT32

B ○ NTFS and FAT32

C ○ NTFS and CDFS

D ○ NTFS only

5 On a domain-based Dfs, where is the Dfs topology stored?

A ○ On the Dfs root server

B ○ On all Dfs root servers in the domain

C ○ In the Active Directory

D ○ On the Dfs clients

6 Automatic Dfs folder replication is available on which of the following? (Choose all that apply.)

A ❑ FAT volumes

B ❑ NTFS volumes

C ❑ Domain-based Dfs

D ❑ Standalone Dfs

7 What does Dfs use to automatically synchronize Dfs shared folders in a domain-based Dfs?

A ○ Kerberos

B ○ FRS

C ○ DFSEXEC.EXE

D ○ NTLM

8 In a replica set, some folders use automatic replication while some are synchronized manually. However, the replica set does not seem to synchronize accurately. What should you do?

A ○ Use only automatic synchronization on a domain-based Dfs.

B ○ Use only manual synchronization on a domain-based Dfs.

C ○ Use only automatic synchronization on a standalone Dfs.

D ○ Use either automatic or manual synchronization, but not both.

Answers

1 *C. The Dfs is installed on a FAT volume.* In this scenario, the best answer is C. If automatic replication is not functional on a domain-based Dfs, the Dfs may be installed on a FAT volume, which does not support automatic replication. *Review "Managing a Domain-based Dfs."*

2 *Select the Dfs root, choose Action⇨New Dfs Link, enter the link information, and click OK.* You can easily add Dfs links to the Dfs tree by following these simple steps. *Read "Managing a Standalone Dfs."*

3 *D. 1,800 seconds.* By default, the client *cache timeout value* — that is, the amount of time a Dfs client stores a Dfs link in its cache — is 1,800 seconds. If changes rarely occur on the shared folder, you can reduce network traffic by increasing this value. *Review "Managing a Standalone Dfs."*

4 *A. NTFS, FAT, FAT32.* You can implement Dfs on NTFS or either FAT or FAT32 file systems, although NTFS is the file system of choice due to its advanced security features and support of automatic Dfs replication. *See "Managing a Standalone Dfs."*

5 *C. In the Active Directory.* A domain-based Dfs provides fault tolerance because the Dfs topology is stored in the Active Directory. *Study "Managing a Domain-based Dfs."*

6 *B and C.* Automatic replication for shared folders in Dfs is available only on a domain-based Dfs on NTFS volumes. *Study "Managing a Domain-based Dfs."*

7 *B. FRS.* FRS (File Replication Service) is used in Windows 2000 to perform automatic file synchronization in Dfs. *Study "Managing a Domain-based Dfs."*

8 *D. Use either automatic or manual synchronization, but not both.* On a domain-based Dfs where you have configured replica sets, you can use either automatic or manual synchronization, but you should not use both. *Study "Managing a Domain-based Dfs."*

Part IV

Configuring and Troubleshooting Hardware Devices and Drivers

The 5th Wave   By Rich Tennant

Ready? Begin the test.

MCSE Testing Center

Ready? "Flight of the Bumble Bee."

THE MIGHTY TUBAS
Jazz Ensemble

In this part . . .

In the world of Windows NT, hardware can cause great pain for systems administrators. As I explain in this part of the book, however, Windows 2000 is a plug-and-play operating system that makes your management of hardware much easier. Chapters 12 and 13 can examine the features and functions of hardware in Windows 2000, including installation, troubleshooting, and driver management and signing.

Chapter 12

Installing and Configuring Hardware

- -

Exam Objectives

▶ Configuring hardware devices

▶ Troubleshooting problems with hardware

- -

*F*ortunately, the powers-that-be at Microsoft have smiled on us and provided a plug-and-play operating system in Windows 2000. Instead of forc-
ing you to manually install and configure hardware devices, Windows 2000
automatically detects and attempts to install hardware on your system. Of
course, this plug-and-play system does not eliminate all the possible hardware problems and issues, but it certainly makes administrators' jobs easier.

In this chapter, I tell you what you need to know for the exam questions that
relate to the relatively easy process of convincing Windows 2000 to play nicely
with your hardware. You can review the following topics in this chapter:

✔ Installing hardware devices

✔ Troubleshooting installation problems

✔ Configuring hardware

Quick Assessment

Configuring hardware devices

1   Windows 2000 is a(n) _____ compliant system.

2   If Windows cannot automatically detect a hardware device, use the _____ to install the device.

3   You should always check the _____ before purchasing a hardware device for a Windows 2000 computer.

4   By using _____, you can access Properties dialog boxes for all hardware devices.

5   To determine the status of a hardware device, check the _____ tab in the device's Properties dialog box.

Troubleshooting problems with hardware

6   In addition to guiding you through the installation process, the Add/Remove Hardware wizard also functions as an effective _____ tool.

7   If Windows cannot detect a hardware device, make certain it is _____ to your computer correctly.

8   To find out whether conflicts exist with other hardware devices, check the _____ tab in a device's Properties dialog box.

Answers

1   *Plug-and-Play.* Review "Installing Windows 2000 Hardware."

2   *Add/Remove Hardware wizard.* Study "Installing Windows 2000 Hardware."

3   *HCL.* See "Installing Windows 2000 Hardware."

4   *Device Manager.* Examine "Configuring Hardware Devices."

5   *General.* Review "Configuring Hardware Devices."

6   *Troubleshooting.* See "Installing Windows 2000 Hardware."

7   *Physically Attached.* Read "Installing Windows 2000 Hardware."

8   *Resource.* Study "Configuring Hardware Devices."

Installing Windows 2000 Hardware

Installing hardware devices in Windows 2000 computers involves two steps. First, you physically attach the new hardware device to your computer, following the manufacturer's instructions. To avoid a potential electric shock and damage to your system, remember to turn off the power before you attach a new device.

Second, after you attach the device, boot your system. Windows 2000 should automatically detect the new hardware device and begin the installation wizard. For the most part, hardware installation does not require any intervention from you, with the exception of providing a disk or CD that contains the drivers for the hardware device. In many cases, Windows 2000 can install generic drivers for the device if you do not have the manufacturer's drivers. If possible, of course, you should always use the manufacturer's device drivers for Windows 2000 so the device functions completely and properly.

 Before purchasing a hardware device, check the Windows 2000 Hardware Compatibility List (HCL) to make certain that the device is compatible with Windows 2000. You can find the HCL on your installation CD-ROM or at www.microsoft.com.

Using the Add/Remove Hardware wizard

In some cases, Windows 2000 may not automatically detect a new hardware device that you attach to your system. For example, you may have non-plug-and-play (legacy) devices. In such cases, you can use Control Panel's Add/Remove Hardware wizard. Like Add/Remove Programs, the Add/Remove Hardware wizard scans your system for devices and enables you to install or remove hardware from your system. Using the wizard, you can select an "unknown" device and install the drivers for it, or you can remove the device, if desired.

 You can also use the Add/Remove Hardware wizard to troubleshoot devices. See Chapter 13 to review that process.

 Lab 12-1 reviews the steps for installing a hardware device using the Add/Remove Hardware wizard. Lab 12-2 explains how to uninstall a device.

Lab 12-1	Installing a Device by Using the Add/Remove Hardware Wizard

1. **Launch the wizard by double-clicking its icon in Control Panel.**

2. **Click Next on the wizard's welcome screen.**

3. In the Choose a Hardware Task dialog box, select the Add/Troubleshoot a Device radio button and then click Next.

Windows searches for new hardware and then displays the new hardware along with any problem hardware. As shown in Figure 12-1, you can then choose to install the new hardware or troubleshoot existing hardware.

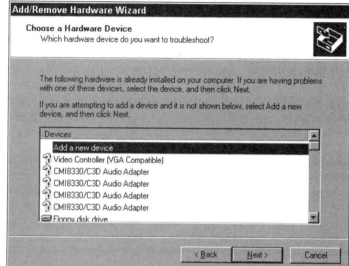

Figure 12-1:
Choosing a hardware device.

4. If Windows did not detect your hardware, select the Add a New Device option so you can manually install the hardware. Click Next.

5. In the resulting Find New Hardware dialog box, select the No button so you can manually install the hardware and then click Next.

6. From the list that appears, select the type of hardware that you want to install and then click Next.

7. In the Select a Device Driver dialog box, select the manufacturer of the device and the model, or click the Have Disk button to install the drivers from a disk or CD.

8. Click Next and then click Finish.

Lab 12-2	Uninstalling a Device by Using the Add/Remove Hardware Wizard

1. Launch the wizard by double-clicking its icon in Control Panel.

2. Click Next on the welcome screen.

3. In the Choose a Hardware Task dialog box, select the Uninstall/Unplug a Device radio button and then click Next.

4. **In the Choose a Removal Task dialog box that's displayed, select either the Uninstall a Device radio button or the Unplug/Eject a Device radio button. Uninstall completely removes the device and its drivers, while the Unplug/Eject option temporarily disables a device. Click Next.**

5. **Select the device that you want to uninstall or unplug and then click Next.**

6. **Click Yes and then click Finish.**

Troubleshooting hardware installations

In a perfect world, you would never have any problems installing hardware on a plug-and-play system. Alas, your network does not live in a perfect world, and hardware installation can pose a few problems.

For the exam, you are expected to know how to troubleshoot hardware installation problems. To help you prepare for those troubleshooting questions, this section describes the common problems and solutions that you are likely to encounter in the real world and on the exam. You should memorize this list before you take the exam:

✔ **The system cannot detect a device:** If your system cannot detect a device, two problems may exist. First, check the device and make certain it is physically attached to your computer correctly. If the device has a separate power supply, make certain the device is turned on. Second, make certain the device is compatible with Windows 2000.

✔ **A manually installed device does not appear on the system:** If you use the Add/Remove Hardware wizard to manually install a device by selecting the device from the list, but the device still does not appear on the system or is not operational, use the Add/Remove Hardware wizard to troubleshoot the device. See Chapter 13 for more details.

✔ **The system cannot detect a device, and the device does not appear in the Add Hardware list:** If the system cannot detect a hardware device, and the device does not appear in the list displayed by the Add/Remove Hardware wizard, the device probably is not compatible with Windows 2000. You can bypass this problem by using the hardware device's installation disk or CD-ROM to install it. If the disk or CD is not available, you probably will not be able to get the device to work with your system.

Configuring Hardware Devices

After you install a hardware device (see the previous sections in this chapter), you can further configure the device so it performs on your system as desired. Depending on the device, you may find an icon for it in Control Panel. If so, you can double-click the icon to open the device's Properties dialog box and make the desired changes.

For example, by double-clicking Phone and Modem Options in Control Panel, you can configure your modem and dialing rules. On the Modems tab in the resulting dialog box, you can access properties for the modem and make any desired changes.

For study purposes, you do not need to know what you can do on each tab in each device's Properties dialog box. You should know how to access a device's properties and you should know about troubleshooting the configuration of each device, which I discuss in this section and in Chapter 13.

For other devices, you can access their properties by using Device Manager, which is a part of the Windows 2000 Computer Management Console. Click Start⇨Programs⇨Administrative Tools⇨Computer Management. In the console's tree pane, click the Device Manager, and a list of all device categories appears in the right pane, as shown in Figure 12-2.

Figure 12-2:
Device
Manager.

If you expand the desired category, you can see a list of devices installed on your system for that category. To configure a device, right-click the device and choose Properties from the pop-up menu.

Each device may have different properties sheets, depending on the device. Also, devices that appear in Control Panel may have more configuration options (such as modems and keyboards). For most devices, the Properties dialog box includes General, Driver, and Resources tabs, as well as others, depending on the device. Chapter 13 tells you all about configuring drivers, so refer to that chapter for more information about the Driver tab.

The General tab for each device gives you information about the device and its status. Figure 12-3 shows the General tab.

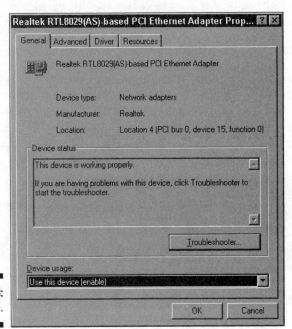

Figure 12-3:
General tab.

If you are having problems with a device, always check the General tab first. If the device is not working properly, the Device Status window tells you so and often points out the problem.

You can also launch the Troubleshooter tool by clicking the Troubleshooter button. This action leads you through a series of steps to help you identify the problem. You can read more about the Troubleshooter in Chapter 13.

Also, at the bottom of the General tab, you can disable the device by selecting that option from the drop-down list. This feature is helpful in troubleshooting as well.

As shown in Figure 12-4, the Resources tab gives you information about which system resources the hardware device uses, such I/O Range and IRQ. Fortunately, Windows 2000 does a good job of assigning system resources to hardware devices automatically, so you typically do not need to manually configure such resource allocations as IRQ and I/O Ranges. You can change these settings, if necessary — for example, if the device has resource conflicts with other devices. The Resources tab tells you about the conflict in the Conflicting Device List box.

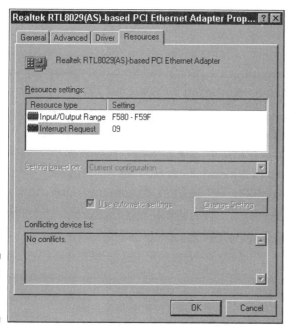

Figure 12-4:
Resources
tab.

Prep Test

1 Windows 2000 can automatically detect and install which type of hardware devices?

A ○ Modems

B ○ Hard Disks

C ○ CD and DVD Drives

D ○ Any Plug-and-Play Hardware

2 You want to install and configure a legacy device on a Windows 2000 computer. What will you probably need in order to complete the installation?

A ○ IRQ Settings

B ○ I/O Settings

C ○ Device Drivers

D ○ Legacy devices cannot be installed on Windows 2000

3 You want to temporarily disable a hardware device. How can you do this without removing the device from the system? (Choose all that apply.)

A ❑ On the General tab in the device's Properties dialog box

B ❑ On the Resource tab in the device's Properties dialog box

C ❑ By manually removing the device from the system

D ❑ By using the unplug option in the Add/Remove Hardware wizard

4 You manually install a legacy device and assign an IRQ for the device. How can you easily determine whether this assignment creates a conflict with another device?

A ○ Use the General tab in the device's properties.

B ○ Use the Resources tab in the device's properties.

C ○ Use the Add/Remove Hardware wizard.

D ○ Uninstall the device to troubleshoot the problem.

5 You want to view properties for several different devices on your Windows 2000 server. How can you use the Computer Management Console to perform this action?

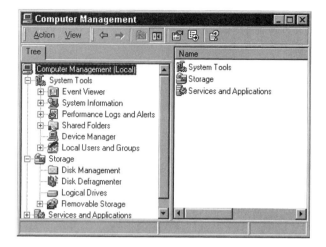

6 You attach a plug-and-play device to your Windows 2000 server, but the system cannot automatically detect it. What should you do first?

A ○ Run the Add/Remove Hardware wizard.

B ○ Make certain the device is physically attached to your computer correctly.

C ○ Check the driver.

D ○ Manually install it.

7 You need to access the complete properties for a scanner attached to your computer. Where can you view the complete properties for the device?

A ○ Device Manager

B ○ Scanner Properties in Hardware profiles

C ○ Control Panel

D ○ Add/Remove Hardware Wizard

8 You are having a problem with a particular device and need to troubleshoot it. You want Windows 2000 to help you troubleshoot the device. Which options can you use to allow Windows 2000 to help you troubleshoot the device? (Choose all that apply.)

A ❑ Click the Troubleshooter button on the General tab in the device's Properties dialog box.

B ❑ Click the Troubleshooter button on the device's Resources tab.

C ❑ Use the Add/Remove Hardware wizard.

D ❑ Access Windows Help files.

Answers

1 *D. Any Plug-and-Play Hardware.* Windows 2000 is a plug-and-play-compliant system that can automatically detect and install plug-and-play devices. *Review "Installing Windows 2000 Hardware."*

2 *C. Device Drivers.* To install a non-plug-and-play device, you need the drivers for the device to manually install it when you run the Add/Remove Hardware wizard. *Read "Installing Windows 2000 Hardware."*

3 *A and D.* You may disable a device for troubleshooting purposes without removing the device from the system. You can accomplish this by disabling the device in the Device Usage drop-down list on the General tab in the device's Properties dialog box, or by using the Add/Remove Hardware wizard to unplug the device. *Review "Installing Windows 2000 Hardware."*

4 *B. Use the Resources tab in the device's properties.* If you believe that a resource conflict exists, such as IRQ or I/O settings, access the Resources tab in the device's Properties dialog box. The Conflicting Device List box automatically lists any conflicting devices. *See "Configuring Hardware Devices."*

5 *Click Device Manager in the console's tree pane, expand the desired device categories in the right pane, right-click the desired device, and then choose Properties from the pop-up menu.* Device Manager is an integrated part of the Computer Management console. After you access the console, you can click Device Manager to access properties for various hardware devices. *Study "Configuring Hardware Devices."*

6 *B. Make certain the device is physically attached to your computer correctly.* If you are installing a plug-and-play device and the system cannot detect it, your first troubleshooting step is to make certain the hardware is physically attached to your computer correctly. Running the Add/Remove Hardware wizard will attempt another detection, but will mainly prompt you to manually install the hardware. *Study "Installing Windows 2000 Hardware."*

7 *C. Control Panel.* Several hardware devices, such as scanners, modems, and keyboards, have icons in Control Panel that you can use to fully configure the device on your system. *Study "Configuring Hardware Devices."*

8 *A and C.* Windows 2000 can assist you in troubleshooting hardware. Use the Troubleshooter button on the General tab in the device's Properties dialog box to start the troubleshooter, or use the Add/Remove Hardware wizard to help you troubleshoot a problem device. *Study "Configuring Hardware Devices."*

Chapter 13

Managing Hardware

· ·

Exam Objectives

▶ Configuring driver signing options
▶ Troubleshooting hardware problems

· ·

*W*indows 2000 makes hardware management easy. With installation wizards and helpful configuration tools, not to mention a plug-and-play operating system, hardware management should no longer consume inordinate amounts of time for system administrators.

In this chapter, I tell you what you need to know for the exam questions that relate to managing hardware. You can review the following topics in this chapter:

✔ Managing drivers and driver signing
✔ Working with hardware profiles
✔ Using troubleshooting tools

Quick Assessment

Configuring
driver sign-
ing options

1 The term *driver* refers to _____ that enables a hardware device to communicate with your operating system.

2 You can easily update a driver for a device by using the _____ tab in the device's Properties dialog box.

3 Windows 2000 provides the _____ to help you install or update drivers.

4 By removing a driver, you effectively remove the _____ from your operating system.

5 _____ is the process manufacturers use to digitally sign a driver.

6 The default driver signing setting in Windows 2000 is _____.

Trouble-
shooting
hardware
problems

7 You can find hardware devices on your system that are not functioning and then determine the problem by using the _____.

8 On a hardware device's General tab, you can click the _____ button to access Windows Help files that guide you to a solution for a particular hardware problem.

Answers

1 *Software.* Review "Managing Drivers."

2 *Driver.* Study "Managing Drivers."

3 *Update Driver Wizard.* See "Managing Drivers."

4 *Hardware Device.* Examine "Managing Drivers."

5 *Driver Signing.* Review "Managing Drivers."

6 *Warn.* See "Managing Drivers."

7 *Add/Remove Hardware Wizard.* Read "Using Hardware Troubleshooting Tools."

8 *Troubleshooter.* Study "Using Hardware Troubleshooting Tools."

Managing Drivers

A *driver* is software that enables the operating system to control a particular hardware device. You can think of a driver as the bridge between the operating system and the hardware. Typically, the company that makes the hardware device also manufactures the driver, which you get on a floppy disk or CD-ROM when you purchase the hardware.

The Windows 2000 operating system also contains an extensive list of generic drivers. When you install a new piece of hardware, Windows searches for the best driver for the device, including drivers that you provide with a floppy disk or CD-ROM. As I explain in the following sections, you manage drivers in two different ways: through the Driver tab in a device's Properties dialog box, or through your computer's system properties.

Using the Driver tab

Each hardware device has a Driver tab in its Properties dialog box. As you can see in Figure 13-1, the Driver tab lists information about the driver and its manufacturer, and you have the options to view driver details, uninstall the driver, or update the driver.

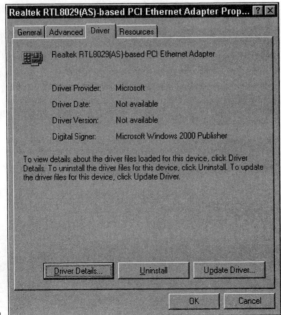

Figure 13-1:
Use the
Driver tab to
uninstall or
update the
device
driver.

To view the driver file, provider, file version, and copyright, click Driver Details.

If you click Uninstall, a warning message appears, telling you that you are about to remove the device from your system. If you remove the driver and then decide that you want to use the device after all, Windows 2000 must repeat the detection-and-installation process to install the hardware device.

For the exam, remember that removing a device's driver effectively removes the device from the system. Hardware cannot function with your operating system without an appropriate driver.

By clicking Update Driver on the Driver tab, you open the Upgrade Device Driver wizard. Due to the constant updates and refinements of device drivers, Microsoft provides this handy wizard so you can update device drivers when updates become available. The wizard prompts you for the location of the new driver, searches for it, and then automatically installs it for the device. This wizard offers an easy way to make driver updates and changes.

Choosing driver signing options

Driver signing is the process manufactures use to digitally sign drivers so you can be assured that they come from the manufacturer and are safe for your system. Similar to the digitally signed software that you can download from the Internet, digitally signed driver files protect you from downloading a hidden virus or some other potentially dangerous piece of code.

By default, Windows 2000 checks all new software — that is, both system software and drivers — for a digital signature. If the system does not find or verify a digital signature, you receive a warning message. To ensure the integrity of your installation CD-ROM, all Windows 2000 CD files are digitally signed and checked during setup.

The exam expects you to know how to change the driver signing options — an easy process. On the desktop, right-click My Computer and then choose Properties. In the Properties dialog box, click the Hardware tab. Notice that you can launch the Hardware wizard and Device Manager, and you can set up Hardware Profiles from this location. Click Driver Signing. As shown in Figure 13-2, Windows displays the Driver Signing Options dialog box.

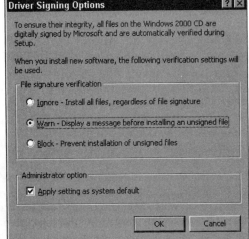

Figure 13-2:
Make
desired
driver
signing
changes in
this dialog
box.

You have the following configuration options, which you should memorize for the exam:

- ✔ **Ignore:** This setting installs all files, regardless of the digital signature or whether one exists.

- ✔ **Warn:** This is the default setting, which gives you a warning message before installing an unsigned file.

- ✔ **Block:** This setting stops the installation of any unsigned file.

- ✔ **Administrator Option:** This option enables you to set the selected setting as the default for all users who log on to the computer. You must be logged on as an administrator to use this option.

Using Hardware Profiles

By using hardware profiles, you can configure the system hardware to meet your needs. Your profile is in effect each time you log on. If another user who accesses the same machine has different needs, you can create a different profile for that user. You often see hardware profiles used on laptop computers. You may have one profile in effect while connected to the network and another for use when you are not connected to the network.

You won't see lots of hardware profile questions on the exam, because servers typically are not used by numerous people requiring different hardware settings.

You access hardware profiles on the Hardware tab of System Properties. To access System Properties, right-click My Computer and then choose Properties. By clicking the Hardware Profiles button on the Hardware tab in the System Properties dialog box, you access a simple interface in which you can easily create new profiles and define settings for laptop computers. As shown in Figure 13-3, you use the radio buttons in this Hardware Profiles dialog box to select the desired boot-up settings so you can choose the hardware profile desired.

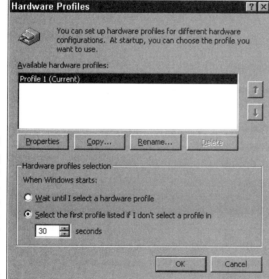

Figure 13-3:
Use the
Hardware
Profiles
interface to
create or
configure
profiles.

That's all you need to know for the exam, so this section does not delve any deeper into the creation of hardware profiles.

Using Hardware Troubleshooting Tools

Windows 2000 attempts to make hardware problem resolution much easier than in previous versions by providing two troubleshooting tools. You can use the Add/Remove Hardware wizard, or the Troubleshooter tool.

Troubleshooting with the Add/Remove Hardware wizard

The Add/Remove Hardware wizard can help you troubleshoot problem hardware. Lab 13-1 shows you how to use the troubleshooting feature of the wizard, and you should be familiar with these steps for the exam.

Lab 13-1	Troubleshooting with the Add/Remove Hardware Wizard

1. **Click Start⇨Settings⇨Control Panel.**

2. **Double-click Add/Remove Hardware.**

3. **Click Next on the welcome screen.**

4. **Click the Add/Troubleshoot a Device radio button and then click Next.**

    Windows searches for new or problem devices and presents you with a list of the devices that it finds.

5. **From the list, select the problem device and click Next.**

    The wizard displays a summary window that identifies the problem with the device, as shown in Figure 13-4.

6. **Click Finish to complete the wizard. After you click Finish, the Troubleshooter opens automatically to assist you.**

Figure 13-4: The Device Status box lists the problem that the device is experiencing.

If the problem involves the device driver, Windows automatically launches the Upgrade Device Driver wizard.

Using the Troubleshooter tool

Windows 2000 provides a Troubleshooter tool to help you resolve problems with hardware devices. The Troubleshooter walks you through a series of questions to attempt to find the problem and its solution.

You can access the Troubleshooter from the problem device's Properties dialog box. On the General tab, click the Troubleshooter button to launch the tool.

The Troubleshooter is a part of the Windows 2000 Help files. As shown in Figure 13-5, the Display Troubleshooter gives you a series of radio buttons. Select the problem you are having and then click Next. You may walk through several of these screens until Windows 2000 determines the problem and presents you with a solution.

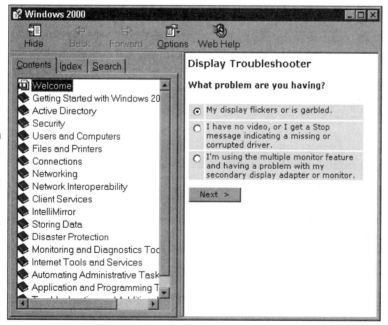

Figure 13-5:
The Trouble-shooter guides you through a series of questions to find the problem with your device.

Prep Test

1 An external CD-ROM drive attached to your server is not functioning properly. What are two actions that you can take to quickly discover the potential problem? (Choose two.)

  A ○ Run HDWSCN.EXE.

  B ○ Use the Add/Remove Hardware wizard.

  C ○ Reattach the device to the system.

  D ○ Check the General tab of the device's Properties dialog box for a status report.

2 You use the Driver tab to remove a driver from a hardware device. What must you do to install a new driver after you remove the old one?

  A ○ Nothing.

  B ○ Click the Update Driver button.

  C ○ Run the Add/Remove Hardware wizard so Windows can detect the device again.

  D ○ Remove the device from your computer and then re-attach it.

3 What is the default Driver Signing option in Windows 2000?

  A ○ Ignore

  B ○ Block

  C ○ Warn

  D ○ Remove

4 You want to change the default driver signing option on your Windows 2000 Server computer. Where can you perform this action?

  A ○ Driver tab

  B ○ Driver Properties

  C ○ System Properties

  D ○ Add/Remove Hardware wizard

5 You want to prevent any unsigned drivers from being installed on your Windows 2000 system, and you want to make certain that this setting applies, regardless of who uses the computer. What do you need to do in the Driver Signing Options dialog box to configure this setup?

```
Driver Signing Options                    ? X

To ensure their integrity, all files on the Windows 2000 CD are
digitally signed by Microsoft and are automatically verified during
Setup.

When you install new software, the following verification settings will
be used.

 ─ File signature verification ──────────────────────────────
  ○ Ignore - Install all files, regardless of file signature

  ● Warn - Display a message before installing an unsigned file

  ○ Block - Prevent installation of unsigned files


 ─ Administrator option ─────────────────────────────────────
  ☐ Apply setting as system default


              [    OK    ]    [   Cancel   ]
```

6 Which of the following actions can you perform using the Hardware tab in System Properties? (Choose all that apply.)

A ○ Launch the Hardware wizard.

B ○ Access Driver Signing Options.

C ○ Launch Device Manager.

D ○ Access the Hardware Profiles dialog box.

7 You are having problems with a network adapter card. The card seems to be functioning and the driver is installed correctly. Which tool can you use to help you discover the solution to the problem?

A ○ Add/Remove Hardware wizard

B ○ General tab

C ○ Resources tab

D ○ Troubleshooter

8 What is the best way to install a new driver for a hardware device using a floppy disk?

A ○ Use the General tab in the device's Properties dialog box.

B ○ Manually place the new driver in the appropriate directory.

C ○ Click the Update Driver button on the Driver tab in the device's Properties dialog box.

D ○ You cannot update a driver from a floppy disk.

Answers

1 *B and D.* You can use the Add/Remove Hardware wizard to troubleshoot a problem device. The wizard can check the device and possibly tell you the problem. Also, you can check the Status section on the General tab in the device's Properties dialog box to identify any problems with the device. *Review "Using Hardware Troubleshooting Tools."*

2 *C. Run the Add/Remove Hardware wizard so Windows can detect the device again.* If you need to update a driver, click the Update Driver button on the Driver tab. If you remove the driver, you effectively remove the device from your system. In that case, you need to run the Add/Remove Hardware wizard so it can detect and reinstall the device. *Read "Managing Drivers."*

3 *C. Warn.* By default, Windows warns you before you install an unsigned device driver. *Review "Managing Drivers."*

4 *C. System Properties.* You can configure driver signing options by accessing system properties, clicking the Hardware tab, and then clicking the Driver Signing button. *See "Managing Drivers."*

5 *Click the Block radio button and then select the Apply Setting as System Default check box.* If you are logged on as an administrator, you can change the default driver signing option and use the Administrator option to make certain that Windows preserves your new setting as the system default. *Study "Managing Drivers."*

6 *A, B, C, and D.* The Hardware tab in System Properties provides an easy access point for all these operations. *Study "Managing Drivers."*

7 *D. Troubleshooter.* If you have device problems that you cannot resolve, launch the Troubleshooter from the General tab in the device's Properties dialog box so Windows 2000 Help can attempt to guide you to a solution. *Study "Using Hardware Troubleshooting Tools."*

8 *C. Click the Update Driver button on the Driver tab in the device's Properties dialog box.* The Update Driver button launches the Update Driver wizard, which enables you to update a device driver from an external source, such as a floppy disk or CD-ROM. *Study "Managing Drivers."*

Part V
Managing Windows 2000 Server

The 5th Wave   By Rich Tennant

"GET READY, I THINK THEY'RE STARTING TO DRIFT."

In this part . . .

I cannot overstate the importance of managing system performance and ensuring that you can recover data. In order to meet the needs of your network, your Windows 2000 server must be able to perform in a satisfactory manner, and you must be able to recover lost data.

In Chapters 14 and 15, you explore the tools and techniques you use for monitoring and optimization, managing priority processes, and managing system state data. You also review the use of Windows Backup and the backup technologies available to you.

Chapter 14

Managing System Performance

• •

Exam Objectives

▶ Monitoring and optimizing usage of system resources

▶ Setting priorities and starting and stopping processes

▶ Optimizing disk performance

▶ Managing and optimizing availability of system state data and user data

• •

*A*s a systems administrator, you need to make certain that your servers are functioning at their peak. This objective includes monitoring your system, solving system resource problems, and even optimizing hard disks. These tasks may not be overwhelming or difficult, but they do require your careful attention to system processes and their performance.

For the exam, you need to know how to manage system and disk performance, as well as how to use Windows 2000 tools, such as Performance Monitor, MSINFO, and even Disk Defragmenter. You can review the following tasks in this chapter:

  ✔ Managing system process and resource usage with Performance Monitor

  ✔ Using MSINFO

  ✔ Configuring performance options and using Task Manager

  ✔ Optimizing disk performance

  ✔ Understanding system state data and user data

Quick Assessment

Monitoring and optimizing usage of system resources

1 To chart system processes in Performance Monitor, you add performance _____.

2 By default, Windows 2000 stores all Performance Monitor logs in _____.

3 To determine whether your system processor is overworked, you use the _____ counter.

4 Use the _____ command to enable Performance Monitor to collect data about logical drives.

Setting priorities and starting and stopping processes

5 On the Advanced tab in the System Properties, you can choose to prioritize either applications or _____.

6 You can use Task Manager's _____ tab to stop system processes.

7 Performance Monitor's Performance tab gives you a percentage reading for both the CPU and _____.

Optimizing disk performance

8 _____ is the process that occurs when your system stores data on the hard disk in a noncontiguous manner.

9 By using _____, you can easily remove old and unnecessary files from your hard disk.

Managing and optimizing availability of system state data and user data

10 The Active Directory services database and the SYSVOL folder are part of system state data only for Windows 2000 _____.

Answers

1   *Counters.* See "Managing System Process and Resource Usage with Performance Monitor."

2   *C:\PerfLogs.* Study "Managing System Process and Resource Usage with Performance Monitor."

3   *Processor \ % Processor Time.* See "Managing System Process and Resource Usage with Performance Monitor."

4   *DiskPerf.* Examine "Managing System Process and Resource Usage with Performance Monitor."

5   *Background Processes.* Review "Configuring Performance Options."

6   *Processes.* See "Using Task Manager."

7   *Memory.* Read "Using Task Manager."

8   *Fragmentation.* Study "Optimizing Disk Performance."

9   *Disk Cleanup.* See "Optimizing Disk Performance."

10   *Domain Controllers.* See "Understanding System State Data and User Data."

Managing System Process and Resource Usage with Performance Monitor

If you have ever used Windows NT on a system admin level, you are familiar with Performance Monitor, which makes a strong return in Windows 2000. Performance Monitor is one of those tools that network administrators tend to avoid (until they need it, anyway), which makes problem resolution much more difficult.

For the exam, you need to know how to use Performance Monitor. Specifically, you need to know which performance counters you should use to monitor various processes and resources. Although you can use Performance Monitor to monitor many system processes, I focus only on what you need to know for the exam in the following sections.

Using Performance Monitor

Like most other tools in Windows 2000, Performance Monitor is an MMC snap-in. It functions in the same manner as all other snap-ins.

To access Performance Monitor, click Start⇨Programs⇨ Administrative Tools⇨Performance. The Performance Monitor snap-in appears, as shown in Figure 14-1.

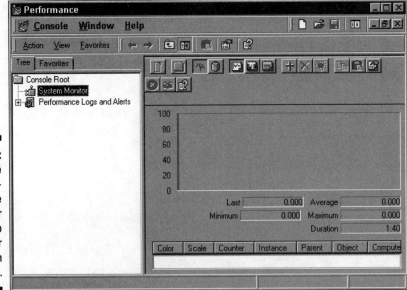

Figure 14-1:
Use the Performance Monitor snap-in to monitor system processes.

You have two basic options when you use Performance Monitor: You can create charts for the System Monitor, or you can generate logs and alerts. As you can see in Figure 14-1, both of these options are available under the console root.

You use the System Monitor tool to monitor processes that are occurring on your system. You create this monitor by creating a chart of system processes that you want to monitor, which you accomplish by adding *counters*. To add counters, click the Add button above the chart in the right console pane (shown as a + sign). After you click the Add button, Performance Monitor displays the Add Counters dialog box, as shown in Figure 14-2.

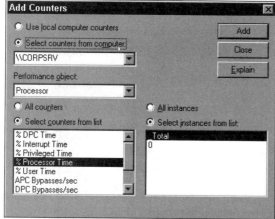

Figure 14-2:
Use the Add
Counters
dialog box
to create
perfor-
mance
charts.

In the Add Counters dialog box, you select the computer that you want to monitor. Then, you select the performance object and either all counters for that object or selected counters. You can select many different performance objects, such as processor, system, memory, paging file, and physical disk. For each object, you select different counters that you want to monitor.

See the next section, "Reviewing important counters," to review specific counters that you need to know for the exam.

After you add the desired counters for the desired object and close the Add Counters dialog box, you can see the charting process taking place, as shown in Figure 14-3. Notice that Performance Monitor assigns a different color for each counter so you can easily track each counter.

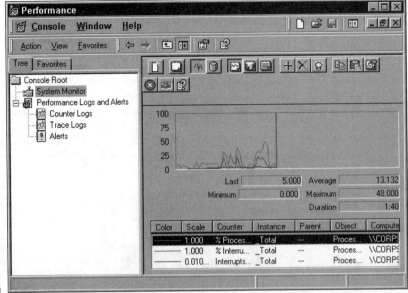

Figure 14-3:
Added
counters are
charted in the
Performance
Monitor
window.

Using the buttons on the toolbar, you can also choose to view the counters in a histogram or report form instead of a chart.

In addition to creating counter charts that you can view, you can create performance logs and configure performance alerts. Expand Performance Logs and Alerts in the console tree, right-click Counter Logs or Trace Logs, assign a new log name, and then create the log file as desired.

Counter log files record activity for counters that you specify, and trace logs are designed to "trace" certain activity, such as I/O or page faults. You do need a tool to parse trace logs so you can extract the data you need (which is a developmental task). For each log type, you can create a new log setting by right-clicking the counter log. When you create a new setting, a window appears in which you can configure the log (either add counters or trace providers) and configure a schedule for the logs to run. By default, all log files are stored in C:\PerfLogs.

In the same manner, you can create alerts so that administrators can be contacted when particular system resources or processes reach a threshold value. Right-click Alerts, choose New Alert Settings, and then provide a name for the new settings. This action opens the Properties dialog box. You can add a counter and then assign a value limit at which an alert will be generated. On the Action tab, you can then determine what action should be taken when the value limit is triggered. You have the following options:

✔ Log an entry in the application event log.

✔ Send a network message.

✔ Start performance data log.

✔ Run a particular program.

Reviewing important counters

For the exam, you need to know the major performance counters. Exam questions may present a particular problem and ask you which performance counters you should use to attempt to find the problem. In the following sections, I examine several counter objects and the counters for those objects that you need to know for the exam. You need to memorize all of these, so make certain you study carefully.

Memory

System memory has an important effect on system performance. Without enough system memory, excessive paging occurs. *Paging* is the process of temporarily writing blocks of data to the hard disk because the system does not have enough RAM available to keep the data in memory. As system resources call for the paged information, the system reads the data from the hard disk back into memory. Paging is an important part of Windows 2000, and you can expect paging to occur. However, excessive paging will slow your system responsiveness, indicating that you need more RAM.

You can use Performance Monitor to track system memory performance by choosing the memory object and using the following counters, which you need to know for the exam:

✔ **Memory \ Available Bytes and Memory \ Cached Bytes:** Use these counters to examine memory usage on your system.

✔ **Memory \ Pages/sec; Memory \ Page Reads/sec; Memory \ Transition Faults/sec; and Memory \ Pool Paged Bytes:** Use these counters to examine memory bottlenecks.

Processor

Your system processor manages all system processing and threads. In networking environments, the demands of the network may outgrow the processing power of your system processor. In many cases, you see an overall system slow-down and a slow-down in services that meet the needs of network clients. In such cases, you can either reduce the load on the server or upgrade to another processor.

You can use Performance Monitor to examine the activity of your system processor. For the exam, you need to know the following counters:

- **Processor \ % Processor Time:** Use this counter to examine the processor usage. A consistently high % Processor Time reading tells you that your processor is overworked and cannot keep up with the demand placed on it.

- **Processor \ Processor Queue Length; Processor \ Interrupts/sec; System \ Processor Queue Length; and System \ Context switches/sec:** You can use all these counters to examine the system processor and determine whether it has become a bottleneck.

Disk

Your hard disk is automatically a Windows 2000 Performance Monitor object, and you can use Performance Monitor to examine its performance.

For the exam, remember that by default, Windows 2000 does not collect logical disk counter data. If you want to get performance data for logical drives for storage volumes, you have to use the **diskperf -yv** command at the command line.

Keep the following disk counters in mind for the exam:

- **Physical Disk \ Disk Reads/sec; Physical Disk \ Disk Writes/sec; and LogicalDisk \ % Free Space:** Use these counters to examine disk usage.

- **Physical Disk \ Avg. Disk Queue Length:** Use this counter to determine whether your disk has become a bottleneck.

Configuring Performance Options

As I explain in the preceding section, you can use Performance Monitor to manage your system performance. To make further configuration choices, you can also access the Advanced tab of the System Properties dialog box.

Right-click My Computer, choose Properties, and then click the Advanced tab. If you click the Performance Options button, you get two choices. First, you can choose to optimize system performance for either applications or background services. By default, the background services option is selected. This option enables your system to provide more priority to background services than to applications that may be running. By clicking the radio button, you can change this setting so that applications have priority. However, doing so may slow down background processes.

You can also click the Change button to make changes to your total paging file size. The minimum paging file size is 2MB, and the recommended size is 1.5 times the amount of RAM on your system. Your paging file is automatically set to the recommended setting, but you can change it if desired.

Windows does a good job of managing its own paging file. If you reduce or increase the paging file too much, you may experience system performance problems. Generally, you should not change this setting.

However, you can optimize the performance of the paging file by moving it to a different disk. For example, if your server contains two hard disks, place the paging file on the disk that does not contain the boot partition. By doing so, you can help system performance.

Using Task Manager

Another important tool that enables you to manage system processes and performance is Task Manager. You access Task Manager by right-clicking an empty area of the taskbar and then choosing Task Manager from the pop-up menu.

Task Manager has three tabs: Applications, Processes, and Performance. The Applications tab shows a list of running applications. You can select any running application and then click End Task, Switch To, or New Task. Typically, you use this tab to end a malfunctioning application.

On the Processes tab, you see a list of all processes running on your system. You can select any process and click End Process to stop the process from running. This feature is also useful in troubleshooting system problems that you believe are caused by a system process.

Finally, the Performance tab shows the percentage amount of CPU usage and memory usage. You can use this tab to see how much CPU or memory resources are currently in use and whether either one appears to be a bottleneck.

Using MSINFO

If you ever took a peek at Windows 98, you may be familiar with the Microsoft Information tool (MSINFO), which Microsoft introduced with that operating system. All Windows 2000 operating systems include MSINFO, and it is an excellent tool for gaining information about your system and troubleshooting problems. Figure 14-4 shows this tool.

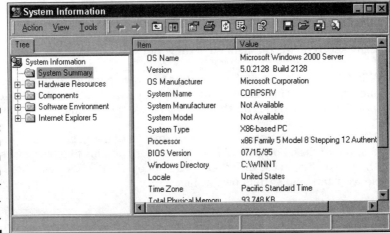

Figure 14-4:
Use System
Information
to gain data
about your
system con-
figuration.

You can access System Information by clicking
Start➪Programs➪Accessories➪System Tools➪System Information.
Alternatively, click Start➪Run, type **MSINFO32**, and then click OK.

System Information gives you an MMC snap-in interface, with categories for
System Summary, Hardware Resources, Components, Software Environment,
and Internet Explorer 5.

You don't have to worry about many exam questions on System Information.
For the exam, you only need to know what information is available in each
category:

- ✓ **System Summary:** The System Summary gives you a complete look at
  your computer system by listing basic system information, including OS
  name, system name, system type, processor, BIOS version, and physical
  memory.

- ✓ **Hardware Resources:** You can check your system's IRQ usage, DMA allocation, memory resources, forced hardware, I/O configuration, and any
  conflicts or sharing that exist on your system.

- ✓ **Components:** This container holds information about your system components, such as multimedia, display, network connections, modems,
  and printing. It also has a category for Problem Devices so you can
  determine the solutions to problems you may be experiencing with
  system components.

✔ **Software Environment:** This container holds information about your system software configuration, such as drivers, environment variables, network connections, running tasks, and services.

✔ **Internet Explorer 5:** This container holds your current settings for IE 5, including file versions, connectivity, cache, content, and security.

Optimizing Disk Performance

Windows 2000 Server contains several tools to help you optimize your disk performance. These easy-to-use tools play important roles in your efforts to manage your Windows 2000 Server. You access some of the tools by clicking Start⇨Programs⇨Accessories⇨System Tools, and you can access all of them by clicking the Tools menu in System Information.

You won't see many questions about these tools, but you do need to know what each of the following tools can do and when you should use each tool:

✔ **Disk Cleanup:** Disk Cleanup is a handy utility you can use to clean out old files on your hard disk in order to free up more storage space. Of course, you can delete these files manually, but Disk Cleanup gives you a quick and easy way to perform the task because Disk Cleanup finds the files that you may want to delete. When you launch Disk Cleanup, the program scans your system and presents you with a list of files you can choose to delete, such as cached Internet files and other files that are no longer in use.

✔ **Dr. Watson:** Dr. Watson is a program error debugger that you may have seen in previous versions of Windows. Dr. Watson logs program errors that you can use to diagnose and solve system problems. Dr. Watson logs errors in a text file called DRWTSN32.LOG whenever an error is detected. Typically, you use Dr. Watson to log errors that you can then send to support personnel for analysis.

✔ **Disk Defragmenter:** Disk Defragmenter is now available in Windows 2000 as an MMC snap-in. Over time, as you create, change, and delete files, information on your hard disk can become *fragmented*. In other words, data is stored in a noncontiguous manner. Pieces of files are stored in any available location on your hard disk, which causes the system to run slower when reading those files from the disk. Disk Defragmenter reorganizes your hard disk data so the data is stored in a contiguous manner. If your system seems slow when reading data from the hard disk, you may need to run this utility.

Understanding System State Data and User Data

For the exam, you need to understand the difference between system state data and user data. *User data* simply refers to data on your system that is accessed by users. Common examples include documents, files, and applications. Your operating system uses system state data, which contains the following, which you need to know for the exam:

- ✔ Registry
- ✔ COM + Class Registration Database
- ✔ System Boot Files
- ✔ Certificate Services Database (if your server is a certificate server)

Windows 2000 domain controllers also contain the Active Directory services database and the SYSVOL directory — member servers do not contain this data because they do not run the Active Directory. Watch out for tricky exam questions concerning the differences between member server and domain controller system state data.

In all likelihood, the exam will ask you about backing up and restoring system state data, which you can read about in Chapter 15.

Prep Test

1 You are experiencing problems with one of your server's hard disks. You decide to set up some Performance Monitor counters so you can examine your disk's read and write time. When you access Performance Monitor's Add Counters dialog box, which performance object do you need to select?

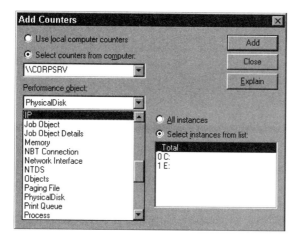

2 Your server seems to be running very slowly, and you believe the system processor may be experiencing problems. You want to set up a Performance Monitor chart so you can track the processor's usage over a period of time. You select the Processor object in the Add Counters dialog box. Which counter would be best to use for this purpose?

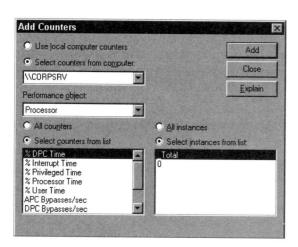

3 Lots of paging seems to be occurring on your system. You want to use Performance Monitor to examine memory usage on your system. Which counters should you use? (Choose all that apply.)

A ❑ System \ Context switches/sec
B ❑ Memory \ Available Bytes
C ❑ Memory \ Cached Bytes
D ❑ Memory \ System Driver Total Bytes

4 You have several logical drives on a storage volume. You want to make certain that disk counters are available for those logical drives in Performance Monitor. What command do you need to run at the command line to enable this object and the counters?

A ○ None — they are available by default
B ○ diskperf -ld
C ○ disperf -dv
D ○ diskperf -yv

5 Which of the following system state data components is unique for Windows 2000 domain controllers?

A ○ Registry
B ○ SYSVOL
C ○ COM + Class Registration database
D ○ System Boot Files

6 Your server has 125MB of system memory, but it seems to run low when several applications are in use. You examine the Virtual Memory dialog box. What is wrong with the settings?

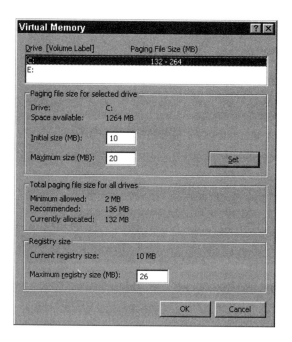

7 Which performance option is in effect by default on Windows 2000 systems for application response?

A ○ Applications

B ○ Pagefile.sys

C ○ Background services

D ○ System processes

8 You manage an administrator trainee employed by your company. After examining the Performance tab of Task Manager for some time, the trainee believes that the instability of the reading may indicate some processor problems. You examine the CPU usage section shown in the following figure. What would you tell the trainee about the CPU readings?

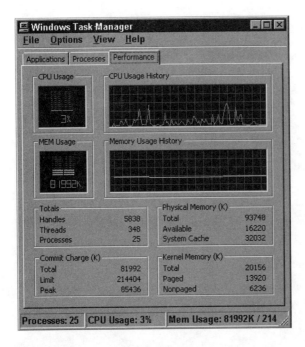

9 You are having problems with a particular device attached to your server. You want to use MSINFO to examine the Problem Devices list so you can look for clues to help you resolve the problem. In which container does the Problem Devices container reside?

A ○ Hardware Resources

B ○ Components

C ○ Software Environment

D ○ Internet Explorer 5

10 Over time, you notice that your hard disk has much slower read time. What action do you need to perform?

A ○ Use Dr. Watson to debug errors.

B ○ Use Disk Cleanup to free up space.

C ○ Use Disk Defragmenter to defragment the drive.

D ○ Examine the DMA allocation in MSINFO.

Answers

1 *Select the PhysicalDisk object.* Using Windows 2000 Performance Monitor, you can select several counters to gain information about the performance of your physical disk. *Review "Managing System Process and Resource Usage with Performance Monitor."*

2 *Select the % Processor Time counter.* The % Processor Time counter gives the percentage of processor usage and is the best counter to examine if you believe your system processor is overworked. *Read "Managing System Process and Resource Usage with Performance Monitor."*

3 *B and C.* To examine excessive paging, you should examine Memory \ Available Bytes and Memory \ Cached Bytes. System \ Context switches/sec is not a memory function, and Memory \ System Driver Total Bytes gives you the number of bytes of pageable memory used by device drivers, which would not help you with the current problem. *Study "Managing System Process and Resource Usage with Performance Monitor."*

4 *D. Diskperf -yv.* The **diskperf -yv** command enables performance counters for logical drives or storage volumes. To view a list of diskperf commands, type **diskperf -?** at the command prompt. *See "Managing System Process and Resource Usage with Performance Monitor."*

5 *B. SYSVOL.* The SYSVOL folder and the Active Directory services database are part of system state data only on Windows 2000 domain controllers. *Study "Understanding System State Data and User Data."*

6 *The virtual memory settings are too low.* You can see in the figure that the recommended size of the paging file for this drive is 136MB (which is generated by multiplying 1.5 times the amount of RAM). A virtual memory setting of 10 to 20MB is too low for this system to use virtual memory correctly. *Study "Configuring Performance Options."*

7 *C. Background services.* Concerning application response, you have the option to select either applications or background services to optimize performance. By default, background services is selected, but you can change this setting by accessing the Advanced tab in the System Properties and then clicking the Performance Options button. *Study "Configuring Performance Options."*

8 *The readings do not show a problem with the CPU.* You can use the Performance tab in Task Manager to examine your CPU activity. Consistently high readings tell you that your CPU cannot handle all the processing requests placed on it by the system and applications. In the figure, the CPU readings are consistently low. *Study "Using Task Manager."*

9 *B. Components.* You can examine any problem devices on your system within MSINFO by expanding the Components container and clicking Problem Devices. *Study "Using MSINFO."*

10 *C. Use Disk Defragmenter to defragment the hard drive.* If your drive provides gradually slower read response, the most likely problem is fragmentation. Run Disk Defragmenter to resolve the problem. *Study "Optimizing Disk Performance."*

Chapter 15

Performing Data and System Recovery

. . . .

Exam Objectives

▶ Recovering system and user data by using Windows Backup

▶ Troubleshooting system restoration by using Safe Mode

▶ Recovering systems and user data by using the Recovery console

. . . .

I cannot overemphasize the importance of backing up data and ensuring that you can recover data when a system fails. You must work tirelessly to ensure that you can recover data at any time a server failure occurs. Windows 2000 helps you back up and recover data with Windows Backup and also provides Safe Mode features to help you troubleshoot and recover a failing system.

The exam expects you to know how to back up and recover data using Windows Backup and Safe Mode. You also need to know how to recover systems and user data by using the Recovery console. In this chapter, you can review these concepts and explore the backup and recovery topics that you need to know for the exam.

Quick Assessment

Recovering system and user data by using Windows Backup

1 _____ is a backup type that backs up only selected files and folders that contain markers, but does not clear the markers.

2 Effective backup strategies often use a(n) _____ of backup types.

3 You can create a backup job either manually or by using the Backup _____.

4 You can recover data using the recovery option in the Windows _____ tool.

Troubleshooting system restoration by using Safe Mode

5 If a configuration problem occurs that prevents you from booting the server, use the _____ option.

6 If you install a new video card and have problems with the system, you can boot your server using the _____ option to load a basic VGA driver.

7 The _____ option enables your server to have networking capabilities while in Safe Mode.

Recovering systems and user data by using the Recovery console

8 You can start the Recovery console by using the Windows 2000 setup disks or the Windows 2000 CD-ROM, or by installing it as a(n) _____ option.

9 By using the _____ command in the Recovery console, you can change the attributes of a file or directory.

10 You can use the _____ command in the Recovery console to manage partitions on your hard drives.

Answers

1   *Differential.* See "Reviewing Backup Concepts."

2   *Combination.* Study "Reviewing Backup Concepts."

3   *Wizard.* See "Using Windows Backup."

4   *Backup.* Examine "Restoring Data."

5   *Last Known Good.* Review "Using Safe Mode."

6   *Enable VGA Mode.* See "Using Safe Mode."

7   *Safe Mode with Networking.* Read "Using Safe Mode."

8   *Startup.* Study "Using the Recovery Console."

9   *Attrib.* See "Using the Recovery Console."

10   *Diskpart.* See "Using the Recovery Console."

Reviewing Backup Concepts

Like Windows NT, Windows 2000 has some different types of backup that you can implement. In fact, both systems support the same backup types, and this section reviews those types for you.

I cannot define only one correct way to back up data. Your backup plan depends on the needs of your network, the type of data used, and the critical nature of the data. You don't need to back up files on a regular basis if those files rarely change, but you do need an effective backup plan for data that changes daily so you can recover the most recent version of that data.

Windows 2000 enables you to use various backup media, such as tape drives, Zip drives, CD-ROM drives, and even hard drives on remote computers.

You need to know the different types of backup for the exam, so you should carefully review the following descriptions:

- ✔ **Normal:** Backs up all files and folders that you select. A normal backup does not use markers to determine which files have been backed up, and it does not remove existing markers. Each file is marked as having been backed up. A normal backup is the easiest type of backup to restore, but it can be slow depending on the amount of data.

- ✔ **Copy:** Backs up all selected files and folders, but does not look at markers and does not clear any existing markers.

- ✔ **Differential:** Backs up only selected files and folders that contain a marker. A differential backup does not clear the existing markers.

- ✔ **Incremental:** Backs up selected files and folders with a marker and then clears the existing marker.

- ✔ **Daily:** Backs up all selected files and folders that have changed during the day. A daily backup does not look at or clear markers, but is an effective way to back up files and folders that have changed during the day.

Creating a backup plan is an important part of the planning process. Most network environments use a combination of normal backups and differential or incremental backups. For example, you may use a normal backup on Monday and then perform incremental backups throughout the rest of the week. The key is finding the balance between ease of data recovery and the amount of time required to perform the backup each day.

Using Windows Backup

Windows 2000 offers an easy-to-use Backup tool. You access the Backup tool by clicking Start⇨Programs⇨Accessories⇨System Tools⇨Backup.

As shown in Figure 15-1, the Backup tool's interface has four tabs. You can start the Backup wizard by clicking a button on the Welcome tab, or you can manually create a backup job by using the other tabs.

For the exam, you need to know how the Backup wizard works. You also need to know how to configure a backup job manually. You can review both processes in the following sections.

Working with the Backup wizard

Lab 15-1 walks you through the steps for using the Backup wizard. You should practice this lab on your server.

Lab 15-1   Using the Windows Backup Wizard

1. **On the Welcome tab, click the Backup Wizard button.**

2. **Click Next on the Welcome screen.**

3. **In the What to Back Up dialog box, specify whether you want to back up everything on the computer, only selected files, drives, or network data, or only system state data. After you select the appropriate radio button, click Next.**

For the exam, you need to know that system state data on a Windows 2000 member server contains the registry, the COM + Class Registration database, system boot files, and the Certificate Services database (if the server is operating as a certificate server). On domain controllers, system state data also includes the Active Directory database.

If you choose to back up only selected files, the wizard displays a dialog box so you can select the files that you want to back up.

4. **If necessary, select the desired files and then click Next.**

5. **Select the backup media that you plan to use by entering the drive path or by clicking the browse button and then selecting the desired path. Click Next.**

6. **In the wizard's completion dialog box, click Advanced to configure additional options.**

7. **In the Type of Backup dialog box, use the drop-down list to select either normal, copy, incremental, differential, or daily backup, as shown in Figure 15-2. You can also click the Backup Migrated Remote Storage Data check box. Make your selections and click Next.**

Windows 2000 supports *remote storage,* which enables your computer to store data in a remote storage location — for example, a tape drive — if the storage space on your hard drive runs low. If you select the backup remote storage option, Windows Backup reads the data stored in remote storage and backs it up as well.

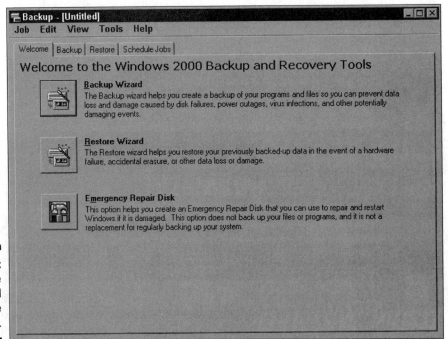

Figure 15-1:
Use the
Backup tool
to configure
backup jobs.

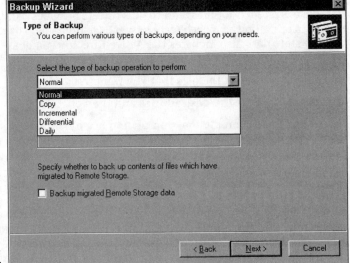

Figure 15-2:
Select the
backup type
as well as
remote
storage data
backup.

In the How to Back Up dialog box, you have options for verifying data after backup and using hardware compression.

You can specify that the system should verify the backup data for integrity before the backup job completes. This option causes your backup job to take more time, but it does ensure that your backup job was successful. If hardware compression is available on your server, you can use hardware compression to reduce the amount of storage space that a backup job consumes. You can only restore compressed backups on drives that support compression. If your hardware does not support compression, this option will be grayed out.

8. **Select the desired backup options and click Next.**

   In the Media Options dialog box, you can choose to append the backup job to existing media, or replace the data on the backup media with this backup. If you choose to replace the media, you can also specify that only the owner or an administrator can have access to the backup data and to backups appended to the replacement data.

9. **Select the desired media options and click Next.**

10. **In the Backup Label dialog box, provide a backup label and media label, if desired, and then click Next.**

11. **In the When to Backup dialog box, indicate whether you want to run the backup now or later by selecting the appropriate radio button. If you choose later, enter a job name and start date. If you click the Set Schedule button, you can enter an exact start time and other minor options, such as beginning the backup when the computer is idle. Make your selections and click Next.**

12. **Click Finish to complete the wizard.**

    Depending on the options you chose, the backup job begins immediately or at the scheduled time.

Performing a manual backup

The Backup wizard is a handy tool to help you configure backup jobs. After you become a pro at creating backup jobs, you may want to perform them manually. This is usually quicker, and you have the same options that the wizard provides.

To manually configure a backup job, access Windows Backup and then click the Backup tab, as shown in Figure 15-3.

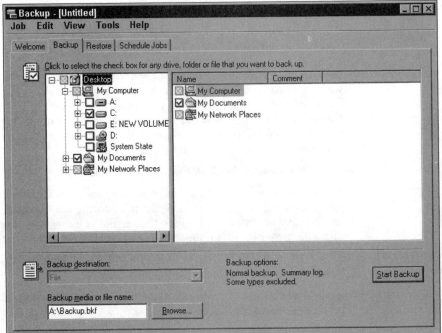

Figure 15-3:
Use the
Backup tab
to manually
configure a
backup job.

Specify what you want to back up by clicking the appropriate check boxes. You can back up individual files, system state data, or entire drives, as desired. At the bottom of the Backup tab, use the Browse button to select the backup media.

If you want to configure additional options for the backup job, choose Tools⇨Options. On the tabs in the resulting Options dialog box, you can select the type of backup, backup log, and other features you also see when using the Backup wizard.

After you select the desired options, you can click the Start Backup button on the Backup tab, or you can click the Schedule Jobs tab to schedule the job. The Schedule Jobs tab displays a calendar on which you can select the backup dates and times.

Restoring Data

You realize the benefits of backing up data after you experience a system or disk failure. After your system becomes operational again, you can use the Windows Backup tool to restore the data that you previously backed up.

To restore data, you can use the Restore wizard on the Welcome tab, or you can use the Restore tab to manually run the restoration process. The wizard displays only a few dialog boxes that enable you to determine what you want to restore and the location of the backup job. You can use the Advanced button to determine where on your hard drive to restore the data and if the restore operation should replace any of the same existing files on your system. The system then restores the data. You can manually select the same options by using the Restore tab.

Creating an Emergency Repair Disk (ERD)

The Emergency Repair Disk (ERD) is a tool you can use to help start and recover your Windows 2000 Server system in the event of a system boot failure. You can easily create an ERD by accessing the Backup utility and clicking the Emergency Repair Disk button on the Welcome tab. You need a blank, formatted floppy disk to create the ERD.

The ERD is not a replacement for a backup plan, and the ERD can only help you repair system files, the partition boot sector, and the startup environment. You can also replace registry files using the ERD in conjunction with the Recovery console.

You should keep a current ERD around at all times. Each time you make a significant system configuration change, you also need to create a new ERD.

Using Safe Mode

All Windows 2000 computers have Safe Mode capabilities (thank goodness!) so you can attempt to solve problems with your server when it will not start.

Windows 2000 provides the following types of Safe Mode, and you need to know them for the exam:

- ✔ **Safe Mode:** Starts Windows 2000 using only basic files and minimal drivers. With this type of Safe Mode, you can start the system so you can troubleshoot and hopefully resolve the problem. If you still cannot start your system using safe mode, you probably need to use the Emergency Repair Disk (ERD) to correct system problems.

- ✔ **Safe Mode with Networking:** Starts Windows 2000 using only basic files and drivers, but also provides a network connection so you can gain access to the network while in Safe Mode.

✓ **Safe Mode with Command Prompt:** Starts Windows 2000 with only basic files and drivers. After you log on, the system displays the command prompt instead of your Windows desktop.

✓ **Enable Boot Logging:** Starts Windows 2000 while logging all the drivers and services that are loaded or not loaded by the system. The log file is called NTBTLOG.TXT, and it is located in the %WINDIR% directory. By using this feature, you can review the boot log and determine the exact cause of your system problem.

✓ **Enable VGA Mode:** Starts Windows 2000 using the basic VGA driver. It is not uncommon to have problems after installing a new video card and driver, so this option installs the basic VGA driver. By using this option, you can resolve the VGA driver problem. Windows always uses VGA mode when you start the system in Safe Mode, Safe Mode with Networking, or Safe Mode with Command Prompt.

✓ **Last Known Good Configuration:** Starts Windows 2000 using the registry information that Windows saved during the last shutdown. (Windows NT also offers this option.) This feature boots the system using the last good configuration that was saved and is only useful when incorrect configuration has caused the problem. Last Known Good does not solve problems with corrupt files or drivers, and any configuration changes made since the last successful startup are lost.

✓ **Debugging Mode:** Starts Windows 2000 while sending debug information to another computer through a serial cable.

Windows 2000 domain controllers also have a Directory Service Restore Mode, which you can use to troubleshoot Active Directory problems or restore the Active Directory database when a failure has occurred. Keep in mind for the exam that this option is available only on domain controllers and not on member servers.

To start your system in Safe Mode, turn on your server and hold down the F8 key. The Safe Mode menu appears, and you can select the type of Safe Mode you want to use by pressing the arrow keys.

Using the Recovery Console

The Recovery Console is a command-line console feature of Windows 2000 that enables you to perform powerful administrative tasks on a system that will not start. Using the Recovery console, you can start and stop services, read and write data to the local drive(s), format drives, and perform many other tasks. The Recovery console is particularly useful if you need to replace corrupt system files with new copies from the installation CD-ROM. Only administrators have rights to use the recovery console.

You can start the Recovery console in two ways. First, if you cannot start your server, you can launch the Recovery console from the setup disks or from your installation CD-ROM (if your computer supports booting from a CD-ROM drive). Second, you can install the Recovery console on your computer so that it is available as a boot menu option.

To install the Recovery console so that it appears as a boot menu option, follow the steps shown in Lab 15-2:

Lab 15-2   Installing the Recovery Console

1. **Insert your Windows 2000 installation CD-ROM into the CD-ROM drive.**

2. **At the command prompt, switch to your CD-ROM drive and then type** \i386\winnt32.exe/cmdcons.

   A message appears, telling you about the Recovery console.

3. **Click Yes to install it as a startup option.**

   File copy begins, and the console is installed.

When you boot your computer using the Recovery console (either by startup disk, CD-ROM, or as a startup option), the basic console is displayed. You are prompted to select which Windows 2000 installation you want to log on to (for dual-boot systems). You then provide your administrator password. You can then perform the desired actions, or you can type **Help** to see a list of available actions and proper syntax.

You don't need to know every syntax option for the exam, but you do need to know the basic options and what you can do with them. Table 15-1 describes those options so you can easily memorize them.

Table 15-1	Recovery Console Tasks
Task	**What It Does**
Disable	Disables system services or device drivers
Enable	Enables system services or device drivers
Exit	Closes the Recovery console and restarts your computer
Fixboot	Writes a new partition boot sector to the system partition
Fixmbr	Writes a new master boot record to the hard drive
Logon	Logs you on to an installation of Windows 2000
Map	Displays a mapping of drive letters to physical device names
Systemroot	Sets the current directory to the systemroot folder

In addition to the basic console tasks listed in Table 15-1, several Recovery console commands are available. Table 15-2 describes these commands, which you should memorize for the exam.

Table 15-2	Recovery Console Commands
Command	*What It Does*
Attrib	Changes the attributes of a file or directory
Batch	Executes the commands specified in a text file
ChDir (CD)	Displays the name of the current directory or changes the current directory
Chkdsk	Checks a disk and displays a status report
Cls	Clears the screen
Copy	Copies a single file to another location
Delete (Del)	Deletes one or more files
Dir	Displays a list of files and subdirectories in a directory
Diskpart	Manages partitions on your hard drives
Expand	Extracts a file from a compressed file
Format	Formats a disk
Listsvc	Lists the services and drivers available on the computer
Mkdir (Md)	Creates a directory
Rename (Ren)	Renames a directory
Rmdir (Rd)	Deletes a directory
Set	Displays and sets environment variables

Prep Test

1 In the Windows Backup wizard, you have the option of verifying the integrity of your backup job after it is complete. Which statement about verification is correct?

  A ○ Verification ensures the integrity of your backup, but increases the time necessary to perform the entire backup operation.

  B ○ Verification ensures the integrity of your backup job, but creates additional disk overhead.

  C ○ Verification ensures the integrity of your backup job, but compresses the data on the backup media.

  D ○ Verification ensures the integrity of your backup job, but removes the file markers.

2 You manually configure a backup job on the Backup tab of Windows Backup. You need this backup to be an incremental backup type. Where on this interface can you configure this option?

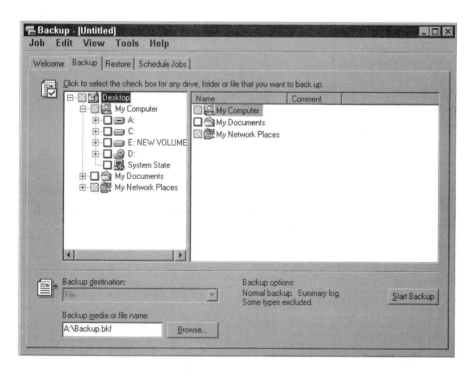

3 You want to implement a backup type that backs up only selected files and folders that contain markers, but you do not want the existing markers cleared. What type of backup do you need to use?

A ○ Normal

B ○ Copy

C ○ Differential

D ○ Incremental

4 You want to implement a backup type that backs up only selected files and folders that contain markers, but you want the existing markers to be cleared. What type of backup do you need to use?

A ○ Normal

B ○ Copy

C ○ Differential

D ○ Incremental

5 Which of the following is not a component of system state data on a Windows 2000 member server?

A ○ Registry

B ○ Active Directory database

C ○ COM + Class Registration database

D ○ System Boot Files

6 When configuring the Advanced options of a backup job, you notice that the hardware compression option is grayed out. Why is this option unavailable?

A ○ The backup job does not support hardware compression.

B ○ Windows 2000 does not support hardware compression.

C ○ Your server hardware does not support hardware compression.

D ○ Your backup media does not support hardware compression.

7 You are having problems with your server. You have tried to boot into Safe Mode, but were not successful. What step should you take next?

A ○ Format the hard drive.

B ○ Reinstall Windows 2000.

C ○ Use the Emergency Repair Disk.

D ○ Boot into command prompt only.

8 You enable Boot Logging on your server to troubleshoot a boot problem. What is name of the log file that Boot Logging generates?

A ○ BOOTLOG.LOG
B ○ NTBTLOG.LOG
C ○ NTBTLOG.TXT
D ○ NTBTLOG.EXE

9 You want to install the Recovery console on an Intel Windows 2000 server. You put the installation CD-ROM in your CD-ROM drive and access the command prompt. What do you need to do now?

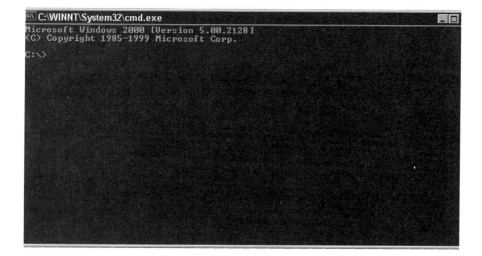

10 When using the Recovery console, you want to view the services and drivers available on the computer. What command do you need to use?

A ○ Diskpart
B ○ Expand
C ○ Ren
D ○ Listsvc

Answers

1 *A. Verification ensures the integrity of your backup, but increases the time necessary to perform the entire backup operation.* Although verification does ensure the integrity of your backup job, it also increases the amount of time that a backup job takes. *Review "Using Windows Backup."*

2 *Choose Tools⇨Options. In the resulting dialog box, click the Backup Type tab and then select the desired backup type from the drop-down list.* When manually creating a backup job, choose Tools⇨Options to access advanced backup options, including backup type selection. *Read "Using Windows Backup."*

3 *C. Differential.* A differential backup backs up selected files and folders that contain markers, but it does not clear the existing markers. *Study "Reviewing Backup Concepts."*

4 *D. Incremental.* An incremental backup backs up selected files and folders that contain markers, and it clears the existing markers. *See "Reviewing Backup Concepts."*

5 *B. Active Directory database.* The Active Directory database is a part of system state data on domain controllers, not member servers. *Study "Using Windows Backup."*

6 *C. Your server hardware does not support hardware compression.* If the hardware compression option is grayed out, the server hardware does not support hardware compression. *Study "Using Windows Backup."*

7 *C. Use the Emergency Repair Disk.* You should maintain a current ERD at all times so that you can attempt to repair Windows 2000 if you cannot boot into Safe Mode. *Study "Using Safe Mode."*

8 *C. NTBTLOG.TXT.* NTBTLOG is stored as a text file in the %WINDIR% directory. *Study "Using Safe Mode."*

9 *Change to your CD-ROM drive letter, type \i386\winnt32.exe/cmdcons, and press Enter.* Use this command-line syntax to install the Recovery console so it is a boot menu option. *Study "Using the Recovery Console."*

10 *D. Listsvc.* You use the Listsvc command to list the services and drivers available on your computer. *Study "Using the Recovery Console."*

Part VI

Managing, Configuring, and Troubleshooting Storage Use

The 5th Wave   By Rich Tennant

"Ah, we're in luck- the Director of IS is available for visitors."

In this part . . .

As an administrator, you must ensure that data remains readily available and protected against failures. Windows 2000's hard disk configuration options and backup protection features differ significantly from those in previous versions.

In Chapters 16 and 17, you explore the management of hard disks and volumes in Windows 2000, including the built-in fault-tolerant features. You also examine disk compression, quotas, and the procedures for recovering from hard disk failures.

Chapter 16

Managing Hard Disks and Disk Volumes

● ●

Exam Objectives

▶ Monitoring, configuring, and troubleshooting disks and volumes

▶ Configuring data compression

▶ Recovering from disk failures

● ●

*A*s a systems administrator, you need to manage hard disks. Fortunately, Windows 2000 handles hard disks much better than Windows NT 4.0 does. However, that means you need to understand some changes and additions in the way that Windows 2000 uses hard disks. Windows 2000 and Windows NT 4.0 have many of the same options, such as fault-tolerance support, but Windows 2000 also gives you some new features that you need to know for the exam and for your job as an IT professional.

For the exam, you need to know how to mange and configure hard disks. You also need to know about data compression and some tactics for recovering from disk failures. You can review the following topics in this chapter:

   ✔ Managing hard disks

   ✔ Configuring volumes

   ✔ Using data compression

   ✔ Configuring mounted volumes

Quick Assessment

Monitoring, configuring, and troubleshooting disks and volumes

1 A dynamic disk can contain any number of disk _____.

2 A storage solution that writes data in a stripe across two or more physical dynamic disks is a(n) _____.

3 A(n) _____ is an effective fault-tolerant solution for dynamic disks, but it doubles the amount of disk space you must have available.

4 The _____ dynamic disk fault-tolerant solution uses a parity bit to reconstruct data lost because of disk failure.

5 A Windows 2000 dynamic disk that is not functioning appears in the Disk Management console as _____.

6 If a dynamic disk has I/O errors, the Disk Management console displays the disk's status as _____.

7 After you upgrade a basic disk to a dynamic disk, you cannot boot previous versions of _____.

Configuring data compression

8 You can choose to compress data on dynamic volumes when you create the volume using the _____ wizard.

Recovering from disk failures

9 If a disk's status is displayed as Healthy (At Risk), you can _____ the disk to attempt to solve the problem.

10 During synchronization between disks in a mirrored volume, the Disk Management console displays the disks' status as _____.

Answers

1 *Volumes.* See "Examining Windows 2000 Disk Basics."

2 *Striped Volume.* Study "Examining Windows 2000 Disk Basics."

3 *Mirrored Volume.* See "Examining Windows 2000 Disk Basics."

4 *RAID-5 Volume.* Read "Examining Windows 2000 Disk Basics."

5 *Offline.* Review "Examining Windows 2000 Disk Basics."

6 *Healthy (Errors).* See "Examining Windows 2000 Disk Basics."

7 *Windows.* Read "Examining Windows 2000 Disk Basics."

8 *Create Volume.* Study "Creating Volumes."

9 *Reactivate.* See "Examining Windows 2000 Disk Basics."

10 *Resynching.* Review "Examining Windows 2000 Disk Basics."

Examining Windows 2000 Disk Basics

As you know, Microsoft loves to change things. Often, however, those changes are for the better, and disk management in Windows 2000 is no exception. You can manage your hard disk needs in Windows 2000 by using the Computer Management tool, which you access by clicking Start⇨Programs⇨Administrative Tools⇨Computer Management. Expand the Storage container and then click Disk Management to access the Disk Management interface, shown in Figure 16-1.

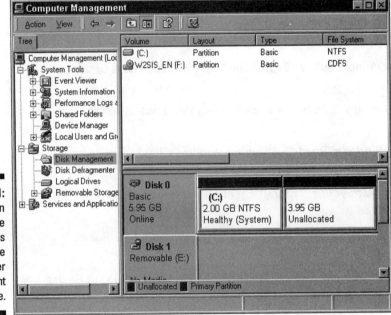

Figure 16-1:
You can configure hard disks through the Computer Management console.

Choosing a file system

Windows 2000 supports FAT, FAT32, and NTFS file systems. The NTFS file system in Windows 2000 is an enhanced version that supports the new security features of the Kerberos protocol. Unless you have a specific reason for using FAT or FAT32, you should format your drives with NTFS so you have the security features of Kerberos and the storage features of Windows 2000, several of which are available only with NTFS.

Understanding basic and dynamic disks

A new feature of Windows 2000 disk management involves the distinction between *basic* and *dynamic* disks. Basic disks consist of partitions and logical drives. If you upgrade from Windows NT 4.0, your disk configuration remains intact and it is a basic disk. With a basic disk, you can manage the partitions and the logical drives, and you can create additional partitions. However, you cannot create any new volume sets, stripe sets, and so on. A dynamic disk is managed by Windows 2000 and contains dynamic volumes, which are simply volumes that you create with the Disk Management console.

Dynamic disks do not contain partitions or logical drives; they contain volumes. With this design, disks are no longer limited to a certain number of partitions, and they can contain multiple volumes. This design gives you greater flexibility for disk management, without the restrictions imposed by previous versions of Windows. Also, you can make changes to your disk configuration on a dynamic disk without having to reboot your computer.

Previous disk management solutions and fault-tolerant solutions are still available on dynamic disks, but the names have changed. (More terminology!) You need to know the differences, so take the time to memorize the following terms:

✔ **Spanned volume:** A spanned volume, formerly called a volume set, is a collection of volume (formerly partition) "pieces" that the system treats as one volume. By using spanned volumes, you can make constructive use of small portions of disk space, but spanned volumes have no inherent fault tolerance.

✔ **Striped volumes:** A striped volume, formerly called a striped set, stores data on two or more physical disks. Striped volumes allocate data evenly (in stripes) across the disks in the striped volume, so you must have the same amount of storage space on each disk. Striped volumes are an excellent storage solution, but they offer no fault tolerance. If one disk in the stripe volume fails, you lose all data on the entire striped volume.

✔ **Mirrored volumes:** Mirrored volumes, formerly called mirror sets, represent a fault-tolerant solution that duplicates data on two physical disks. One disk is the primary disk, while the other disk is the mirror (or a copy of the primary disk). If one disk fails, you can reconstruct data using the mirror. In fact, in Windows 2000, if one of the disks fails, your system continues to operate as though nothing has happened by using the mirror. You can replace the failed disk and recreate the mirror for continued fault tolerance. Mirrored volumes are effective fault-tolerant solutions, but do have a high cost in terms of megabytes (50 percent).

In other words, if you want to mirror a 2GB disk, you must have another 2GB disk available. This configuration requires twice as much disk space as you would normally use without the mirror. So, in terms of disk expense (expressed in terms of megabytes), you get to use only half of your total storage space.

✔ **RAID-5 volumes:** A RAID-5 volume, formerly called a stripe set with parity, requires at least three physical disks. Data is written in a stripe fashion across the disks and includes a parity bit that the system can use to reconstruct data in case of a disk failure. If a disk fails within the RAID-5 volume, the data can be regenerated with the parity bit. You cannot mirror or extend RAID-5 volumes after you create them, but they are an effective fault-tolerant solution.

In order to manage your disks in Windows 2000, you need to upgrade each disk from basic to dynamic. You can perform this action by right-clicking the disk (not the partitions) in the Disk Management console and then choosing Upgrade to Dynamic Disk. You need to reboot your computer for the upgrade to take effect.

After you upgrade to a dynamic disk, you cannot boot previous versions of Windows on the dynamic disk, because these operating systems cannot access dynamic volumes. So, dynamic disks are a Windows 2000-only solution, but you should implement them as soon as possible to take advantage of the features that dynamic disks offer.

When you upgrade a basic disk to a dynamic disk, you must have 1MB of unformatted free space at the end of the disk, which Windows uses for administrative purposes. To maintain previous volume sets, striped sets, and so on from a basic disk, you must upgrade all the basic disks to dynamic disks. Also, keep in mind that you cannot upgrade removable media to dynamic disks.

Understanding online and offline disks

In addition to the distinction between basic and dynamic disks, Windows 2000 introduces two more disk-related terms: *online* and *offline*. The Disk Management console displays this status for each disk. *Online* means the disk is up and running. In contrast, an *offline* disk has errors and is not available.

You can access the properties of either an online or offline disk by simply right-clicking the disk in Disk Management and then choosing Properties. From the Properties dialog box for an offline disk, you can use the disk tools to attempt to repair the disk. Alternatively, you can attempt to repair the offline disk by right-clicking it and then choosing Reactivate Disk.

Understanding disk status

The Disk Management console provides several pieces of information about each disk volume, such as layout, type, file system, status, capacity, and free space. For the exam, you need to know about disk status and the possible status indicators that can occur.

You need to memorize these status indicators for the exam:

- **Healthy:** The volume is accessible and has no problems.

- **Healthy (At Risk):** The volume is accessible, but I/O errors have been detected. The underlying disk — that is, the physical disk on which the volume is located — is displayed as Online (Errors). Usually, you can solve this problem by reactivating the disk (right-click the disk and choose Reactivate Disk).

- **Initializing:** The volume is being initialized and will be displayed as Healthy after initialization is complete. This status does not require any action.

- **Resynching:** The system is resynchronizing mirrored volumes. After Windows 2000 completes the resynchronization, the status is displayed as Healthy, and no action is necessary from you.

- **Regenerating:** Data on RAID-5 volumes is being regenerated from the parity bit. This process occurs after a disk failure and disk replacement by an administrator. No action is required.

- **Failed Redundancy:** The underlying disk is offline on fault-tolerant disks. In this case, you no longer have any fault tolerance on either mirrored or RAID-5 volumes. You need to reactive or repair the disk to avoid potential data loss if one of the disks fails.

- **Failed Redundancy (At Risk):** This status is the same as Failed Redundancy, but the status of the underlying disk is Online (Errors). Reactivate the disk so that it returns to Online status.

- **Failed:** The system cannot start the volume automatically, and you need to repair the volume.

Creating Volumes

You can easily create new volumes on your dynamic disks in Windows 2000 in the Disk Management console. Simply right-click the free space where you want to create a new volume and then choose Create Volume. This action launches the Create Volume wizard.

You can create any volume, spanned volume, striped volume, mirrored volume, or RAID-5 volume (assuming you have the number of drives required) by using the Create Volume wizard.

The Create Volume wizard is rather straightforward and easy to use, but the exam does expect you to understand how the wizard works. Review Lab 16-1, which creates a simple volume, to make certain you understand how the wizard works.

Lab 16-1   Creating a Simple Volume

1. **In the Disk Management console, right-click the area of free space where you want to create the volume and then choose Create Volume.**

2. **Click Next on the Create Volume Welcome screen.**

3. **Select Simple Volume from the list of options and click Next.**

   If you want to create a different kind of volume, select the desired type and click Next.

4. **Select the desired disk and click Add. As shown in Figure 16-2, you can also adjust the MB size for the volume, as desired. Click Next.**

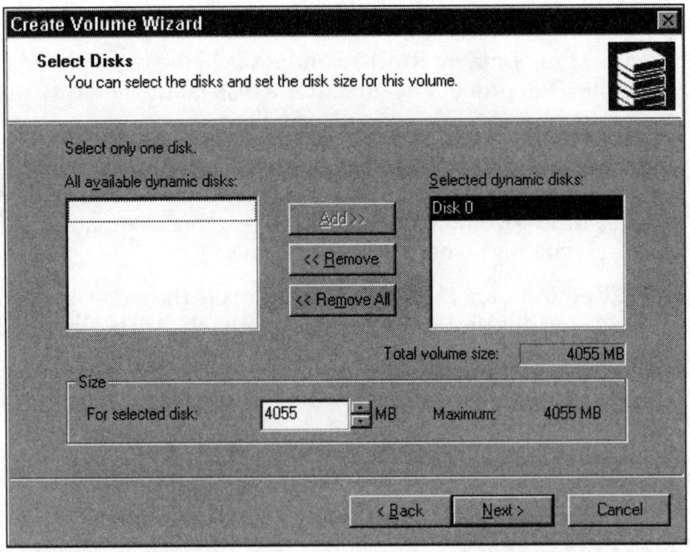

Figure 16-2:
Select the disk and volume size and then click Next.

5. **Select a drive letter for the volume or choose to mount the volume to an empty folder. You can also choose not to assign a drive letter or drive path at this time. Make your selection and click Next.**

See the section "Using Mounted Volumes," later in this chapter, for more information about mounted volumes.

6. **Indicate whether you want to format the volume. If you choose to format it now, select a file system, an allocation unit size, and a volume label. You can also choose to perform a quick format and enable file and folder compression, if desired.**

   The data compression option enables the Disk Management console to compress data on the volume so that more storage space is available.

7. **Click Finish to complete the wizard.**

   The system creates the volume and formats it (if specified).

Checking Out Common Management Tasks

After you configure your volumes in the desired manner, disk management requires very little time on your part. Your basic tasks include occasional management and troubleshooting.

You can manage your disk volumes through the Disk Management tool. By right-clicking a dynamic disk or disk volume, you can perform several tasks. These tasks may vary depending on the type of disk or volume, but you should understand the following basic management actions, which you need to remember for the exam:

- **Open/Explore:** Enables you to open the disk or volume and view its contents.

- **Extend Volume:** You can dynamically extend a disk volume to incorporate more space from free disk space. You can only extend volumes with other NTFS volumes — not FAT or FAT32.

- **Change Drive Letter and Path:** You can dynamically change a volume's drive letter and path by entering the desired change.

- **Reactivate Volume/Disk:** Use the Reactivate feature to correct Online (Error) status readings.

- **Delete Volume:** Removes the volume from your computer.

- **Properties:** In the Properties dialog boxes for disks and volumes, you can see general information about the disk and its hardware, and you can access disk tools, such as Error Checking and Disk Defragmenter.

Using Mounted Volumes

By using mounted volumes in Windows 2000, you can easily replace drive letters so that a disk volume appears as a folder. In other words, by mounting a drive to a folder, you can give the drive a friendly name and you do not run out of available drive letters. To create the mounted volume, you create an empty folder with a desired name and then mount the desired volume to the folder using Disk Management.

To create a mounted volume, follow the steps that I describe in Lab 16-2.

Lab 16-2   Creating a Mounted Volume

1. **Right-click the volume you want to mount and choose Change Drive Letter and Path from the pop-up menu.**

2. **In the Change Drive Letter and Path dialog box, click Add.**

3. **As shown in Figure 16-3, click the Mount in This NTFS Folder option, enter the path to the shared folder, and click OK. (You can also click Browse and then navigate to the shared folder.)**

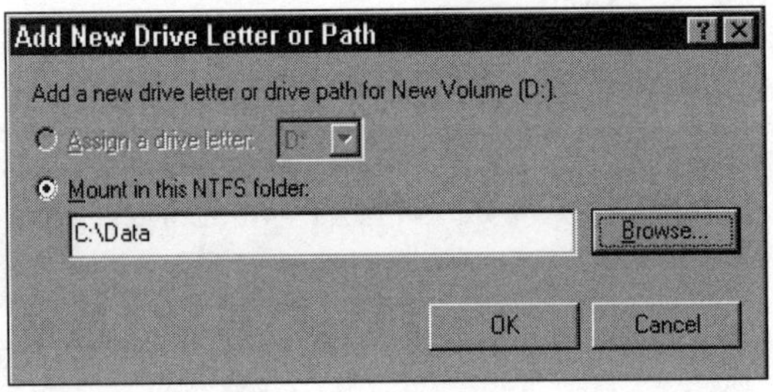

Figure 16-3:
Enter the name of the NTFS folder and click OK.

> **Add New Drive Letter or Path** [?] [X]
>
> Add a new drive letter or drive path for New Volume (D:).
>
> ○ Assign a drive letter: [D:] [▼]
>
> ● Mount in this NTFS folder:
>
> [C:\Data] [Browse...]
>
> [OK] [Cancel]

After you mount the volume to the NTFS folder, the folder appears as a drive on your system, as shown in Figure 16-4.

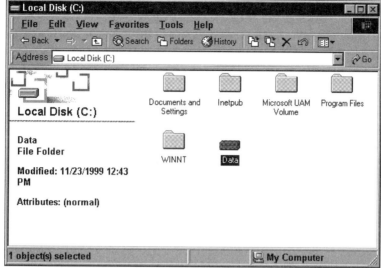

Prep Test

1 Your server has three dynamic physical disks. Each disk has just over 1MB of free space. What storage solution can you implement that makes the best use of this free space?

A ○ Spanned Volume

B ○ Striped Volume

C ○ Mirrored Volume

D ○ RAID-5 Volume

2 You have four dynamic physical disks on your server. You want to implement a fault-tolerant solution that provides the best performance and uses the least amount of megabyte cost available. What solution do you need to implement?

A ○ Spanned Volume

B ○ Striped Volume

C ○ Mirrored Volume

D ○ RAID-5 Volume

3 You want to use a fault-tolerant solution that creates an exact copy of your primary hard drive. You have three physical disks on your computer. Which fault-tolerant solution should you use?

A ○ Spanned Volume

B ○ Striped Volume

C ○ Mirrored Volume

D ○ RAID-5 Volume

4 You want to upgrade a removable media drive to dynamic so you can take advantage of volumes on the removable media. You examine the removable media drive in Disk Management, as shown in the figure, but it does not appear to be either basic or dynamic. Why?

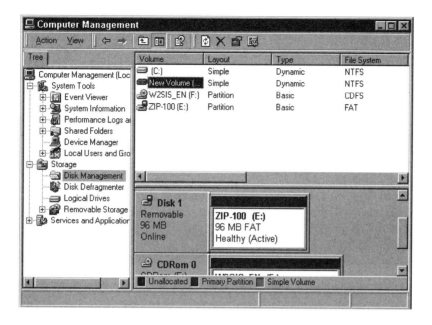

5 You notice that your RAID-5 volume is displayed as Regenerating after a recent disk failure. What action to you need to take?

A ○ No action is required.

B ○ Reactivate the disk.

C ○ Make the disk online.

D ○ The disk is not usable and needs to be replaced.

6 You notice that a particular volume is displayed as Healthy (At Risk). What action do you need to take?

A ○ No action is required.

B ○ Reactivate the disk.

C ○ Make the disk online.

D ○ The disk is not usable and needs to be replaced.

7 When creating a new volume, NTFS is the preferred file system. What other options do you have? (Choose all that apply.)

A ❑ FAT

B ❑ FAT32

C ❑ VFAT

D ❑ CDFS

8 You have a FAT32 volume that you want to extend, but the option does not seem to be available. What is the problem?

A ○ The disk is offline.

B ○ The disk needs to be reactivated.

C ○ You can only extend volumes formatted with NTFS.

D ○ The drive is mounted.

9 You want to mount a volume to a folder. What folder requirements must be met in order to accomplish this task? (Choose all that apply.)

A ❑ It must be an NTFS folder.

B ❑ The folder must be empty.

C ❑ The folder must reside in the root of C.

D ❑ There are no folder requirements.

Answers

1 *B. Striped Volume.* Because you have three disks with slightly more than 1MB each, your best solution is to create a striped volume, which makes better use of the storage space and provides the best performance. *Review "Examining Windows 2000 Disk Basics."*

2 *D. RAID-5 Volume.* You need at least three physical disks to create a RAID-5 volume, which stripes data across the disks and writes a parity bit for data regeneration in the case of a disk failure. The only other choice is a mirrored volume, which has a 50-percent megabyte cost and slower write and read time, so your best answer choice is D. *Read "Examining Windows 2000 Disk Basics."*

3 *C. Mirrored Volume.* A mirrored volume creates a *mirror,* or exact copy, of one hard disk on another hard disk. In the case of a failure, you can recover the data from the copy. *Study "Examining Windows 2000 Disk Basics."*

4 *You cannot upgrade removable media to dynamic.* Windows 2000 does not support dynamic removable media. *See "Examining Windows 2000 Disk Basics."*

5 *A. No action is required.* The Regenerating status indicator tells you that data on a RAID-5 volume is being regenerated. After regeneration is complete, the status will appear as Healthy, and you do not need to take any action. *Study "Examining Windows 2000 Disk Basics."*

6 *B. Reactivate the disk.* When a volume is displayed as Healthy (At Risk), you need to reactivate the disk by right-clicking it and then choosing Reactivate Disk. *Study "Examining Windows 2000 Disk Basics."*

7 *A and B.* NTFS is the file system of choice, but when you create a new volume, the Create New Volume wizard also allows you to choose FAT and FAT32, if desired. *Study "Creating Volumes."*

8 *C. You can only extend volumes formatted with NTFS.* Although you can use volumes formatted with FAT, only volumes formatted with NTFS can be extended. *Study "Checking Out Common Management Tasks."*

9 *A and B.* You can mount a volume to a folder, but the folder must be an NTFS folder and it must be empty. *Study "Using Mounted Volumes."*

Chapter 17

Configuring Profiles and Disk Quotas

Exam Objectives

▶ Configuring and managing user profiles

▶ Monitoring and configuring disk quotas

Windows 2000's user profiles and disk quotas enable you to manage what users can do — and what they cannot do — with their systems. In a networking environment, user profiles and disk quotas help you control user activity and the use of system resources. You can expect to see at least a few exam questions about these powerful tools.

For the exam, you need to know how to configure user profiles and disk quotas. You can expect the exam to ask profile questions, but especially questions about disk quotas because this technology is new in Windows 2000.

Quick Assessment

1 A(n) _____ user profile is stored on the hard drive of the user's computer.

2 A(n) _____ user profile is stored on the server's hard drive and is applied to the user's account, regardless of which computer the user employs for logging on to the system.

3 A(n) _____ user profile is required and does not allow the user to make changes to the profile.

4 A roaming user profile can reside on any Windows 2000 _____.

5 Disk quotas can only function on _____ volumes.

6 Users cannot implement data _____ to increase their available disk quota space.

7 When you create quota entries, you configure both the quota limit and the _____ level.

8 You cannot delete a quota entry until all the user's _____ have been removed from the hard disk.

Answers

1   *Local.* See "Configuring and Managing User Profiles."

2   *Roaming.* Study "Configuring and Managing User Profiles."

3   *Mandatory.* See "Configuring and Managing User Profiles."

4   *Server.* Examine "Configuring and Managing User Profiles."

5   *NTFS.* Review "Configuring Disk Quotas."

6   *Compression.* See "Configuring Disk Quotas."

7   *Warning.* Read "Configuring Disk Quotas."

8   *Folders and Files.* Study "Configuring Disk Quotas."

Configuring and Managing User Profiles

User profiles are not new in Windows 2000, but they are easier to manage and configure than in previous versions. Implementing user profiles can offer various benefits. With user profiles, several users can use the same computer while retaining their individual settings, and any changes to the desktop and system settings do not affect other users who access the same computer. You can even require settings for the user through roaming user profiles.

Windows 2000 supports three kinds of user profiles, and you need to know them for the exam:

- ✔ **Local:** The first time a user logs on to a computer, Windows 2000 creates a local user profile on that computer's hard disk. Any changes the user makes to the desktop and system settings are saved on the hard disk and reapplied when the user logs on again.

- ✔ **Roaming:** Roaming user profiles are saved on the server and they *roam* with the user. In other words, a user can log on to any Windows 2000 computer on the network, and that user's profile is downloaded from the server. For example, with a roaming user profile, a user with extremely poor taste could log on to several different computers during the day and see the same bright purple desktop on each machine.

- ✔ **Mandatory:** A mandatory user profile is a required profile for the user. In other words, it is mandated by the administrator. Users cannot change mandatory user profiles. The mandatory user profile can also be a roaming user profile so that mandatory settings remain in effect regardless of which computer the user employs for logging on to the network. The user can adjust configuration or desktop settings, but those settings are not saved. The next time the user logs on, the mandatory settings are applied once again.

Setting up roaming user profiles

With a roaming user profile, a user can log on to any computer running Windows 2000 within that user's domain. After the Active Directory authenticates the roaming user profile, Windows 2000 copies the roaming user profile to the local computer. The server stores any changes the user makes to the profile settings. Consequently, the server can download the up-to-date profile to the local computer, regardless of which computer the user employs for logging on to the network.

The roaming user profile path location can be on any server — it does not have to reside on a domain controller. When a user logs on, the Active Directory checks the user's account to determine whether a roaming user profile path exists. That path can point to a member server, and the user profile information is then copied from that server to the client computer.

To set up a roaming user profile, follow the steps I describe in Lab 17-1.

Lab 17-1   Setting Up a Roaming User Profile

1. **On the desired server, create a share with an intuitive name (such as profiles). The share should have the UNC path of *servername**sharename*.**

2. **Open the Active Directory Users and Computers tool and enter the UNC path for the roaming profile on the user account's Profile tab. You must be an Active Directory administrator to perform this step.**

   The next time the user logs on, the user profile is copied from the local computer and saved to the server via the UNC path.

Copying profiles

You manage the user profiles on a Windows 2000 computer by right-clicking My Computer, choosing Properties, and then accessing the User Profiles tab, shown in Figure 17-1.

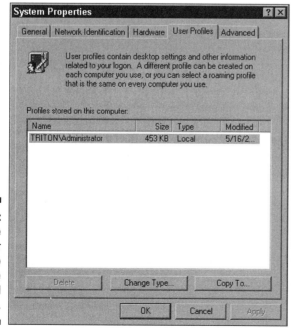

Figure 17-1:
Use the User Profiles tab to manage local profiles.

To copy a profile to another location and even change the user who is permitted to use the profile, select the desired profile and then click Copy To. This feature is useful if you want to use a particular profile as a template for other user profiles.

Creating a mandatory user profile

Windows 2000 stores profiles in the registry as NTUSER.DAT. The .DAT extension means that users can make changes to their profiles as desired. If you want to make the profile mandatory, change NTUSER.DAT to NTUSER.MAN. The .MAN extension makes the profile read-only so that changes a user makes cannot be saved to the profile. You can make this change directly by editing the registry, but the preferred method is to use the Active Directory Users and Computers tool to access the user's account and change the .DAT extension to the .MAN extension on the Profile tab.

Configuring Disk Quotas

Disk quotas track and control disk space on Windows 2000 volumes. (For more information about Windows 2000 volumes, see Chapter 16.) You can configure disk quotas to establish a limit of disk space usage and even log events when users exceed their disk space limit. In effect, using disk quotas controls the user of disk space and encourages network users to remove outdated information that they do not need to keep in storage.

Disk quotas function only on NTFS volumes on Windows 2000 computers. NTFS volumes on Windows NT computers do not support disk quotas.

When you configure disk quotas, you establish the actual disk usage limit and you establish a warning level. For example, a user may have a disk space limit of 100MB and a warning level of 90MB. You can also allow users to exceed their disk space limit. In this case, you can use disk quotas to track individual user disk usage, without actually restricting the user's storage space.

For the exam, remember that data compression does not affect disk quotas. If a user has only 50MB of storage space, compression does not allow the user to store more than 50MB of data.

Disk quotas affect individual users and their disk usage. For example, if one user has 25MB of storage space on a disk, and another user also has 25MB of storage on the same disk, one user's consumption of 25MB does not affect the other user. In other words, each user has a quota. This design is particularly useful for network volumes where multiple users have a quota they can use on that volume.

Disk quotas apply to volumes — not the file or folder structure on the underlying disk. It doesn't matter how many folders or files a user saves — all the data collectively equals the storage space used. Also, disk quotas can apply to spanned volumes. Because the quota applies to the volume, it doesn't matter how much data is stored on each physical disk — the quota applies to the entire volume. Disk quotas are based on file ownership, so if a user takes ownership of a file, that file counts toward the user's disk quota.

Enabling disk quotas

To enable disk quotas for a particular volume, access the volume through either My Computer or Disk Management, right-click the volume, and then choose Properties. In the Properties dialog box, click the Quota tab. To enable quotas on the volume, click the Enable Quota Management check box, as shown in Figure 17-2.

After you enable quotas for the volume, you can set the following options on the Quota tab, which you need to remember for the exam:

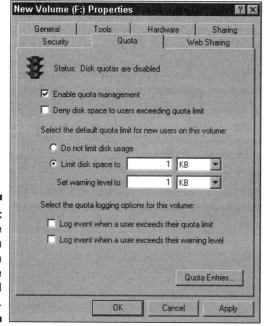

Figure 17-2:
Enable quotas on the Quota tab of the desired volume.

Part VI: Managing, Configuring, and Troubleshooting Storage Use

✔ **Decide whether to deny disk space to users exceeding the quota limit.**
Remember that you do not have to deny disk space to users exceeding
their limits, but you can use the disk quotas for monitoring purposes.
However, you can deny disk space by selecting this check box.

✔ **Indicate whether you want to limit disk space.** If you choose to establish a limit, enter the limit and the warning level values in the provided
boxes.

✔ **Specify whether to log an event when a user exceeds the quota limit
or when a user exceeds the warning level.** You can choose either of
these options, both of them, or neither.

Configuring quota entries

On the Quota tab, you can click the Quota Entries button to configure quota
entries for the volume. Quota entries define the quota limits and warning
levels for users of that volume. If you click the Quota Entries button on the
Quota tab, the Quota Entries dialog box appears, as shown in Figure 17-3.

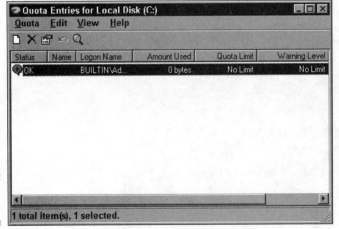

Figure 17-3:
Quota
entries
enable you
to set
quotas for
users.

To configure a new quota entry, choose Quota⇨New Quota. This action
opens the user list from the Active Directory. From this list, you can select
the user for whom you want to create the quota entry. Select the user, click
Add, and then click OK. The Add New Quota Entry dialog box appears, as
shown in Figure 17-4. In this dialog box, you can configure the disk space limit
and warning level.

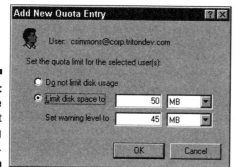

Figure 17-4:
Setting the
quota limit
and warning
for the user.

After you configure quota entries, you can easily edit them by selecting the user in the Quota Entries dialog box and clicking the Properties button on the taskbar. This action enables you to change the quota limit and the warning level. You can also perform standard management tasks such as copying and deleting users from the list.

For the exam, remember that you cannot delete a quota entry until all the user's files and folders have been removed from the volume, or until another quota entry has taken ownership of them.

Prep Test

1 For a particular user, you want to specify profile settings that the user cannot change. What kind of profile do you need to implement for the user?

A ○ Local

B ○ Roaming

C ○ Mandatory

D ○ Required

2 To make a standard profile mandatory, what do you need to do to the profile's file extension so that the file becomes read-only?

A ○ Change the extension to .DAT.

B ○ Change the extension to .MAN.

C ○ Change the extension to .REQ.

D ○ Change the extension to .TXT.

3 You want to configure a roaming user profile for a particular user. A shared folder has been created on your Windows 2000 member server to hold the user profile. What do you need to do now?

A ○ Edit the user's account on your member server.

B ○ Edit the user's account in the Active Directory.

C ○ Change the profile path on the user's computer.

D ○ Delete the user's local profile from the user's computer's hard drive.

4 You want to configure disk quotas on a particular volume with these settings:

✔ Refuse disk space to users who exceed their limit.

✔ Provide a default limit of 50MB and a warning of 45MB.

✔ Log an event when a user exceeds the warning level.

What do you need to do on the Quota tab to configure these options?

```
New Volume (F:) Properties                          ? X

   General    |    Tools    |    Hardware   |    Sharing
      Security      |      Quota      |      Web Sharing

        Status:  Disk quotas are disabled

    [✓] Enable quota management
    [ ] Deny disk space to users exceeding quota limit

    Select the default quota limit for new users on this volume:

        ( ) Do not limit disk usage
        (•) Limit disk space to        1    KB     ▼
            Set warning level to       1    KB     ▼

    Select the quota logging options for this volume:

        [ ] Log event when a user exceeds their quota limit
        [ ] Log event when a user exceeds their warning level

                                    Quota Entries...

                OK           Cancel          Apply
```

5 In a FAT disk's Properties dialog box, you notice that the Quota tab is not available. Why?

A ○ Disk quotas are not installed on your system.

B ○ The FAT volume is not configured for disk quotas.

C ○ Disk quotas are not available on FAT volumes.

D ○ You need to enable disk quotas on the General tab.

6 You have a spanned volume that includes space on three physical disks. You want to implement disk quotas on this spanned volume, but you want to make sure that users have a total storage limit of only 30MB on the spanned volume — not on each physical disk. What do you need to do after configuring the quota for the spanned volume?

A ○ Set limits on each physical disk.

B ○ Set limits on each volume in the spanned volume.

C ○ Install disk quotas for spanned volumes using Add/Remove Programs.

D ○ You do not need to do anything else.

7 You want to remove a quota entry for a particular volume, but you cannot remove the entry. What is the most likely problem?

A ○ The user account is not available.

B ○ You need to edit DISKQT.TXT to manually remove the user.

C ○ The user's files and folders must be removed from the volume.

D ○ There is a general system error.

Answers

1 *C. Mandatory.* Mandatory profiles turn the profile file into a read-only file, which prevents the user from making changes to the profile. *Review "Configuring and Managing User Profiles."*

2 *B. Change the extension to .MAN.* Typical profiles are named NTUSER.DAT in the registry. To make the profile read-only, change NTUSER.DAT to NTUSER.MAN. *Read "Configuring and Managing User Profiles."*

3 *B. Edit the user's account in the Active Directory.* To set up a roaming user profile, you must change the user's account Profile Properties tab to point to the roaming profile location. Use the Active Directory Users and Computers tool on a Windows 2000 domain controller to accomplish this task. *Study "Configuring and Managing User Profiles."*

4 *Click the Deny Disk Space to Users Exceeding Quota Limit check box, click the Limit Disk Space radio button and enter the value of 50MB, enter the value of 45MB in the Warning box, and click the Log Event When a User Exceeds Their Warning Level check box. See "Configuring Disk Quotas."*

5 *C. Disk quotas are not available on FAT volumes.* Disk quotas are available only on Windows 2000 NTFS volumes. *Study "Configuring Disk Quotas."*

6 *D. You do not need to do anything else.* Disk quotas apply to volumes — not physical disks. A spanned volume is treated as any other volume. In this case, after you set up disk quotas on the spanned volume, the users cannot exceed their quota limit, regardless of how the data is stored across the spanned volume. *Study "Configuring Disk Quotas."*

7 *C. The user's files and folders must be removed from the volume.* Before deleting a quota entry, you must remove the user's files and folders from the volume, or another user must take ownership of them. *Study "Configuring Disk Quotas."*

Part VII

Configuring and Troubleshooting Windows 2000 Network Connections

The 5th Wave   By Rich Tennant

Network Help Desk at Disney Corp.

In this part . . .

Windows 2000 Server provides numerous networking technologies that you can use to meet the needs of your environment, and you need to understand those technologies for the exam. In Chapters 18 and 19, you examine the configuration of protocols, connections, and remote access in Windows 2000. In Chapter 20, you explore the implementation of Terminal Services and how those services can benefit your environment.

Chapter 18

Managing Protocols and Connections

●●●

Exam Objectives

▶ Installing, configuring, and troubleshooting network protocols

▶ Configuring the properties of a connection

▶ Installing and configuring network services

▶ Installing, configuring, and troubleshooting shared access

▶ Installing, configuring, and troubleshooting network adapters and drivers

●●●

At its basic level, a protocol is a rule that determines how computers communicate with each other. Just as humans must speak a common language for communication to take place, different computers must use a common protocol in order for communication to occur. Protocols provide the foundation for network communication and interoperability.

Fortunately, Windows 2000 does not have too many new surprises concerning protocols and connections, and this chapter focuses only on what you may see on the exam. You can review the following topics in this chapter:

✔ Installing and configuring protocols

✔ Installing and configuring services

✔ Configuring shared access

✔ Installing and managing network adapters and drivers

Quick Assessment

Installing, configuring, and troubleshooting network protocols

1 You can install a new protocol for a network interface card by accessing the connection's _____ pages.

2 A common problem when using the NWLink protocol is an incorrect _____.

Configuring the properties of a connection

3 On the General tab in the Properties dialog box for a network connection, you can install protocols and _____ for that connection.

4 You can establish a new ISDN connection using the _____ wizard.

Installing and configuring network services

5 When you install a new network service using a connection's Properties dialog box, you install the service for that particular _____.

Installing, configuring, and troubleshooting shared access

6 You can share a(n) _____ connection in a small office or home network so that other computers can access the Internet.

7 Windows 2000 assigns a new, static _____ address to the server on which you establish a shared connection.

Installing, configuring, and troubleshooting network adapters and drivers

8 You can manage a network adapter card's driver using the _____ tab of the NIC's Properties dialog box.

Answers

1 *Properties.* Review "Installing and Configuring Protocols."

2 *Frame Type.* Study "Installing and Configuring Protocols."

3 *Services.* See "Installing Network Services."

4 *Make New Connection.* Examine "Installing Other Connections."

5 *Network Interface Card.* Read "Installing Network Services."

6 *Dial-Up.* Review "Configuring Internet Connection Sharing (ICS)."

7 *IP.* See "Configuring Internet Connection Sharing (ICS)."

8 *Driver.* Study "Managing Network Adapters and Drivers."

Installing and Configuring Protocols

You install and configure network protocols for any network interface card (NIC) that you have installed on your server. If you have multiple NICs, you can configure different protocols and services for each NIC, depending on how you want to use it for network communication. The process for installing and configuring protocols is rather easy, and the following sections point out what you need to know for the exam. You can also read more about protocols and services in Chapter 2.

The following sections focus solely on standard networking protocols. You can study much more about other networking and authentication protocols in Chapter 19. Also note that other chapters address specific protocol configurations. For example, Chapter 5 covers DHCP and MADCAP.

Installing protocols

You install new protocols for a NIC by accessing that NIC's Properties dialog box. To access a NIC's Properties dialog box, right-click My Network Places on your desktop and then choose Properties. Windows 2000 opens the Network and Dial-up Connections dialog box, which shows Local Area Network (LAN) connections or NICs installed on your server.

To install and configure protocols for a NIC, right-click its icon and choose Properties. Windows 2000 opens the Local Area Connection Properties dialog box for that NIC, as shown in Figure 18-1.

To install a new protocol, follow the steps in Lab 18-1. You should remember how to perform this process for the exam.

Lab 18-1   Installing a Protocol

1. **In the NIC's Local Area Connection Properties dialog box, click Install.**

2. **In the resulting Select Network Component Type dialog box, select Protocol and then click Add.**

3. **In the Select Network Protocol dialog box, select the protocol you want to install and click OK. If you want to install a different protocol that does not automatically appear, click Have Disk. (You must have a disk or CD-ROM containing the protocol to use this option.)**

   Windows 2000 installs the protocol on your system. The protocol now appears in the list that's displayed in the Local Area Connection Properties dialog box.

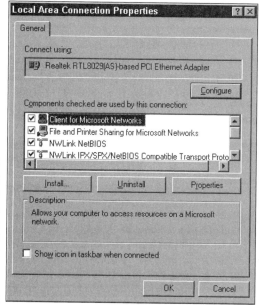

Figure 18-1:
Use the
Local Area
Connection
Properties
dialog box
to install
protocols.

Configuring protocols

To configure a protocol after you install it, select the protocol in the Components window in the Local Area Connection Properties dialog box and then click Properties.

If you select a protocol and the Properties button appears gray (unavailable), that protocol has no configurable options. For example, NetBEUI does not have any configurable options, so you cannot access a Properties dialog box for that protocol.

After you click the Properties button, various sheets may appear, depending on the protocol you select. For example, the Properties dialog box for Internet Protocol (TCP/IP) has a General tab where you can configure the IP address, subnet mask, and default gateway, as well as preferred DNS server IP addresses. You can also configure TCP/IP to obtain its IP address from a DHCP server (see Chapter 5). If you select NWLink and click Properties, you see a General tab where you can manually enter the internal network number and frame type.

The exam expects you to know the major options that you can configure for the more common protocols. You don't need to know all the details about each setting, but you do need to have a general understanding of what you may need to configure. Table 18-1 points out the major configuration options for each major protocol. You should memorize this information for the exam.

Table 18-1	Protocol Configuration
Protocol	*Configuration Options*
TCP/IP	Used for communication in a TCP/IP network. Configurable options are IP address, subnet mask, default gateway, DHCP option, and additional options such as DNS or WINS servers.
NWLink	Used for communication with IPX/SPX networks (NetWare). Configuration options are the internal network number and frame type in use. (Typically, your server detects them automatically, but you can manually configure these settings for troubleshooting purposes.)
AppleTalk	Used for communication with Macintosh computers. The configurable option is the AppleTalk zone.

TCP/IP is the *de facto* standard for communication on the Internet. Because of its wide adaptation, most major networks today use the TCP/IP protocol. TCP/IP functions by using a unique IP address for each network client. This address is then used for communication among computers on the network.

TCP/IP networks can be *subnetted,* or divided, into different sections for greater manageability and to control network traffic. The default gateway on the subnet enables traffic to flow from one subnet to another. Details about TCP/IP and subnet configuration certainly go beyond the scope of this book and the exam, but the exam expects you to be familiar with TCP/IP networking.

Windows 2000 networks are built on TCP/IP, and implementation of the Active Directory requires a TCP/IP network.

NWLink is Microsoft's implementation of the IPX/SPX protocol used for communication in NetWare networks. As you might expect, Microsoft wants NetWare networks to be able to connect with Microsoft networks. NWLink, along with Services for NetWare, enables Windows 2000 clients to access client and server applications available on a NetWare server through NWLink. In the same manner, NetWare clients can use NWLink to access client and server applications running on Windows 2000 servers, and Microsoft clients can even use NWLink to communicate with IPX/SPX network devices (like printers) and even to communicate with each other.

An important aspect of NWLink that you are likely to see on the exam concerns frame type. The frame type determines the way a NIC formats data to be sent over the network to NetWare computers or other computers using

NWLink. In order for network communication to occur, the Windows 2000 server must use the same frame type as the NetWare computer. Incorrect frame types are a common problem that prevents network communication with NWLink.

AppleTalk is the protocol used by Apple Macintosh computers. Windows 2000 Server provides this protocol to enable Macintosh and Windows 2000 computers to communicate with each other. AppleTalk networks function by using *zones,* which are simply logical groupings that make network resource access and browsing easier (comparable to a Windows domain).

In addition to the protocols that I describe in Table 18-1, an exam question may mention DLC or Network Monitor Driver. You use DLC (Data Link Control) for older Hewlett-Packard JetDirect cards that do not support TCP/IP. The Network Monitor Driver works in conjunction with Network Monitor to enable Network Monitor to receive frames from your NIC.

Removing protocols

To boost network communication performance, you should remove any protocols that you no longer use or need on your system. To remove a protocol, simply select it in the Components window of the Local Area Connection Properties dialog box and then click Uninstall. Click Yes in the dialog box that appears, and you will be prompted to reboot your system after Windows 2000 uninstalls the protocol.

Troubleshooting common protocol problems

Generally, protocols are not problematic system components. For the exam, you need to know two basic problems and solutions for TCP/IP and NWLink.

First, in a TCP/IP network, you must have an appropriate IP address and subnet mask configured (if you are not using DHCP). If your server has a static IP and subnet mask, but you do not have connectivity, the odds are pretty good that you have configured an incorrect IP address or subnet mask. If DHCP is in use, this information is automatically supplied to the server (see Chapter 5).

If you are using NWLink to communicate in a NetWare environment, and you cannot gain connectivity, the most likely problem is an incorrect frame type. Windows 2000 does a good job of automatically detecting this information, but if you have connectivity problems, check the frame type and make certain that the NetWare servers use the same one.

Installing Network Services

Depending on the configuration of your server, you can install additional client and service features on your server for a particular NIC. To access the NIC's Properties dialog box, right-click My Network Places and then choose Properties. Then, right-click the NIC's icon and choose Properties to access the Local Area Connection Properties. Click Install, select either Client or Service, and then click Add. From the list that appears, select the type of service you want to install and then click OK.

The network services you can install from this location are specific services for the NIC. To explore other server services, such as DHCP, WINS, and RAS, see Part III in this book.

Installing Other Connections

Windows 2000 Server can support many types of connections other than a typical network connection using a NIC. For example, you can install modem connections, VPN connections, serial, parallel, or infrared ports, and ISDN lines to accommodate your networking needs.

You can easily install these connections by first installing necessary hardware and using the Add/Remove Hardware wizard, or by using the Make New Connection wizard in the Dial-up and Network Connections dialog box, which you access by right-clicking My Network Places and then choosing Properties. You can read more about installing these connections by reviewing Chapters 2, 12, and 13.

Configuring Internet Connection Sharing (ICS)

Windows 2000 servers can share access points with other computers on your network. Namely, Windows 2000 offers *Internet connection sharing (ICS)* so that other computers can access information on the Internet using the share on the server. The server then provides the connection, address-translation, and name-resolution functions to retrieve the Internet information and return it to the client that requests it.

This Windows 2000 feature provides some of the functionality of a proxy server and is designed for small-office or home networks. By configuring the server with the dial-up connection and modem, ISDN hardware, DSL connection, or some other kind of connection technology, only one computer on your network must have the hardware or configuration and all others can use it through the share.

Essentially, ICS enables a single Windows 2000 Server machine (or even a Windows 2000 Professional computer) to act as a single point of access, or a gateway. Through this gateway, the other computers on your network can access the Internet. This process is accomplished through Network Address Translation (NAT) routing. Only the gateway computer is issued a TCP/IP address from the Internet Service Provider (ISP), which means to the ISP and the Internet, only one computer is connected. All other computers connecting through the gateway have nonroutable addresses. Using NAT, the gateway computer performs routing functions so that local network computers can access the Internet, retrieve information, and have that information routed back to them through the computer with ICS enabled.

In the past, NAT could be quite complicated and required various routers; however, Windows 2000 Server includes software that enables your server to act like a NAT router. ICS is easy to configure and offers a great solution for small-office and home networks.

ICS is not difficult to configure, but it is a new feature of Windows 2000 Server, so you can expect some exam questions on this topic. This section explores only the ICS topics that you are likely to see on the exam.

Setting up shared access

To set up shared access for an Internet connection, follow the steps in Lab 18-2.

Lab 18-2   Setting Up Shared Access

1. **Right-click My Network Places and then choose Properties.**

2. **In the Network and Dial-up Connections dialog box, right-click the connection you want to share and choose Properties.**

3. **In the resulting Properties dialog box, click the Sharing tab, shown in Figure 18-2.**

4. **To enable shared access, click the Enable Internet Connection Sharing For This Connection check box.**

If desired, you can also select the Enable On-demand Dialing check box. On-demand dialing enables your server to automatically establish a dial-up connection when a user accesses the shared connection. For example, assume that a user needs to retrieve an Internet document through the shared connection. When the user accesses the shared connection, the server automatically establishes a dial-up connection to service the user's needs.

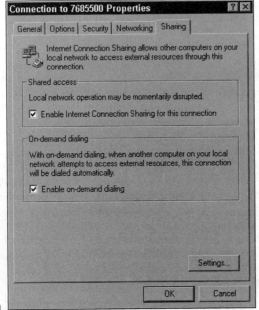

Figure 18-2:
Use the
Sharing tab
to configure
shared
connec-
tions.

After you select the desired settings on the Sharing tab, click OK to share the connection. Windows 2000 Server displays a message telling you that your NIC will be set to use the IP address 192.168.0.1, which may cause your server to lose connectivity with other computers on the network. The 192.168.0.1 address is a nonroutable address. At this point, your server enables a DHCP allocator service to hand out IP addresses in this nonroutable range. You simply enable all other computers on your network to receive their IP addresses from the DHCP server. The ICS-enabled server gives out IP addresses in the 192.168.0.*x* range, and your clients have TCP/IP connectivity on your local network and use the ICS-enabled server to access the Internet.

The message you receive during configuration tells you that you may lose connectivity on your network. This occurs until all computers receive a new 192.168.0.*x* IP address from the ICS-enabled server. For example, assume that you are using an address range of 10.0.0.*x* on your network. When you enable ICS, the server's IP address changes to 192.168.0.1, so your clients will lose IP connectivity with the server until they have the new IP address range supplied by DHCP.

On the exam, you may see a question about a small-office network that implements Internet connection sharing and then loses IP connectivity with the server. The problem involves the use of the new IP address of 192.168.0.1. Clients simply need to be configured to obtain a new IP address from DHCP, which will give them a 192.168.0.*x* address, and then connectivity will be restored. Obviously, you cannot have other DHCP servers in operation, handing out addresses in a different class/range.

You can also configure applications and services for use with the shared connection. On the Sharing tab, click Settings. On the Applications and Services tab in the dialog box that's displayed, click Add or use the Edit and Delete buttons as needed to enable the use of various applications via the connection. The applications feature is designed for applications that you may have installed that can be shared over the Internet with another office or user. The services feature enables you to determine which services (such as FTP and SMTP) can be used over the connection. These features enable you to configure the connection sharing to meet the needs of your network users. Because of the NAT routing features of ICS, some applications or games will not work until they have been configured to work with NAT routing.

ICS is designed for very small networks or home networks. It is not intended for use in networks with other Windows 2000 domain controllers or where DNS and DHCP servers are in use. ICS does not provide the security features necessary for larger networks and it does not enable you to manage your TCP/IP internal network addressing. Likewise, you cannot manipulate the ICS settings, such as turning off the DHCP allocation of 192.168.0.x addresses, the DNS proxy that is used with the service, and other features. Because of these issues, larger environments that want to use a gateway to the Internet should configure it through Network Address Translation (NAT) as a part of Routing and Remote Access Service. (See Chapter 19 for more information about Routing and Remote Access.)

Watch out for tricky exam questions that combine the use of Internet connection sharing with large networks. This is not the intended use of ICS, and this configuration is certain to cause connectivity and even security problems.

Managing Network Adapters and Drivers

You manage network interface (adapter) cards (NICs) and drivers for those cards in the same manner as any other hardware device attached to your computer. If you access the NIC's properties in the Network and Dial-up Connections dialog box, you can click Configure to access the NIC's Properties dialog box. You can troubleshoot problems and manage the driver for the NIC using the Driver tab.

I need to play traffic cop for a moment and direct your attention to a few other places in this book that address issues concerning NICs and drivers. First, the previous sections in this chapter examine configuring protocols and ICS for a NIC, so refer to those sections for more information. Also, Chapter 12 explores hardware installation and configuration. You install NICs like all other Plug-and-Play devices in Windows 2000, so refer to that chapter for more information about installation and troubleshooting. Finally, Chapter 13 explores the configuration, management, and upgrade issues for hardware drivers you need to know for the exam.

With that said, I need to point out two remaining NIC-related issues in this section. For the most part, installing and configuring a NIC is very easy, especially if you choose a Plug-and-Play-compatible NIC that Microsoft lists on the HCL. However, you should know about two special issues:

✓ If you have a Plug-and-Play-compatible ATM (Asynchronous Transfer Mode) NIC, Windows 2000 should automatically detect and install it. Remember, however, that you can install only four ATM NICs on a single Windows 2000 computer. After you install the ATM NIC, Windows 2000 automatically installs Windows ATM Services.

✓ If you have more than one NIC in your server and you want to use Network Monitor to capture frames on those NICs, you need to install an instance of Network Monitor Driver on each NIC. As I explain in the section "Configuring protocols," earlier in this chapter, the Network Monitor Driver works in conjunction with Network Monitor to enable Network Monitor to receive frames from your NIC.

Prep Test

1 You have several protocols installed for a particular network interface card. You want to configure one of the protocols, but the Properties button in the Local Area Connection Properties dialog box is grayed out. What is causing this?

   A ○ The protocol is not installed correctly.

   B ○ The protocol is not operative.

   C ○ The protocol is not configurable.

   D ○ The protocol is not functioning.

2 You want to install the QoS Control feature on a particular network adapter card. What do you need to do in this window to install the feature?

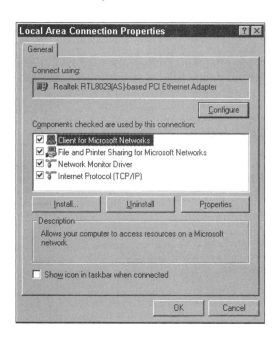

3 You are having problems communicating on a TCP/IP network. All other computers and servers in your IP subnet can communicate with each other, but your computer cannot communicate with other computers, and they cannot communicate with yours. The NIC is installed and functioning correctly, and TCP/IP is installed. What is the most likely problem.

A ○ Incorrect DNS Server

B ○ Incorrect Default Gateway

C ○ Incorrect Frame Type

D ○ Incorrect Subnet Mask

4 An inexperienced administrator needs to install NWLink on a member server that will communicate with a NetWare server, but the administrator cannot find the internal network ID number and is hesitant to install the protocol. When the administrator comes to you for help, what advice should you offer?

A ○ Find the ID number on the NetWare server and use it for the Windows 2000 server.

B ○ The Windows 2000 server should be able to automatically detect the internal network ID number.

C ○ The Windows 2000 server does not need an internal network ID number.

D ○ The Windows 2000 server does not need NWLink to communicate with the NetWare server because this capability is built into Windows 2000 servers.

5 You have a small office network with one Windows 2000 server and ten Windows 2000 Professional clients. You have an ISDN connection established for the server but no connections for the clients. The clients need Internet connectivity, but you do not want the cost of installing ISDN hardware on all the client machines. What is an inexpensive solution?

A ○ Install modems on the client computers.

B ○ Use the server for all Internet communication.

C ○ Share the ISDN connection.

D ○ Create a multilink the clients can use.

6 An administrator plans to share an ISDN connection to the Internet so that clients on a particular IP subnet in a medium-sized network environment can use the connection. The administrator comes to you for advice. What is the first thing you should tell the administrator?

A ○ Make certain you use an appropriate IP address.

B ○ Make certain you have a specific subnet mask.

C ○ Connection sharing should be used only in small office or home networks and is not designed for normal LAN environments.

D ○ Configure all clients with the connection sharing software.

7 In a small office network, you want to make certain that clients who access a shared ISDN connection can use FTP to connect to an FTP server on a remote network. What do you need to do to configure this option?

A ○ Nothing. Clients can automatically perform this action.

B ○ On the Sharing tab, click the FTP check box.

C ○ On the Sharing tab, click Settings. Then, click the FTP check box on the Application tab and configure the FTP information.

D ○ On the Sharing tab, click Settings. Then, click the FTP check box on the Services tab and configure the FTP information.

8 When you configure shared access on a Windows 2000 server for a modem, what happens to your NIC card?

A ○ Nothing.

B ○ The NIC becomes inoperative.

C ○ The NIC is assigned a different, static IP address.

D ○ The NIC is assigned a different subnet mask.

Answers

1 *C. The protocol is not configurable.* Some protocols, such as NetBEUI, do not have Properties dialog boxes because you cannot configure these protocols. In these cases, the Properties button is grayed out. *Review "Installing and Configuring Protocols."*

2 *Click Install. In the dialog box that's displayed, select Service and then click Add. Then, select QoS in the list that appears and click OK.* QoS is a feature of Windows 2000 that helps control communication depending on network traffic issues. QoS is a service, so if you want to install it on a connection, you install it as you would any other service. *Read "Installing Network Services."*

3 *D. Incorrect Subnet Mask.* In this scenario, the only possible answer is an incorrect subnet mask. Incorrect DNS server and default gateway settings would not halt IP communication, and incorrect frame types refer to problems with the NWLink protocol. *Review "Installing and Configuring Protocols."*

4 *B. The Windows 2000 server should be able to automatically detect the internal network ID number.* Windows 2000 requires NWLink to communicate with NetWare servers, but can generally auto-detect the internal network ID and frame type. The administrator should install the protocol and then perform troubleshooting if connectivity cannot be established. *See "Installing and Configuring Protocols."*

5 *C. Share the ISDN connection.* You can share dial-up connections so that small offices or home networks can have one connected computer and the other computers can share the connection. *Study "Configuring Internet Connection Sharing (ICS)."*

6 *C. Connection sharing should be used only in small office or home networks and is not designed for normal LAN environments.* Connection sharing should not be used in networks that have other Windows 2000 servers. It is designed for small office or home networks, and should not be used in this scenario. *Study "Configuring Internet Connection Sharing (ICS)."*

7 *D. On the Sharing tab, click Settings. Then, click the FTP check box on the Services tab and configure the FTP information.* You can set up numerous services using the Services tab, such as FTP, SMTP, and POP3. *Study "Configuring Internet Connection Sharing (ICS)."*

8 *C. The NIC is assigned a different, static IP address.* When you enable shared access, your NIC card is automatically assigned a static IP address of 192.168.0.1. *Study "Configuring Internet Connection Sharing (ICS)."*

Chapter 19

Implementing Remote Access and Virtual Private Networks

. . . .

Exam Objectives

▶ Configuring, monitoring, and troubleshooting remote access

▶ Configuring inbound connections

▶ Creating a remote access policy

▶ Configuring a remote access profile

▶ Installing, configuring, and troubleshooting a virtual private network (VPN)

. . . .

*R*emote access and virtual private networks (VPNs) both give remote users access to the LAN. With the widespread use of laptop computers and telecommuting, the need for remote access and VPNs has exploded in the past several years. Remote Access Service (RAS) in Windows NT gained the reputation of being difficult to configure and troubleshoot. Windows 2000 simplifies the management of remote access, but you still have many different options.

You can expect several questions about remote access and VPNs on the exam. From a member server perspective, many member servers in Windows 2000 networks function as remote access servers to manage dial-in clients, so you need to study this chapter well. You can review the following topics in this chapter:

   ✔ Understanding Routing and Remote Access Service (RRAS)

   ✔ Enabling RRAS

   ✔ Configuring policies and profiles

   ✔ Configuring VPN connections

Quick Assessment

Configuring, monitoring, and troubleshooting remote access

1 _____ is installed by default in Windows 2000 Server, but you do have to enable it.

2 The _____ service provides a central authentication database for multiple remote access servers.

3 The _____ authentication protocol provides encryption keys used during RRAS authentication negotiation.

Configuring inbound connections

4 To configure an inbound connection, you configure the desired _____ for the connection media.

Creating a remote access policy

5 A remote access policy defines certain _____ that a client follows in order to gain a RRAS connection.

6 By a policy definition, you can either _____ or _____ access to the RRAS server according to the policy configuration.

Configuring a remote access profile

7 On the profile _____ tab, you can allow clients to access a DHCP server for an IP address, or you can specify an IP address from a range.

8 For multilink configuration within a profile, you can use _____ to automatically drop unneeded links.

Installing, configuring, and troubleshooting a VPN

9 In Windows 2000, VPNs support the _____ protocol, which is used with IPSec.

10 You can use _____ with VPNs to support smart-card logon.

Answers

1   *Routing and Remote Access.* Review "Understanding Remote Access."

2   *RADIUS.* Study "Enabling Remote Access."

3   *MS-CHAP V2.* See "Configuring Server Properties."

4   *Port.* Examine "Configuring Inbound Connections."

5   *Rules.* Review "Creating a Remote Access Policy."

6   *Grant; Deny.* See "Creating a Remote Access Policy."

7   *IP.* Read "Configuring a Remote Access Profile."

8   *BAP.* Study "Configuring a Remote Access Profile."

9   *L2TP.* Review "Configuring Virtual Private Networks."

10   *EAP.* Study "Configuring Virtual Private Networks."

Understanding Remote Access

Routing and Remote Access Service (RRAS) enables remote network clients to establish a remote connection with a RRAS server. After the connection is established, the remote client functions just like a locally connected network client. The user can browse the network, use permitted resources, connect to other servers — anything a locally connected client can do — provided that the RRAS client has appropriate permissions. In recent years, RRAS has grown in importance as increasing numbers of users work from laptops in different locations.

Windows NT offers remote access, and an NT add-on component enables the routing features. Windows 2000 combines these technologies as Routing and Remote Access.

The exam objectives do not focus on the configuration of routing interfaces on a Windows 2000 server. Instead, they focus on the remote access configuration. Consequently, this chapter focuses primarily on the remote access portion of Routing and Remote Access, even though the term *RRAS* refers to both routing and remote access.

Enabling Remote Access

The Setup program installs RRAS by default on Windows 2000 servers when you perform an initial installation. However, Setup does not enable RRAS. In order to set up and implement RRAS, you have to enable it by using the Routing and Remote Access Server Setup wizard.

You need to know this wizard's options for the exam. To practice setting up RRAS using the Routing and Remote Access Server Setup wizard, follow the steps in Lab 19-1.

Lab 19-1   Enabling Routing and Remote Access

1. **Click Start⇨Programs⇨Administrative Tools⇨Routing and Remote Access.**

2. **In the console, select your server and then choose Action⇨Configure and Enable Routing and Remote Access.**

3. **Click Next on the wizard's welcome screen.**

4. **In the wizard's Common Configurations dialog box, select the type of remote access server you want to install and then click Next. For this lab, select Remote Access Server, as shown in Figure 19-1.**

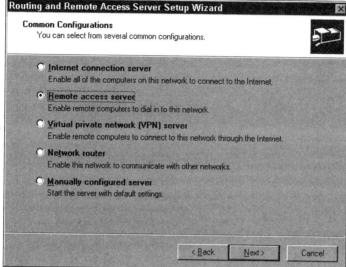

Figure 19-1:
You have
several
remote
access
server
options.

5. **Verify the required protocols in the list provided. Typically, you need TCP/IP, but you may need others depending on your network clients. Click Next.**

6. **In the IP Address Assignment dialog box, specify how you want IP addresses assigned to remote clients — either automatically or from a specified range — and then click Next.**

   If you choose to have IP addresses assigned automatically, remote clients get an IP address through DHCP (see Chapter 5). If you want to have the addresses assigned from a specified range, enter an IP address range to assign to remote clients.

7. **Indicate whether you want to enable RADIUS and then click Next.**

   Remote Authentication Dial-In User Service (RADIUS) provides a central authentication database for multiple remote access servers and collects accounting information about remote connections. You can set up this remote access server to use an existing RADIUS server if you so choose.

8. **Click Finish.**

   Windows 2000 starts the Routing and Remote Access Service.

Configuring Server Properties

After you enable RRAS, you can further configure the server by accessing its Properties dialog box. In the Routing and Remote Access console, select your server and then choose Action⇨Properties.

You need to know the configuration options on the Properties tabs that I explore in the following sections. Depending on your network configuration, you may have other tabs, such as AppleTalk for Macintosh clients, but the following sections explore only those tabs that you need to know for the exam.

Configuring the General tab

The General tab in the server's Properties dialog box gives you two options. First, you can choose to enable your server as a router. If you select this option, you can choose to allow only local LAN routing, or you can choose to allow LAN and demand-dial routing. Next, you can choose to enable your server as a remote access server. These options simply enable you to use your server as both a routing server and a remote access server, or either one, as desired.

Configuring the Security tab

On the Security tab in the server's Properties dialog box, you can select the security and accounting provider. You can select either Windows authentication and accounting or RADIUS authentication and accounting. If you choose to implement RADIUS, click Configure to connect to a RADIUS server.

For Windows authentication, click Authentication Methods and then select the type of Windows authentication you want to use for remote access. You have the following options, and you need to know them for the exam:

- **Extensible authentication protocol (EAP):** Allows the use of third-party authentication software and is also used for smart-card logon.

- **MS-CHAP V2:** Generates encryption keys during RRAS authentication negotiation.

- **MS-CHAP:** An earlier version of CHAP that provides secure logon.

- **Shiva Password Authentication Protocol (SPAP):** Used by Shiva clients connecting to a Windows 2000 RRAS Server. SPAP is more secure than clear text, but less secure than CHAP.

- **Unencrypted password (PAP):** No encryption required.

- **Unauthenticated access:** No authentication used.

Configuring the IP tab

On the IP tab in the server's Properties dialog box, you can enable IP routing and allow IP-based remote access and demand-dial connections. You can choose to implement DHCP IP leases for remote clients or you can enter a static IP address pool. These are the same options you configure with the RRAS Setup wizard, but you can use this tab to make changes as necessary.

Configuring the PPP tab

The PPP tab in the server's Properties dialog box gives you three main check boxes for Point to Point Protocol features you can enable.

You need to know these options for the exam:

- ✔ **Multilink Connections:** Enables you to use multilink, which connects several modems or adapters together to increase bandwidth. You can also choose to use dynamic bandwidth control with Bandwidth Allocation Protocol (BAP) or Bandwidth Allocation Control Protocol (BACP). These protocols allow the multilink connection to dynamically add or drop PPP links as necessary for the traffic flow.

- ✔ **Link Control Protocol (LCP) extensions:** Used to managed LCP and PPP connections.

- ✔ **Software Compression:** Uses the Microsoft Point to Point Compression Protocol (MPPC) to compress data sent on the remote access or demand-dial connection.

Configuring the Event Logging tab

The Event Logging tab in the server's Properties dialog box provides an effective way to monitor your remote access server through the use of log files.

The Event Logging tab has several radio buttons so you can choose to log the kind of information desired, such as errors, warnings, and PPP logging. If you are experiencing problems with your remote access server, these different logging options can help you pinpoint the problem.

Monitoring Remote Clients

You can monitor the clients currently connected to the remote access server by using the Routing and Remote Access console. In the console tree, expand your server and then click the Remote Access Clients icon. The details pane lists the remote access clients by user name, duration, and the number of ports in use. You can use this interface to manually disconnect clients, if desired.

Configuring Inbound Connections

Inbound connections enable remote clients to connect to your remote access server. To enable the clients to connect, you must configure the hardware, such as a modem or ISDN adapter, to accept the inbound connection.

To configure the inbound connection, expand your server in the Routing and Remote Access console, select Ports, and then choose Action⇨Properties. The resultant dialog box lists the routing and remote access devices attached to your computer. Select the desired device and click Configure. The Configure Device dialog box appears, as shown in Figure 19-2.

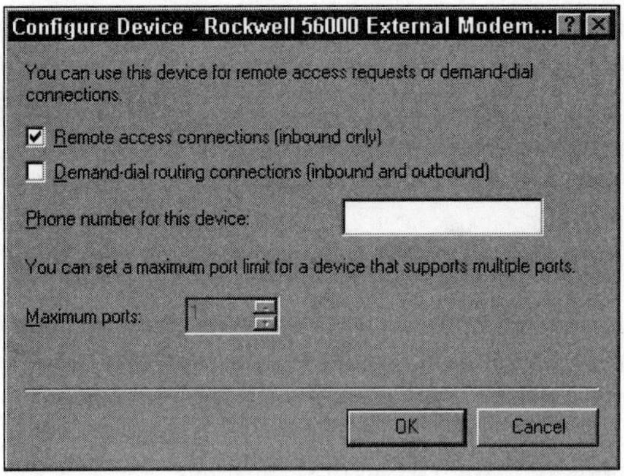

Figure 19-2:
Configuring
a device to
accept
inbound
connec-
tions.

> **Configure Device - Rockwell 56000 External Modem...** ? ☒
>
> You can use this device for remote access requests or demand-dial connections.
>
> ☑ Remote access connections (inbound only)
>
> ☐ Demand-dial routing connections (inbound and outbound)
>
> Phone number for this device: [＿＿＿＿＿＿＿]
>
> You can set a maximum port limit for a device that supports multiple ports.
>
> Maximum ports: [＿＿]
>
> [OK]   [Cancel]

To allow the device to accept only inbound connections, click the appropriate check box. You can also choose to use the device for demand-dial routing connections. After you enable the device for inbound connections, users can dial the specified phone number to contact the device for inbound access.

Creating a Remote Access Policy

Remote access policies define how remote clients can use remote access. The policies create rules that the clients must follow for different remote access rights and permissions. For example, you specify certain dial-in numbers, dial-in hours, and even telephone numbers from which a user must dial in for remote access.

Lab 19-2 guides you through the steps for creating a new remote access policy. Review this lab carefully, because you need to know how to perform this task for the exam.

Lab 19-2	Creating a Remote Access Policy

1. **Select Remote Access Policy in the tree pane of the Routing and Remote Access console and then choose <u>A</u>ction⇨<u>N</u>ew Remote Access Policy.**

2. **Enter a friendly name for the policy and click Next.**

3. **In the Conditions dialog box, click Add to see a list of conditions you can use to create the policy. In the resulting dialog box, shown in Figure 19-3, select the desired condition(s) and click Add. You may be asked to enter additional information, depending on the option you selected. Click Next.**

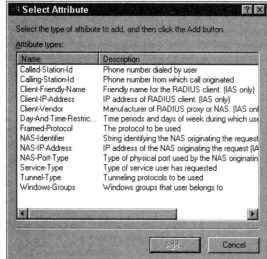

Figure 19-3: Selecting the desired policy attribute.

4. **In the Permissions dialog box, specify whether to grant or deny remote access permission, based on your attribute selection. Click Next.**

5. **Click Finish.**

   The new policy appears in the details pane of the Routing and Remote Access console.

Editing a Remote Access Policy

After you create desired policies, you can easily edit them and change them, as necessary.

To edit a policy, click the Remote Access Policies icon in the console tree and then select the desired policy in the details pane. Choose Action⇨Properties. As shown in Figure 19-4, the resulting Properties dialog box has a single Settings tab, which shows how the policy is defined.

Use the Add, Remove, or Edit buttons to make changes to the existing policy attribute. You can also change the grant or deny feature for the policy by selecting the desired radio button. Editing a policy gives you the same options you have when creating a new policy, and you can easily change existing policies without removing and then recreating them.

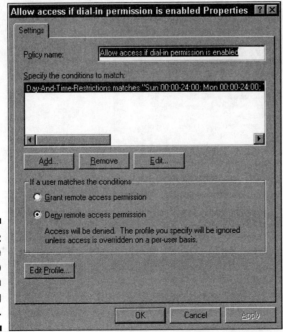

Figure 19-4:
Use the Settings tab to edit an existing policy.

Configuring a Remote Access Profile

For each remote access policy, you can configure the remote access profile. The profile defines settings for users who match the conditions you specify in the policy.

You can create or edit a profile when you first create a policy by clicking the Edit Profile button during the policy steps. You can also edit it by accessing the policy's properties and clicking Edit Profile.

This action opens the Edit Dial-in Profile dialog box, which contains six tabs. For the exam, you need to know the configuration options that each tab offers. The following sections point out what you need to know for the exam.

Configuring the Dial-in Constraints tab

You use the Dial-in Constraints tab in the Edit Dial-in Profile dialog box to set restrictions for the dial-in policy. As shown in Figure 19-5, you can choose to disconnect the connection if it remains idle for a certain period of time, restrict the maximum session time, or restrict access to certain days and times. You can also choose to restrict the kind of dial-in media used by the client.

Configuring the IP tab

You use the IP tab in the Edit Dial-in Profile dialog box to set a specific profile for the policy, such as server-assigned or client-requested IP address. By default, the Server Settings Define Policy radio button is selected.

Configuring the Multilink tab

On the Multilink tab in the Edit Dial-in Profile dialog box, you can define multilink settings for the particular profile, as shown in Figure 19-6. By default, the profile uses the server settings, but you have the option to define multilink settings for the profile. You can choose to allow or disable multilink and use BAP, if desired. If you choose to use BAP, you specify when a link is dropped by the percentage of bandwidth usage and period of time. Additionally, you can require BAP for dynamic multilink requests.

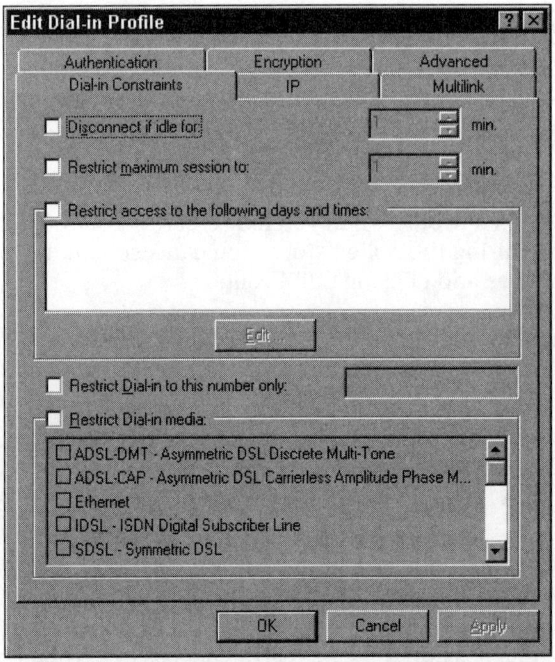

Edit Dial-in Profile   ? X

| Authentication | Encryption | Advanced |
| Dial-in Constraints | IP | Multilink |

☐ Disconnect if idle for: [1] ⇕ min.

☐ Restrict maximum session to: [1] ⇕ min.

☐ Restrict access to the following days and times:

```
┌──────────────────────────────────────┐
│                                        │
│                                        │
│                                        │
│                                        │
│              [ Edit ]                  │
└──────────────────────────────────────┘
```

☐ Restrict Dial-in to this number only: [   ]

☐ Restrict Dial-in media:

☐ ADSL-DMT - Asymmetric DSL Discrete Multi-Tone
☐ ADSL-CAP - Asymmetric DSL Carrierless Amplitude Phase M...
☐ Ethernet
☐ IDSL - ISDN Digital Subscriber Line
☐ SDSL - Symmetric DSL

[OK]   [Cancel]   [Apply]

Figure 19-5:
Use the
Dial-in
Constraints
tab to place
restrictions
on the
remote user.

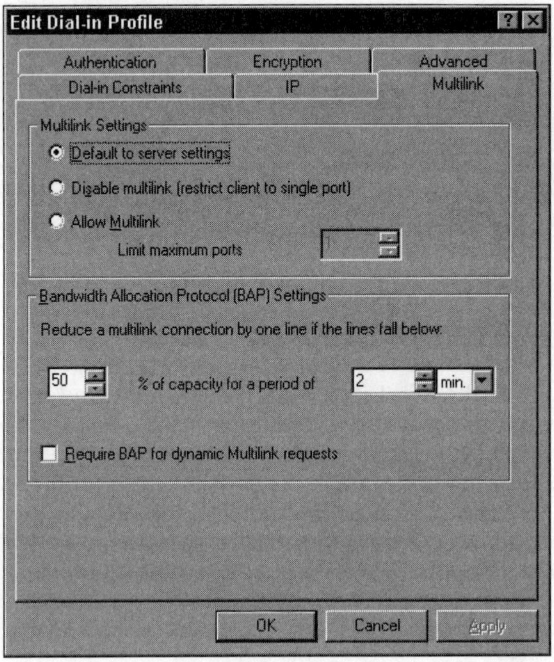

Edit Dial-in Profile   ? X

| Authentication | Encryption | Advanced |
| Dial-in Constraints | IP | Multilink |

Multilink Settings
  ⦿ Default to server settings
  ○ Disable multilink (restrict client to single port)
  ○ Allow Multilink
        Limit maximum ports   [1] ⇕

Bandwidth Allocation Protocol (BAP) Settings
Reduce a multilink connection by one line if the lines fall below:

[50] ⇕ % of capacity for a period of   [2] ⇕ min. ▼

☐ Require BAP for dynamic Multilink requests

[OK]   [Cancel]   [Apply]

Figure 19-6:
Use the
Multilink tab
to configure
multilink
settings for
the profile.

Configuring the authentication and encryption settings

You configure authentication and encryption settings for the RRAS server by accessing the server's properties. You can also configure authentication and encryption settings for a policy's profile. With this feature, you can implement different encryption and authentication settings for each profile, if desired. The Authentication and Encryption tabs in the Edit Dial-in Profile dialog box both provide a series of check boxes from which you can select the desired authentication and encryption settings. These are the same as the server properties, and you can review them in the section "Configuring Server Properties," earlier in this chapter.

Configuring the Advanced tab

The Advanced tab in the Edit Dial-in Profile dialog box enables you to specify additional attributes to be returned to the remote access sever. If you click Add, you see a lengthy list of attributes that you can select, as shown in Figure 19-7.

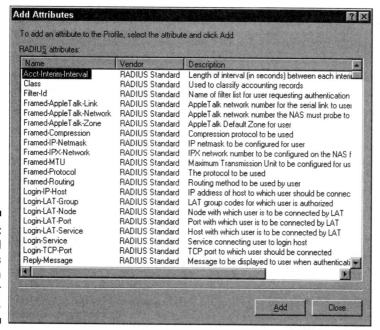

Figure 19-7: Additional attributes that you can specify for a profile.

The Add Attributes option enables you to specify additional information for certain network client configurations. You don't need to know these attributes for the exam, but do keep in mind that you can configure specific client options on the Advanced tab in the Edit Dial-in Profile dialog box.

Configuring Virtual Private Networks

A VPN is an extension of a local private network that contains links across public networks, such as the Internet. With a VPN, you can establish a link between two computers across a public network and send information as if it were through a private point-to-point link.

To emulate this private link, data is encapsulated in a frame that provides routing information so the data can travel over the public network to its destination. At the receiving end, the outer frame is removed to reveal the actual data inside. The data in the frame is encrypted for safety as it travels over the private network.

VPNs offer effective solutions for many scenarios in which one office needs to send data intermittently to another office without maintaining an expensive WAN link. By using the Internet as a transport mechanism, data can be transmitted safely and inexpensively.

Windows 2000 has several new features of VPNs. You should remember these new features for the exam:

- ✔ **Layer Two Tunneling Protocol (L2TP):** Windows 2000 supports both Point to Point Tunneling Protocol (PPTP) and L2TP, which is used with Windows 2000's Internet Protocol Security (IPSec). This combination creates very secure VPNs.

- ✔ **Remote Access Policies:** You can use remote access policies to set connection conditions for VPNs. This feature enables you to enforce different kinds of authentication and security features.

- ✔ **MS-CHAP V2:** With MS-CHAP V2, VPNs are greatly strengthened in terms of security because you can send encrypted data that requires the use of encryption keys for decoding.

- ✔ **Extensible Authentication Protocol (EAP):** Windows 2000 supports EAP for VPN connections. EAP enables you to use new authentication methods with RRAS and VPNs, specifically smart-card logon.

- ✔ **Account Lockout:** Windows 2000 supports account lockout after a specified number of failed VPN connection attempts, but this feature is disabled by default.

After you install routing and remote access, you can enable VPN usage on the RRAS server by accessing the Ports option in the console tree. Select Ports and then choose Action⇨Properties. In the Ports Properties dialog box, you see a PPTP and L2TP Miniport available, as shown in Figure 19-8.

Figure 19-8: Use the Ports Properties dialog box to configure the PPTP and L2TP ports.

As with other ports, select the desired port and click Configure to allow remote access connections and demand-dial connections (inbound and outbound). This feature enables your server to accept PPTP or L2TP connections for data transmission.

After you configure your VPN ports, you can create VPN policies and profiles, as desired, to manage your VPN connections. For more information about policies and profiles, see the section "Configuring a Remote Access Profile," earlier in this chapter.

1 You need to set up routing and remote access on your Windows 2000 server. You access routing and remote access through Administrative Tools. What do you need to do now in this interface to configure and enable it?

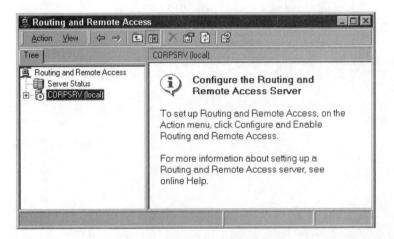

2 After installing your server as a remote access server, you also want to enable it to be a LAN router. Where can you enable this feature?

A ○ Server Properties, General tab

B ○ Server Properties, IP tab

C ○ Server Properties, Security tab

D ○ Server Properties, PPP tab

3 You want your RRAS server, which is configured for multilink connections, to dynamically drop unneeded links. Which protocols are used for this purpose? (Choose all that apply.)

A ❑ IPSec

B ❑ BAP

C ❑ BACP

D ❑ L2TP

4 Which protocol is used to enable software compression on a remote access server?

A ○ BAP

B ○ L2TP

C ○ MPPC

D ○ MS-CHAP

5 For a particular remote access profile, you want to make certain that all connected clients gain access by using encryption keys. On the Authentication tab for this profile, what do you need to do?

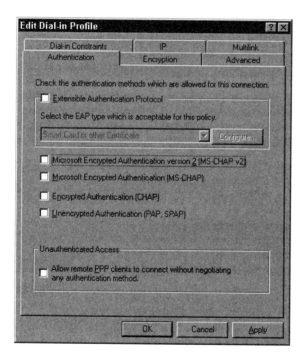

6 You want to make certain that if RRAS clients dial a particular phone number, they are granted remote access, assuming they provide authentication. What do you need to do?

A ○ Create a policy.

B ○ Create a profile.

C ○ Use MS-CHAP.

D ○ Use MS-CHAP V2.

7 For a particular profile, you want to limit access times to Monday through Friday, from 8:00 a.m. to 6:00 p.m. Where can you configure this option?

A ○ Profile properties, Dial-in Constraints tab

B ○ Profile properties, IP tab

C ○ Profile properties, Multilink tab

D ○ Profile properties, Authentication tab

8 By default, how is a policy's IP tab configured?

A ○ For DHCP IP assignment

B ○ For manual IP address range assignment

C ○ For client-requested IP address assignment

D ○ By the server's default settings

9 Which VPN protocol is used with IPSec to create highly secure VPN transmissions?

A ○ MS CHAP

B ○ EAP

C ○ L2TP

D ○ IEAP

10 Which Windows 2000 feature of VPNs refuses to authenticate a remote user after a specified number of failed logon attempts?

A ○ EAP

B ○ L2TP

C ○ MS CHAP

D ○ Account Lockout

Answers

1 *Select your server, choose Action⇨Configure and Enable Routing and Remote Access, and then complete the setup wizard.* Routing and remote access is installed by default in Windows 2000, but you have to configure and enable the service before you can use it. *Review "Enabling Remote Access."*

2 *A. Server Properties, General tab.* You can use the General tab to enable either remote access, router, or both. *Read "Configuring Server Properties."*

3 *B and C.* Bandwidth Allocation Protocol and Bandwidth Allocation Control Protocol are used to dynamically drop unneeded links during a multilink session. *Review "Configuring Server Properties."*

4 *C. MPPC.* Microsoft Point to Point Compression protocol is used to enable software compression for remote access transmissions. *See "Configuring Server Properties."*

5 *Click the MS-CHAP V2 check box and click OK.* MS-CHAP V2 provides encrypted logon through the use of encryption keys. *Study "Configuring a Remote Access Profile."*

6 *A. Create a policy.* You can use policies to configure numerous connection items that either grant or deny access, such as particular phone numbers and times of day. *Study "Creating a Remote Access Policy."*

7 *A. Profile properties, Dial-in Constraints tab.* The Dial-in Constraints tab enables you to restrict access by days and times, as well as other restrictions such as Disconnect If Idle and Restrict Maximum Session. *Study "Configuring a Remote Access Profile."*

8 *D. By the server's default settings.* By default, a profile's IP tab uses the server's settings for client IP configuration. *Study "Configuring a Remote Access Profile."*

9 *C. L2TP.* Layer 2 Tunneling Protocol is used with IPSec to provide highly secure VPN transmissions. *Read "Configuring Virtual Private Networks."*

10 *D. Account Lockout.* Windows 2000 VPNs support account lockout. *See "Configuring Virtual Private Networks."*

Chapter 20

Implementing Terminal Services

· ·

Exam Objectives

▶ Installing, configuring, monitoring, and troubleshooting Terminal Services

▶ Remotely administering servers by using Terminal Services

▶ Configuring Terminal Services for application sharing

▶ Configuring applications for use with Terminal Services

· ·

*T*erminal Services enable you to manage servers from remote locations by opening a terminal window on virtually any machine in your network. You can also use Terminal Services to share applications, with users connecting to a terminal server on which the application runs. In Windows 2000, you typically install and use Terminal Services on member servers, so you can expect the exam to ask you a few questions.

The exam expects you to know how to install and implement the Remote Administration and Application Server modes of Terminal Services. You can review the following topics in this chapter:

   ✔ Understanding Terminal Services

   ✔ Using Remote Administration and Application Server modes

   ✔ Configuring connections

   ✔ Understanding Terminal Services commands

Quick Assessment

Installing, configuring, monitoring, and troubleshooting Terminal Services

1 Terminal Services provides a terminal _____ window for client computers.

2 You can install Terminal Services in either Remote Administration mode or _____ mode.

3 You use the Terminal Services _____ to make client installation disks.

4 You can change the properties of a Terminal Services connection by using the _____ tool.

Remotely administering servers by using Terminal Services

5 In Remote Administration mode without licenses, you can have _____ concurrent connections.

6 For remote administration, you should only install Terminal Services on a server on a(n) _____ partition.

Configuring Terminal Services for application sharing

7 You can only share applications if Terminal Services is running in _____ mode.

8 Although you can install Terminal Services Application Server mode with permissions for legacy applications, this feature has serious _____ risks.

9 Terminal Services running in Application Server mode can provide unlicensed clients access for _____ days.

Configuring applications for use with Terminal Services

10 After you install the Application Server mode, you can install applications using either the `change user` command, or more simply through _____, which manages multisession support for you.

Answers

1 *Emulation.* Review "Understanding Terminal Services."

2 *Application Server.* Study "Installing Terminal Services."

3 *Client Creator.* See "Reviewing Terminal Services Administrative Tools."

4 *Terminal Services Configuration.* See "Reviewing Terminal Services Administrative Tools."

5 *Two.* Review "Using Terminal Services Remote Administration Mode."

6 *NTFS.* See "Using Terminal Services Remote Administration Mode."

7 *Application Server.* Read "Using Terminal Services Application Server Mode."

8 *Security.* Study "Using Terminal Services Application Server Mode."

9 *90.* Review "Using Terminal Services Application Server Mode."

10 *Add/Remove Programs.* Study "Using Terminal Services Application Server Mode."

Understanding Terminal Services

Terminal Services provides remote access to a server desktop through software that serves as a terminal emulator. This feature transmits the user interface to the client. The client then manages the interface through keyboard entries and mouse clicks that are returned to the server for processing. A terminal server can host many sessions at one time, and each session user sees only his or her manipulation of the interface.

Terminal Services for clients can run various platforms, including Windows platforms and even Macintosh and UNIX platforms with additional third-party software.

You can deploy Terminal Services in either Remote Administration mode or Application Server mode, but not both at the same time. In Remote Administration mode, you can access and administer your server from any remote terminal on your network. In Application Server mode, terminals that may not be able to run Windows can connect to the terminal server and run applications as needed.

Terminal Services has several benefits, with a major one being the use of Windows 2000 and Windows 2000 applications on older computers that cannot support Windows 2000. By using this feature, users can get acquainted with Windows 2000 before you implement it on all client computers.

Reviewing Terminal Services Administrative Tools

Several administrative tools enable you to manage Terminal Services on your Windows 2000 server.

For the exam, you need to know what you can do with each of these tools:

- ✔ **Terminal Services Manager:** You use this interface to manage and monitor users, sessions, and processes on any server running Terminal Services on the network.

- ✔ **Terminal Services Configuration:** You use this interface to change the Terminal Services TCP/IP connection that clients use to access the terminal server. You can perform such tasks as naming a connection, specifying a connection transport and its properties, and enabling or disabling logons.

✔ **Active Directory Users and Computers and Local Users and Groups Extensions:** This feature extends the Active Directory Users and Computers on domain controllers and local users and groups so you can control Terminal Services features for each user.

✔ **Terminal Services Licensing:** This tool registers and tracks licenses for Terminal Services clients.

✔ **System Monitor Counters:** Terminal Services extends System Monitor by adding User and Session objects and their counters.

✔ **Task Manager Additional Fields:** Terminal Services provides two additional fields to Task Manager for monitoring and ending processes for all sessions.

✔ **Client Creator:** You use this tool to make disks that you use to install the Terminal Services client.

✔ **Client Connection Manager:** The Client Connection Manager is installed on the client computer when you install Terminal Services.

✔ **Multi-user Support in Add/Remove Programs:** This feature ensures that applications are installed for use in a multisession environment.

Installing Terminal Services

You install Terminal Services just as you do any other Windows 2000 component: by using either Add/Remove programs in Control Panel or the Configure Your Server tool. For specific instructions for installing this or any other Windows 2000 service, see Chapter 2.

When you choose to install Terminal Services, a dialog box appears asking you to select one of two modes, either Remote Administration mode or Application Server mode. You can choose to install either one, but the exam expects you to know about both of them. You can read about using both of these Terminal Services modes in the following sections of this chapter. After you install Terminal Services, you need to reboot your computer.

Using Terminal Services Remote Administration Mode

You use Terminal Services Remote Administration mode to manage your Windows 2000 server from virtually any computer on your network.

When you choose to install this mode, you should install it only on Windows 2000 servers on an NTFS partition, and you don't need to enable Terminal Services Licensing for remote administration. Keep both of these points in mind for the exam.

After you install Terminal Services in Remote Administration mode, you can install Terminal Services on the desired client computer so that you can remotely administer your server.

To install Terminal Services on the client, you need to make the installation disks by clicking Start⊅Programs⊅Administrative Tools⊅ Terminal Services Client Creator. Follow the instructions that appear. You need two floppy disks for the 32-bit client creator. Terminal Services also provides a 16-bit client creator for backward compatibility. To use the 16-bit client creator, you need four disks.

Use the two floppy disks to install the Terminal Services Client on the desired client computers. After you complete the installation, launch the Terminal Services Client application from the Programs menu and then enter an administrator user name and password. The terminal appears on the remote computer where you can administer the terminal server. With appropriate administrator permissions, you can configure the server just as if you were sitting at it.

You can manage sessions in progress by using the Terminal Services Manager on the terminal server, as shown in Figure 20-1. You start the Terminal Services Manager by clicking Start⊅Programs⊅ Administrative Tools⊅Terminal Services Manager.

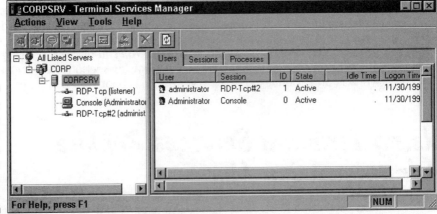

Figure 20-1:
Use
Terminal
Services
Manager to
manage
sessions.

By selecting the desired user and clicking the appropriate commands in the Action menu, you can disconnect the user, send the user a message, reset the connection, log the user off, and examine the status. Although these actions are all simple, they are considered important monitoring features and you should keep them in mind for the exam.

You don't have to worry about licensing when using Terminal Services Remote Administration mode. Two concurrent connections are allowed, and you do not need licenses for the connections.

Using Terminal Services Application Server Mode

Application Server mode enables users to connect to your terminal server and run applications. Keep in mind that the server performs all the processing, and users are simply provided a graphical interface. Although this feature is effective and very useful, you should consider the impact on system resources that running several sessions can create. With numerous clients connecting to the terminal server, your processor and system RAM must be able to run multiple applications and processes. In short, use the Application Server mode on a server that has plenty of system resources and no responsibility for running lots of other network tasks.

When you choose to install Terminal Services Application Server mode, a dialog box appears in which you can select permissions compatible with Windows 2000 users or permissions compatible with Terminal Server 4.0 users. The Windows 2000 option provides the most secure environment. By default, users have the same permissions as members of the Users group, which may prevent them from running some legacy applications. If you use legacy applications, you can choose to use permissions compatible with Terminal Server 4.0 users.

If you select this option, users have full access to critical registry and file system locations, which many legacy applications require. As you know, this can be a dangerous scenario.

After you make your selection, you see a dialog box that lists any programs that may not function properly in Application Server mode. Take note of those applications. Also, you are prompted for the location of the license server database, which is automatically installed by default in C:\WINNT\System32\Lserver.

For the exam, remember that terminal server licensing for the Application Server mode can apply to either an enterprise or a domain, depending on which option you select during setup. Keep in mind that terminal servers can only access domain license servers if they are in the same domain as the license server. Terminal Services has its own method for licensing clients that log on to the terminal server. Clients must receive a valid license before they can log on in Application Server mode. The license must be activated by Microsoft, which uses Microsoft Clearinghouse, a database for maintaining and activating licenses.

However, Terminal Services allows unlicensed clients to connect for 90 days. After that time, terminal servers will not allow clients to connect without appropriate licenses. You can use the Terminal Server Licensing tool available in Administrative Tools to active the license with the Microsoft database.

Configuring Application Sharing

After you have Terminal Services set up and ready to go, you need to install and configure applications for sharing and multisession access. With this setup, multiple users can access the same application at the same time.

You can configure application sharing in either of two ways. First, you can use Add/Remove Programs in Control Panel to install the desired applications. You can also use the `change user` command at the command prompt before and after installing the program. The `change user` command ensures that program files are installed in the systemroot rather than in the Windows subdirectory of the user's home directory. The `change user` action makes the program available for multisessions. The `change user / install` command places the system in install mode and turns off the .INI file mapping. After you install the program, the `change user / execute` command returns the system to execute mode, restores the .INI file mapping, and redirects user-specific data to the user's home directory.

Add/Remove Programs automatically runs the `change user` command in the background, so it is the preferred method for installing applications on a terminal server for multisession use.

After you install the applications, Terminal Services clients can connect to the terminal server and open multiple sessions of the program.

Any applications that you installed before you installed Terminal Services Application Server mode need to be reinstalled so they will be available to users in multisession mode. Keep this in mind for the exam.

When installing applications on your terminal server, you should disconnect any users to avoid potential problems. Also, remember to test your application installations. Some 16-bit programs may have problems working with Terminal Services, so you should test all installations and note any problems.

Managing Terminal Services Connections

The Terminal Services Configuration tool provides an MMC interface with which you can configure your Terminal Services connections and server settings. The Server Settings container gives you the attributes you configured during setup, which you can change from this location, if desired. You access the Terminal Services Configuration tool by clicking Start⇨Programs⇨Administrative Tools⇨Terminal Services Configuration.

For the exam, you are most likely to see a question or two about configuring your connections. If you click the Connections container in the console tree, you see an RDP-TCP connection in the details pane. Microsoft Remote Desktop Protocol (RDP) is the protocol used for Microsoft Terminal Services. If you use other terminal servers, you may use a different protocol, in which case, you should check the third party's documentation.

To create a new connection, select the Connections container and then choose Action⇨Create New Connection. A wizard assists you in creating the connection, but you only need to create one if you are using third-party terminal services. If you only use Microsoft Terminal Services, you only need the RDP-TCP connection.

To access the properties of the RDP-TCP connection, select the connection in the tree pane and then choose Action⇨Properties.

The resulting Properties dialog box has several tabs available, but the following sections examine only the ones that you need to know for the exam.

Configuring the General tab

The General tab in the RDP-TCP Properties dialog box reports to you the type of connection and the transport (TCP). This tab also has a box in which you can enter a comment. The important point about the General tab is that you can change the Encryption settings by clicking the drop-down list. Terminal Services in Windows 2000 Server supports the use of encrypted data between the client and the server.

You have three levels of encryption, which you need to know for the exam:

- **Low:** Only data sent from the client to the server is protected by encryption, based on the server's standard key strength.

- **Medium:** All data sent between the client and the server is protected by encryption, based on the server's standard key strength.

- **High:** All data sent between the client and the server is protected by encryption, based on the server's maximum key strength.

Configuring the Sessions tab

On the Sessions tab in the RDP-TCP Properties dialog box, you can configure default settings to manage user sessions. By default, all these settings are turned off, but you can use them to place certain restrictions on users.

To create the restrictions, simply click the desired check boxes, drop-down lists, and radio buttons to configure the restrictions as desired. For example, you can choose to end a disconnected session after a certain period of time, limit active sessions, create an idle session limit, and even override user settings. Figure 20-2 shows the Sessions tab in the RDP-TCP Properties dialog box.

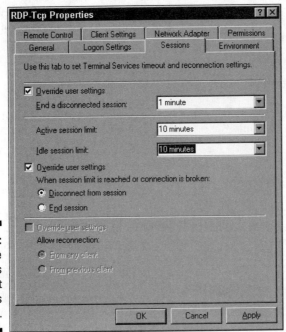

Figure 20-2:
Use the
Sessions
tab to set
sessions
limits.

Configuring the Environment tab

The Environment tab in the RDP-TCP Properties dialog box enables you to override settings from the user's profile and Client Connection Manager.

When you override the settings, you can choose to start a program when the user logs on, and you can choose to disable wallpaper, which can greatly conserve server resources.

Reviewing Terminal Server Commands

Terminal Services has several commands you can use to manage the terminal server. You need to know these commands for the exam, so you should carefully review Table 20-1.

Table 20-1	Terminal Server Commands
Command	*What It Does*
change logon	Temporarily disables logons to the terminal server
change port	Changes COM port mappings for MS-DOS program compatibility
change user	Changes the .INI file mapping for the current user
cprofile	Removes user-specific file associations from a user's profile
dbgtrace	Enables and disables debug tracing
flattemp	Enables or disables flat temporary directories
logoff	Ends a client's session
msg	Sends a message to one or more clients
query process	Displays information about processes
query session	Displays information about Terminal Services sessions
query termserver	Lists terminal servers on the network
query user	Displays information about users logged on to the system
register	Registers a program so that is has special execution characteristics

(continued)

Table 20-1 *(continued)*

Command	What It Does
reset session	Enables you to reset a session from the terminal server
shadow	Enables you to monitor or remotely control an active session of another user
tscon	Connects a client from a Terminal Services session
tsdiscon	Disconnects a client from a Terminal Services session
tskill	Terminates a process
tsprof	Copies user information and changes the profile path
tsshutdn	Shuts down a Terminal Services server

Prep Test

1 If you have Terminal Services installed on a Windows 2000 member server, which Windows 2000 utility has two fields added that enable you to monitor and end processes?

A ○ Event Viewer

B ○ Task Manager

C ○ Active Directory

D ○ Dskchk

2 You want to install both Remote Administration and Application Server modes on the same server, but you can't seem to do so. Why?

A ○ Your server is not configured for Application Server mode.

B ○ Remote Administration is active at the time of installation.

C ○ There is a conflict between multisessions.

D ○ You cannot install both modes on one server.

3 You need to create some client installation disks for terminal services using the Client Creator utility. How many floppy disks do you need?

A ○ 1

B ○ 2

C ○ 3

D ○ 4

4 How many client licenses do you need to implement Remote Administration mode?

A ○ None

B ○ 2

C ○ 6

D ○ 10

5 In your network, you want to implement Application Server mode so that numerous users can connect to the server and run a particular legacy application. When you install Application Server mode, which licensing option do you need to select?

A ○ Windows 2000 users

B ○ Terminal Server 4.0 users

6 By default, where does Windows 2000 Server store the license server database for Terminal Services Application Server mode?

A ○ C:\WINNT\System32\Lserver

B ○ C:\WINNT\System32\Tserver

C ○ C:\WINNT\Terminal\license

D ○ C:\WINNT\System\license

7 How is Application Server mode licensing activated?

A ○ ISV Provider

B ○ Microsoft Clearinghouse

C ○ It is internally generated

D ○ Activation is not required

8 Which is the preferred method for installing applications on a Terminal Server running in Application Server mode?

A ○ change user

B ○ The program's setup executable

C ○ Add/Remove Programs

D ○ Manual installation

9 Which type of connection does Windows Terminal Services use?

A ○ MS-CHAP

B ○ EAP

C ○ L2TP

D ○ RDP-TCP

10 With which terminal server command can you remotely control the session of another user?

A ○ register

B ○ shadow

C ○ tdiscon

D ○ tskill

Answers

1 *B. Task Manager.* Upon installation, Terminal Services adds two additional fields to Task Manager so you can monitor and end user sessions through Task Manager. *See "Reviewing Terminal Services Administrative Tools."*

2 *D. You cannot install both modes on one server.* You can install either Remote Administration or Application Server mode, but not both on the same server. *Read "Installing Terminal Services."*

3 *B. 2.* You need two floppy disks to create the client installation disks. *Review "Using Terminal Services Remote Administration Mode."*

4 *A. None.* In Remote Administration mode, two concurrent sessions are allowed and no licensing is required. *See "Using Terminal Services Remote Administration Mode."*

5 *B. Terminal Server 4.0 users.* For legacy applications, choose to install permissions for Terminal Server 4.0 users. This option provides compatibility with legacy applications, but is a less secure configuration. *Study "Using Terminal Services Application Server Mode."*

6 *A. C:\WINNT\System32\Lserver.* If desired, you can change this default location for the Terminal Services licensing database. *Study "Using Terminal Services Application Server Mode."*

7 *B. Microsoft Clearinghouse.* You activate Terminal Services licensing by connecting to Microsoft Clearinghouse, a database that manages licensing. *See "Using Terminal Services Application Server Mode."*

8 *C. Add/Remove Programs.* You can install programs on a Terminal Server by using either the change user command or Add/Remove programs. *Study "Configuring Application Sharing."*

9 *D. RDP-TCP.* Microsoft Remote Desktop Protocol (RDP) is a TCP protocol that uses the IP transport in Microsoft Terminal Services environments. *Read "Managing Terminal Services Connections."*

10 *B. Shadow.* By using the shadow command, you can monitor or remotely control an active session of another user. *See "Reviewing Terminal Server Commands."*

Part VIII

Implementing, Monitoring, and Troubleshooting Security

The 5th Wave   By Rich Tennant

"Careful Sundance. This one's been locked up studying for his MCSE exam allll week, and he's gotten pretty mean."

In this part . . .

*A*s networks have grown more complex, the security needs of those networks have become just as complex. Windows 2000 provides many security features, and in this part, you review those features that you need to know for the exam. In Chapters 21 and 22, you explore the Encrypting File System (EFS), local and system policies, the Security Configuration Tool Set, auditing, and the troubleshooting process for these security features in Windows 2000 Server.

Chapter 21

Configuring Encrypting File System and Policies

Exam Objectives

▶ Encrypting data on a hard disk by using Encrypting File System (EFS)

▶ Implementing, configuring, managing, and troubleshooting local policy in a Windows 2000 environment

▶ Implementing, configuring, managing, and troubleshooting system policy in a Windows 2000 environment

*T*his chapter examines two security features in Windows 2000 Server — one is new and the other is not. The new feature — Encrypting File System (EFS) — enables users to encrypt files and folders so that other users cannot read, move, or delete them. This chapter also gives you an overview of local and system policies in Windows 2000. Policies enable you to manage both local and network systems by providing standardized configurations. For the most part, you manage policies in Windows 2000 through Group Policy, but this chapter makes sure you have your feet on solid ground with respect to local and system policies.

Quick Assessment

Encrypting data on a hard disk by using EFS

1 EFS functions only on _____ volumes.

2 EFS does not protect a file from being _____.

3 You cannot encrypt _____ files, folders, or drives.

4 You cannot encrypt _____ files.

5 If you move an encrypted file or folder to a FAT volume, the encryption is _____.

6 You can encrypt files using the _____ command.

7 You can use a recovery _____ to recover encrypted files.

Implementing, configuring, managing, and trou- bleshooting local policy

8 Local policies apply to the computer at which you are _____.

Implementing, configuring, managing, and trou- bleshooting system policy

9 Most Windows 2000 networks use _____ policy instead of system policy.

Answers

1 *NTFS.* Review "Understanding Encrypting File System."

2 *Deleted.* Study "Understanding Encrypting File System."

3 *Compressed.* See "Understanding Encrypting File System."

4 *System.* Examine "Understanding Encrypting File System."

5 *Lost.* Review "Understanding Encrypting File System."

6 *Cipher.* See "Encrypting a File or Folder."

7 *Agent.* Read "Recovering Encrypted Data."

8 *Logged On.* Study "Understanding Policies."

9 *Group.* See "Understanding Policies."

Understanding Encrypting File System

Encrypting File System (EFS) is a powerful new security feature in Windows 2000. With EFS, you can encrypt your files and folders.

However, EFS functions only on NTFS volumes. Before you try to implement EFS, you should convert any FAT or FAT32 volumes to NTFS.

EFS is invisible to the user. You specify that you want to encrypt a file or folder, but you work with the file or folder just as you normally do. In other words, you don't have to decrypt a file to use it and then re-encrypt it. You can open and close your files, move them, rename them — any action — without having to be aware of the encryption. However, if an intruder attempts to open, move, copy, or rename your file or folder, the intruder receives an access-denied message.

For the exam, you need to know the following important points about EFS:

- ✔ Only files or folders on NTFS volumes can be encrypted.

- ✔ You cannot encrypt compressed files or folders. You must expand the file or folder before you encrypt it. Similarly, you must expand a compressed volume before you encrypt any files or folders on the volume.

- ✔ Only the user who encrypts the file or folder can open it.

- ✔ Encrypted files cannot be shared.

- ✔ Encrypted files moved to a FAT or FAT32 volume lose their encryption.

- ✔ You cannot encrypt system files.

- ✔ Encrypted files are not protected against deletion. Anyone with delete permission can delete an encrypted file.

- ✔ Encrypt your Temp folder so that files remain encrypted while you edit them. This action keeps temporary files created by some programs encrypted while they are in use. Also, encrypt the My Documents folder.

- ✔ You can encrypt or decrypt files and folders stored on a remote computer that has been enabled for remote encryption. However, the data is not encrypted while it is in transit over the network. (Other protocols, such as IPSec, can provide this feature.)

- ✔ You can't drag and drop files into an encrypted folder for encryption purposes. If you want to put files into an encrypted folder, use the copy-and-paste method so that the files will be encrypted in the folder.

Encrypting a File or Folder

You can encrypt a file or folder by accessing its Properties dialog box. On the General tab, click Advanced. In the resulting Advanced Attributes dialog box, select the Encrypt Contents to Secure Data check box, as shown in Figure 21-1.

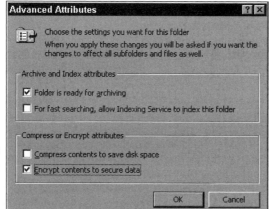

Figure 21-1:
Enabling
encryption.

In the same manner, you can also decrypt a file or folder. Simply access the Advanced Attributes dialog box for the file or folder and then uncheck the Encrypt Contents to Secure Data check box. Keep in mind that you do not have to encrypt or decrypt your files and folders to work with them — the encryption feature is invisible to you.

When you encrypt a folder, Windows 2000 asks whether you also want to encrypt all files and subfolders within the folder. When you encrypt a file, the system asks whether you also want to encrypt the folder that contains the file.

You can also encrypt files and folders using the `cipher` command at the command line. To see a list of options, type the following command:

```
cipher /?
```

Recovering Encrypted Data

The security policy for your system includes data recovery for EFS. Windows 2000 automatically generates a recovery policy when you encrypt your first file or folder. If you lose the file encryption certificate and private key (for example, because of a disk failure), a recovery agent can decrypt the file or folder for you.

By default, when you log on to the system for the first time as an administrator, you become the default recovery agent. If an employee leaves the company, the recovery agent can log on to the employee's machine and recover any encrypted data. The recovery agent feature is part of the security policy.

As the recovery agent, you have a special certificate and associated private key that enable you to recover data. You can recover data by using the Export and Import commands from the Certificates MMC, which enables you to back up the recovery certificate and associated private key to a secure location. The default recovery policy is configured locally for standalone computers. For networked computers, the administrator configures the recovery policy at either the domain, organizational unit, or individual computer level, and that policy applies to all Windows 2000 computers within the scope.

You can specify a recovery agent for a local computer by opening the Group Policy MMC snap-in in Local Computer mode. Select Public Key Policies, right-click Encrypted Data Recovery Agents and then click Add. This action opens a wizard that enables you to specify the user who is the recovery agent for the local computer.

Understanding Policies

Security settings determine how the system implements and enforces various security behaviors. A *policy* is a collection of settings that an administrator applies to a computer to control which security features are in effect.

In a Windows 2000 network, security policies remain an important aspect of your overall security plan, as they were in Windows NT. However, in Windows 2000, you define security policies through Group Policy, a powerful feature that enables you to manage the security settings of computers within a domain or organizational unit.

Local policies apply to a particular computer. They are based on the computer where you logged on and the rights you have on that local computer. Local policies affect numerous security components, such as the enabling or disabling of security settings, digital signing of data, user logon rights and permissions, and the audit policy.

Account policies apply to the user account and the rules of security behavior for that account.

Finally, system policies apply to the computer system. In Windows NT 4.0, system policies are based on registry settings, and you make them using the System Policy Editor. For the most part, Windows 2000 relies on Group Policy rather than the System Policy Editor. However, the System Policy Editor remains useful in some circumstances — specifically, the management of Windows NT 4.0 computers, Windows 9*x* computers, and even the management of standalone computers running Windows 2000.

Windows 2000 computers have a local Group Policy object. With this feature, you can store group policy settings on individual computers, even if they are not in an Active Directory environment. However, the local group policy settings can be overwritten by group policy objects on the site, domain, or organizational unit level.

You can make group policy settings for the local computer by opening the Group Policy snap-in and selecting the local computer. From this interface, shown in Figure 21-2, you can configure local settings for the computer for both the computer configuration and the user configuration.

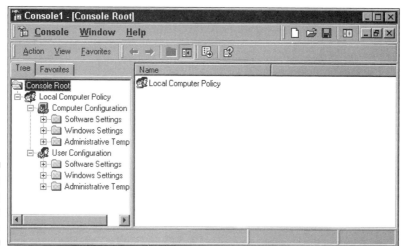

Figure 21-2:
Group
Policy
snap-in.

Prep Test

Configuring EFS and Policies

1 You want to implement EFS on a compressed volume. You can't seem to make this work, even though the volume is formatted with NTFS. What is the problem?

A ○ EFS does not work with compression.

B ○ You are not using Microsoft compression.

C ○ You need to install the EFS compression protocol.

D ○ The volume is formatted with Windows NT 4.0's version of NTFS.

2 You want to use the command prompt to enable encryption on certain folders. Which command can you use to gain a full list of command-line compression options?

A ○ Compress /?

B ○ Encrypt /?

C ○ Cipher /?

D ○ Protect /?

3 Which type of file on your computer cannot be encrypted?

A ○ System

B ○ DLL

C ○ CAB

D ○ All files can be encrypted

4 Aside from the recovery agent and the user who encrypts the files, which other users can open encrypted files by default?

A ○ None

B ○ Backup Operators

C ○ EFS Operators

D ○ Replication Administrators.

5 By default, who is the recovery agent?

A ○ Microsoft

B ○ RA Admin

C ○ Administrator

D ○ EFS Admin

6 Which answer choice best describes the preferred method of policy management in Windows 2000 networks?

A ○ Security Policy

B ○ Local Policy

C ○ Group Policy

D ○ Active Directory

Answers

1 *A. EFS does not work with compression.* You cannot encrypt compressed volumes, folders, or files. Before you can encrypt the volume, folder, or file, you must remove the compression. *Review "Understanding Encrypting File System."*

2 *C. Cipher /?.* The Cipher command enables you to compress data at the command line. *Read "Encrypting a File or Folder."*

3 *A. System.* You cannot encrypt system files. *Review "Understanding Encrypting File System."*

4 *A. None.* Only the user who encrypts the file can open it, along with the recovery agent. *See "Understanding Encrypting File System."*

5 *C. Administrator.* By default, the administrator who logs on to the machine is the recovery agent. *Study "Recovering Encrypted Data."*

6 *C. Group Policy.* Group Policy is an Active Directory-integrated component that enables an administrator to tightly manage policies in a Windows 2000 network. *Study "Understanding Policies."*

Chapter 22

Managing Auditing and Security Configuration

· ·

Exam Objectives

▶ Implementing, configuring, managing, and troubleshooting auditing

▶ Implementing, configuring, managing, and troubleshooting local accounts

▶ Implementing, configuring, managing, and troubleshooting account policy

▶ Implementing, configuring, managing, and troubleshooting security by using the Security Configuration Tool Set

· ·

*W*indows 2000 offers numerous security features to meet the security needs of your network. The Windows 2000 Server exam expects you to know about some specific issues that fall within the broader concept of security. This chapter explores the exam-specific topics of auditing, local accounts and account policy, and the use of the Security Configuration Tool Set.

The exam expects you to know about these security features, so study this chapter carefully. I discuss only what you need to know for the exam, and you can review the following topics in this chapter:

> ✔ Managing auditing
>
> ✔ Managing local accounts
>
> ✔ Using security tools

Quick Assessment

Implementing, configuring, managing, and troubleshooting auditing

1 The auditing process stores audit entries in the _____.

2 You can configure an audit policy through the _____ snap-in.

3 For each audit policy, you choose to audit the policy based on _____ or _____.

4 By default, files and folders _____ any auditing policies from the parent.

Implementing, configuring, managing, and troubleshooting local accounts

5 On a Windows 2000 member server, you configure local accounts using the _____ console.

Implementing, configuring, managing, and troubleshooting account policy

6 You can create an account policy by using the _____ snap-in for the local computer.

7 By creating an account policy, you can configure settings for password policy, account lockout policy, and _____ policy.

Using the Security Configuration Tool Set

8 The _____ tool enables you to analyze your computer's security settings.

Answers

1 *Security Log.* Review "Using Auditing."

2 *Group Policy.* Study "Using Auditing."

3 *Success; Failure.* See "Using Auditing."

4 *Inherit.* Examine "Using Auditing."

5 *Computer Management.* Review "Managing Local Accounts and Account Policy."

6 *Group Policy.* See "Managing Local Accounts and Account Policy."

7 *Kerberos.* Read "Managing Local Accounts and Account Policy."

8 *Security Configuration and Analysis.* Study "Using Security Configuration Tools."

Using Auditing

Auditing is the Windows 2000 Server security feature that monitors security events on your server. By using auditing, you can determine whether intruders or other security breaches are affecting your server.

You can audit many events on your system, including access to files and folders, management of user and group accounts, and log-on and log-off activity.

The Windows 2000 auditing feature generates an audit trail to help you keep track of the security administration events that occur on the system. This feature is particularly useful because you can see how auditing has occurred. You can also determine whether other administrators with access to your server have changed any auditing of events.

To implement auditing on your server, you complete three major steps:

1. **Determine which categories of events you want to audit by turning on auditing for those events.**

2. **Determine the size of the security log the auditing process will generate, as well as certain characteristics of the log.**

3. **Modify the security descriptors for certain objects that you plan to audit, such as folders or files.**

Configuring an audit policy

To start setting up auditing, you configure an audit policy. The policy tells the system what you want to audit.

To configure an audit policy, open an MMC and then add the Group Policy snap-in. Expand Computer Configuration, Windows Settings, Security Settings, and Local Policies, and then select Audit Policy, as shown in Figure 22-1.

You can see in the details pane the different audit policies that you can configure. By default, auditing is turned off for all of them.

To enable auditing, double-click the desired audit policy and then click either the success or failure check box to audit the event, based on success or failure, as shown in Figure 22-2.

Continue down the list and enable auditing for each event desired.

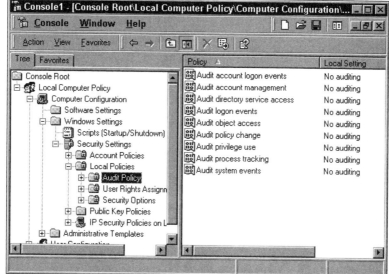

Figure 22-1:
Use the
Group
Policy
snap-in to
configure an
audit policy.

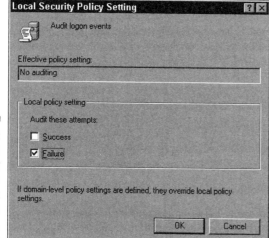

Figure 22-2:
Use the
Success or
Failure
check box
to enable
auditing.

Auditing access to files and folders

You can audit access to files and folders on NTFS partitions. Before you configure the file or folder for auditing, you must enable the Audit Object Access event in the Group Policy snap-in (see the previous section).

To configure auditing for a particular file or folder, follow the steps that I describe in Lab 22-1.

Lab 22-1   Configuring Auditing for a File or Folder

1. **Right-click the desired file or folder and choose Properties.**

2. **In the Properties dialog box, click the Security tab and then click Advanced.**

3. **Click the Auditing tab and then click Add.**

4. **Select a user or group account for which you want to audit access to the file or folder and then click OK.**

5. **In the Auditing Entry dialog box, shown in Figure 22-3, select the events you want to audit by clicking the Successful or Failed check boxes. Click OK.**

The auditing options you configured appear in the Access Control Settings dialog box, as shown in Figure 22-4.

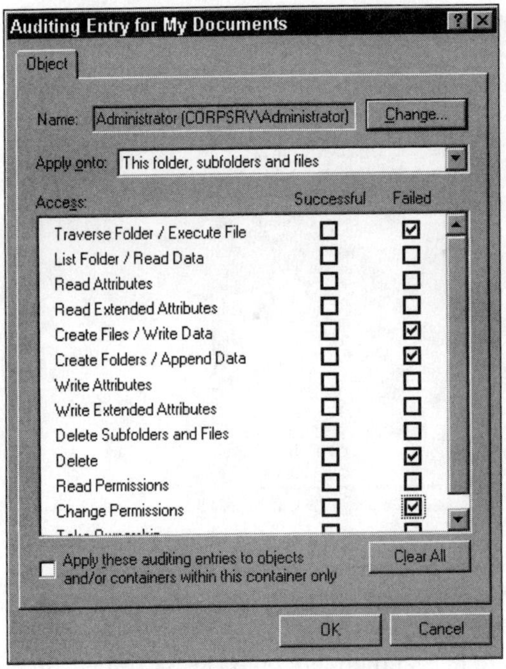

Figure 22-3:
Click the
Successful
or Failed
check boxes
to configure
auditing for
the file or
folder.

> **Auditing Entry for My Documents**   ? X
>
> | Object |
>
> Name: Administrator (CORPSRV\Administrator)   Change...
>
> Apply onto: This folder, subfolders and files
>
> Access: Successful   Failed
> Traverse Folder / Execute File   □   ☑
> List Folder / Read Data   □   □
> Read Attributes   □   □
> Read Extended Attributes   □   □
> Create Files / Write Data   □   ☑
> Create Folders / Append Data   □   ☑
> Write Attributes   □   □
> Write Extended Attributes   □   □
> Delete Subfolders and Files   □   □
> Delete   □   ☑
> Read Permissions   □   □
> Change Permissions   □   ☑
>
> □ Apply these auditing entries to objects   Clear All
>   and/or containers within this container only
>
>   OK   Cancel

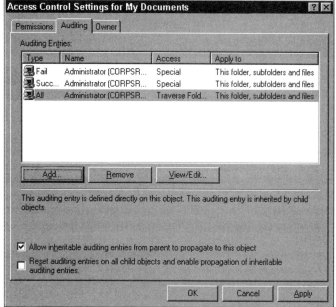

Access Control Settings for My Documents

Permissions | Auditing | Owner

Auditing Entries:

Type	Name	Access	Apply to
Fail	Administrator (CORPSR...	Special	This folder, subfolders and files
Succ...	Administrator (CORPSR...	Special	This folder, subfolders and files
All	Administrator (CORPSR...	Traverse Fold...	This folder, subfolders and files

Add... | Remove | View/Edit...

This auditing entry is defined directly on this object. This auditing entry is inherited by child objects.

☑ Allow inheritable auditing entries from parent to propagate to this object

☐ Reset auditing entries on all child objects and enable propagation of inheritable auditing entries.

OK | Cancel | Apply

Figure 22-4:
Auditing
entries
appear in
the Access
Control
Settings
dialog box.

By selecting a check box at the bottom of the Access Control Settings dialog box, you can allow inheritable auditing entries from the parent to propagate to this object, or you can choose to reset auditing entries on all child objects and enable propagation. With these features, both the parent and the child objects can inherit auditing entries. You can disable both or either of these options by clearing the check boxes.

Viewing the security log

After you implement auditing, you can view the security log by clicking Start⇨Programs⇨Administrative Tools⇨Event Viewer and then clicking Security Log in the left console pane. You see the list of audited events, which you can use to determine whether your system has security problems or issues that you need to address.

The security log is limited in size, so you should choose carefully which events you want to audit.

Managing Local Accounts and Account Policy

You configure local accounts on Windows 2000 member servers for users who log on to the local machine. Accounts on domain controllers are stored in the Active Directory.

On a Windows 2000 member server, you create and manage local accounts by using the Computer Management tool, which is available in Administrative Tools. In the Computer Management console, expand Local Users and Groups to see the Users and Groups containers. If you click either container, you see a list of users and groups in the details pane, as shown in Figure 22-5. By default, a Windows 2000 server has an administrator account and a guest account, which is disabled by default.

To create a new user or group account, select the desired container and then choose either Action⇨New User or Action⇨New Group. In the dialog box that's displayed, you can enter the user name and password, and determine the following password-related settings:

- ✔ User must change password at next logon.
- ✔ User cannot change password.
- ✔ Password never expires.
- ✔ Account is disabled.

Weak management of passwords translates directly into weak security. Microsoft recommends that all passwords should be at least seven characters long, they should not contain a user's name, and they should use a mixture of upper- and lowercase letters, numbers, and symbols. For example, xjjb34!2 is an appropriate password in Windows 2000.

After you create user accounts, you can add them to groups as desired, and you can configure account properties. Right-click a user account and choose Properties to open the Properties dialog box for that account.

For the exam, you don't need to worry about the specifics of the Properties dialog boxes for user and group accounts. Just remember that you can configure account properties and manage the account's password, group memberships, and profile from these dialog boxes.

In addition to creating accounts and configuring their properties, you can configure the Account Policy for your server.

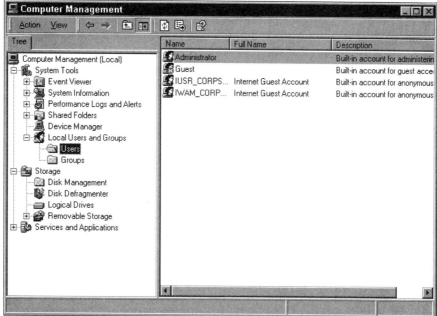

Figure 22-5:
Use
Computer
Manage-
ment to
configure
local user
and group
accounts.

To configure your Account Policy, open an MMC and add the Group Policy snap-in. Expand Computer Configuration, Windows Settings, and Security Settings, and then select Account Policies. As shown in Figure 22-6, you see the policy entries in the details pane.

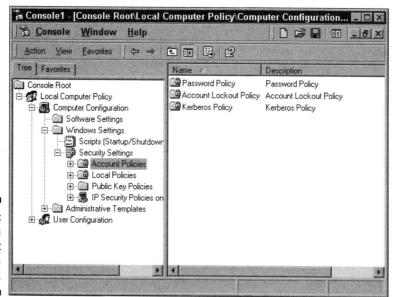

Figure 22-6:
Configuring
the Account
Policy for a
server.

Double-click either the Password Policy container, the Account Lockout Policy container, or the Kerberos Policy container, and then double-click the entries to configure the desired policy settings. You can define various policy settings, such as account lockout duration, account lockout threshold, enforce password history, and maximum password age.

Using Security Configuration Tools

Windows 2000 Server includes a tool set that you can use to manage your security configuration. You have a Security Configuration and Analysis snap-in and a Security Templates snap-in that you can manually add to an MMC.

You need to know about both of these snap-ins for the exam, and the following sections explain the issues that you are likely to see on the exam.

Using the Security Configuration and Analysis snap-in

You use the Security Configuration and Analysis tool to analyze and configure local computer security. The tool uses a security database, which you need to create before you use the tool for the first time. Right-click the Security Configuration and Analysis object and choose Open Database. In the dialog box that's displayed, click Open. In the resulting dialog box, select the database template to open and then click Open.

After you open a database, you can perform three major tasks. Select the Security Configuration and Analysis object in the console and then click the Action menu. By choosing options in the Action menu, you can perform the following tasks, which you need to remember for the exam:

- ✔ **Analyze Computer Now:** This process analyzes your security configuration and reports issues or potential problems to the database. This feature is an excellent troubleshooting tool.

- ✔ **Configure Computer Now:** This process applies any templates you have chosen to your computer.

- ✔ **Import Template:** This action enables you to import a security template that you want to apply to your system. After importing a desired template, choose <u>A</u>ction⇨<u>C</u>onfigure Computer Now.

Using the Security Templates snap-in

The Security Templates snap-in contains a list of security templates you can edit to configure your system security as desired. You can also create new templates and import other templates into this snap-in. For each template, you can define account policies, local policies, event log, restricted groups, system services, the registry, and file system. For each category, you can open the templates and adjust the settings as desired.

Like the Security Configuration and Analysis snap-in, the Security Templates snap-in gives you an all-in-one location where you can implement and configure the desired security settings for your server.

Prep Test

1 What auditing feature does Windows 2000 generate so you can keep track of auditing events or audit policy changes?

A ○ Audit.log

B ○ Audit file

C ○ Audit trail

D ○ Audit list

2 You want to audit access to a particular folder. You access the advanced settings from the Security tab in the folder's Properties dialog box, but you receive an error message when you try to configure auditing. What did you forget to do?

A ○ Configure Event Viewer.

B ○ Configure the Audit Object Access event.

C ○ Configure the Audit Folder Access event.

D ○ Install auditing.

3 Which tool can you use to view the security log?

A ○ Group Policy snap-in

B ○ Event Viewer

C ○ Task Manager

D ○ Configure Your Server

4 When auditing a particular file, where can you block inherited auditing entries from the parent?

A ○ Security tab

B ○ Computer Management

C ○ Access Control Settings dialog box

D ○ Group Policy snap-in

5 What is Microsoft's recommended minimum password character length?

A ○ 5

B ○ 6

C ○ 7

D ○ 8

6 Which two accounts are configured on a Windows 2000 member server by default? (Choose two.)

A ❑ Administrator
B ❑ Backup Operator
C ❑ IUSR
D ❑ Guest

7 What can you use to configure account policy?

A ○ Computer Management
B ○ Group Policy snap-in
C ○ Configure Your Server
D ○ Security Configuration snap-in

8 You want your computer to configure the policy templates you have decided to use. Which tool can automatically perform this action for you?

A ○ Templates snap-in
B ○ Group Policy snap-in
C ○ Security Configuration and Analysis snap-in
D ○ Active Directory Users and Computers snap-in

Answers

1 *C. Audit Trail.* Windows 2000 generates an audit trail that keeps track of audited events and changes to the audit policy. *Review "Using Auditing."*

2 *B. Configure the Audit Object Access event.* Before you can audit a file or folder, you have to enable the Audit Object Access policy in the Group Policy snap-in. *Read "Using Auditing."*

3 *B. Event Viewer.* Use Event Viewer to examine the security log. *Review "Using Auditing."*

4 *C. Access Control Settings dialog box.* The Access Control Settings dialog box contains check boxes that enable you to block inheritance from parent objects and to child objects. You can block inheritance by clearing the check boxes. *See "Using Auditing."*

5 *C. 7.* Microsoft recommends that all passwords have at least seven characters, with a mixture of letters, numbers, and keyboard symbols. *Study "Managing Local Accounts and Account Policy."*

6 *A and D.* The Administrator and Guest accounts are configured by default, but the guest account is also disabled by default. *See "Managing Local Accounts and Account Policy."*

7 *B. Group Policy snap-in.* You can use the Group Policy snap-in to configure account policies, as well as other policies for the local Windows 2000 computer. *Read "Managing Local Accounts and Account Policy."*

8 *C. Security Configuration and Analysis snap-in.* This tool can analyze your computer's security settings and configure your computer's security template settings. *Study "Using Security Configuration Tools."*

Part IX
The Part of Tens

The 5th Wave   By Rich Tennant

Bill and Irwin discover The Land of Lost Files

My God, Hathfield, we've found it! Answer sheets to the entire MCSE exam!

In this part . . .

*H*ere it is . . . The Part of Tens. This is the place in the book where you gather some additional tidbits of information to help you on exam day.

In Chapter 23, I explore ten great test tips you should remember before you take the exam. In Chapter 24, I answer ten common questions about the Windows 2000 Server exam. Use these chapters to help you get a handle on your upcoming test day experience.

Chapter 23

Ten Great Test Day Tips

. . . .

In This Chapter

▶ Take it easy

▶ Read everything

▶ Manage your time — don't let it manage you

▶ Remember that scratch paper is your friend

▶ Study the answers

▶ Make educated guesses if you're not sure

▶ Avoid reading too much

▶ No crying, please

▶ Check out the instructions

. . . .

*T*he glorious day finally arrives. You know this book better than you know the alphabet, you passed the practice exams, and you're ready to conquer the Windows 2000 Server exam. Before you take the test, however, you should consider some practical test-day tips that can help you to increase your chances for success when you slide into that exam chair and click the Start button. Based on my personal testing experience and my experience in training other MCSE candidates, here are the tried-and-true actions that can help you.

Relax

Sure, telling you to relax sounds easy enough, but many test takers have a serious case of exam butterflies — myself included. The problem with those exam butterflies is that they super-charge your adrenaline, which can often lead to serious test-taking problems. When you are anxious, you tend to think and move quickly — both of which can cause big mistakes on the exam.

To master those tricky exam questions, you need to slow down and think carefully about each question to ensure that you choose the right answer. It is a proven fact that most test takers miss several questions because they are nervous. You can avoid this problem by taking deep, relaxing breaths and reminding yourself throughout the exam to calm down and think carefully.

Read Carefully

MCSE exam questions are often tricky. They may give you lots of convoluted information, much of which you may not even need in order to answer the question correctly. To sift through each question, you should read the question all the way through, including the answer choices, and then read the question again with an analytical eye. In this way, you ensure that you understand the question before you try to answer it. Many test takers miss several questions due to misreading — don't be one of them!

Time Is the Enemy

Unfortunately, you have a limited amount of time to answer the questions before the exam forces you to exit. Inexperienced test takers typically worry about the time limit and therefore work too quickly. Actually, few test takers run out of time. If you read at a normal pace, you have plenty of time to master the exam without rushing. Of course, you can't dilly-dally, but you don't have to kick yourself into overdrive either.

Remember the time limit, watch it as you go to make sure that you stay on track, and don't let it stress you out so much that you aren't paying careful attention to the exam questions.

Use Scratch Paper

When you take a Microsoft exam, you can use scratch paper to make notes or create sketches. The testing center administrator will provide you with paper if you ask. Use your scratch paper to help you organize the key elements of difficult questions so you can draw logical conclusions. If you are a visual learner, like me, drawing quick pictures or sketches can also help you make sense of tricky test questions. Remember, scratch paper is your friend!

If You Know the Answer . . .

Sometimes, you read an exam question and think, "I know the answer, no problem." You then scan the answer choices quickly and find the right answer. Right? Wrong! In many cases, a question has two similar answers, and one is "more correct" than the other. Even if you are certain you know the answer to a question, make sure you examine all the answer choices before making a selection. Remember, you are not always looking for the right answer. Sometimes, you need the one that is "most correct."

If You Don't Know the Answer . . .

You will encounter exam questions for which you do not know the answer. However, this does not necessarily mean that you are doomed to missing the question. Try to look at the question logically and rule out possible answers that you know are incorrect. The exam is a game of odds, and you can increase your odds of selecting the correct answer by ruling out answers that you know aren't right.

Don't Fall into the Re-reading Loop

On the Windows 2000 Server exam, you can easily fall into the "re-reading loop." The re-reading loop occurs when you read a question for which you don't know the answer, so you re-read it, and then re-read it, and re-read it, and . . . . You get the idea.

If your exam uses adaptive technologies, you can't skip the question and come back to it later, so you must make a decision. If you don't understand the question or you can't find an answer you like, re-reading over and over will not help. Take an educated guess and move on because the longer you stay in the re-reading loop, the more exam time you burn.

Avoid Crying Fits (And Other Acts of Desperation)

The Microsoft gods do not smile on crying fits or other acts of desperation during the exam. If you feel you are getting completely overwhelmed, try these tactics instead:

✔ Close your eyes, take deep, slow breaths, and count to 10. This technique can help you to relax and refocus your mind on the exam.

✔ Stop for a moment, use your scratch paper, and write the word *relax* several times. This may seem like a silly trick, but just writing the word a few times will refocus your mind and help you regroup.

✔ If time permits, take a short break. You are allowed to take a break during the exam if desired, but you do have to be careful with your time limit if you choose this option.

Read the Instructions

The Windows 2000 exams make use of several new testing technologies, which you can read more about in Chapter 1. If you are a pro at certification exams, you may have a tendency to skip over the instructions for different types of questions. However, because many questions are "new" in terms of style and approach, make certain you read the instructions so you are answering the questions in a manner required by the exam. Not doing so wastes lots of time and could cause you to miss questions.

Avoid Celebration Cheers (Until You Leave the Testing Center, Anyway)

When you pass the test, make sure you don't jump up and down, sing, yell, clap, or show any emotion in the sight of the testing center administrator! Save the celebration until you are in the parking lot, and make sure you give yourself a pat on the back for a job well done.

Chapter 24

Ten Common Questions and Answers about the Windows 2000 Server Exam

● ●

In This Chapter

▶ What can I expect?

▶ Will I see lots of questions?

▶ Will this exam ask only multiple-choice questions?

▶ Can I get help on the Internet?

▶ Should I study the Windows 2000 Server interface?

▶ What can I do if I fail the test?

▶ Will my score report help?

▶ When should I take the test?

▶ What can I take to the testing center?

▶ How should I schedule my test?

● ●

*M*icrosoft certification exams are no picnic, and test takers usually have lots of questions about the exam. In this chapter, I list the ten most common questions (and answers!) about the Windows 2000 Server exam. These questions and answers help you know what to expect and how to devise a successful plan for the exam day.

What Kind of Exam Is 70-215?

The Windows 2000 Server exam (70-215) uses various testing technologies that Microsoft has implemented. You can expect to see standard multiple-choice questions, interface questions, case-study questions, and even select-and-paste items. (See Chapter 1 for more information about these testing technologies.) By using many testing technologies, Microsoft can present unique exams to individual test takers. Fortunately, you can download samples of the different testing technologies so the exam won't surprise you. Go to www.microsoft.com/mcp to get the samples and practice using them before you take the exam.

How Many Questions Will I See on My Exam?

The exam has no set number of questions. Depending on the testing technologies used on your exam, you may see 30 to 50 questions, or you may get only 15 questions before you are declared a winner! The exams are designed to be "smart" exams that determine your skill level as you go. After the exam determines whether you have passed or failed, the testing software ends the test.

Will All Exam Questions Give Me Multiple-Choice Items?

Not all exam questions use a multiple-choice format. Depending on the type of question you receive, you may see multiple-choice responses, but other options also exist. For example, some questions ask you to drag and drop items to a correct location, some ask for an open-ended response, and others present a dialog box from the operating system and ask you to configure it. Your best bet? Be prepared for anything!

What Online Resources Can Help Me Prepare?

Several online resources can help you prepare for the Windows 2000 Server exam. Some of these sites provide discussion areas about the exam, and others provide general information or even products. Here are some of the better sites for information about the Windows 2000 Server exam:

- www.microsoft.com/mcp: Watch this page for changes and for general certification information.
- www.mcpmag.com: This is a good site for keeping up with all kinds of certification news.

✔ www.transcender.com: This site provides practice test software.

✔ www.microsoft.com/train_cert: This site provides information about Microsoft training and certification programs, as well as a good list of helpful links.

✔ www.saluki.com/mcp: This is a great MCP site, full of information about Microsoft certification.

Perform an Internet search because new sites pop up all the time.

Do I Need to Know the Windows 2000 Interface for the Exam?

Absolutely! One of Microsoft's goals is to test hands-on experience. Consequently, you need to spend some time working on a Windows 2000 server. Interface and select-and-place questions test your real-world knowledge of the server software.

What Should I Do If I Don't Pass the Exam?

If you don't pass the Windows 2000 Server exam on the first try, you need to regroup and restudy. The best approach is to think carefully about the exam experience and restudy the issues or questions you didn't know. Also, you need to make certain that you can pass the practice exams before attempting the real exam a second time.

Can I Use My Score Report to Identify Weak Areas?

Unfortunately, no. Unlike previous versions of the MCSE certification exams, the new testing technologies do not give you test categories with your percentage score. The new testing technologies really do not lend themselves to this kind of information, so if you don't pass the exam on the first try, you can't expect to have the score report to assist your study efforts.

When Is the Best Time to Take an Exam?

Plan to take the exam at a time during the day when you are most alert. If you are, by nature, a morning person, schedule the exam for the morning hours; if you wake up during the afternoon, take the exam during the afternoon. Also, try to choose an exam day that isn't loaded with other activities and pressures. You want to be able to focus on the exam and not have too many other distractions.

What Should I Take to the Testing Center?

You aren't allowed to take any materials into the testing center, including pagers or cellular phones. If you want scratch paper, the test center administrator can provide paper for you. You need two forms of ID, one with a photo, and I advise you to wear layered clothing in case the testing center is cold.

How Do I Schedule an Exam?

You can schedule an exam by calling Sylvan Prometric at 800-755-EXAM or Virtual University Enterprises (VUE) at 888-837-8616. You can also register online at www.2test.com or www.vue.com. You need to pay for the exam by credit card at the time you register, and you will need to provide your social security number. Exams cost $100.00 each, whether you pass or fail.

Part X
Appendixes

The 5th Wave
By Rich Tennant

"We sort of have our own way of mentally preparing our people to take the MCSE exam."

In this part . . .

Your study is done, you know Windows 2000 Server
like the back of your hand . . . . Now it's time to put in
some practice.

In this part, you find two full-length practice exams so you
can test your skills. For each question, you can check
your answer, read an explanation, and take a look at the
objective and chapter cross-reference. Also in this part,
you find installation instructions and information about
the practice questions and other content on the CD-ROM.

Appendix A

Practice Exam 1

• •

Practice Exam Rules

▶ 90 minutes to complete the exam

▶ 50 questions

▶ At least 38 correct answers to pass the exam

▶ No cheating! (Don't use your book to find answers, because you won't have this luxury on exam day)

• •

*H*ere's an opportunity to practice for the Windows 2000 Server exam. As you work through this practice exam, read each question carefully and make certain that you read all the answer choices before making a final decision.

In addition to regular multiple-choice questions, this practice exam has some interface questions. On those questions, I ask you about some configuration option and then show you a picture of an element from the Windows 2000 Server user interface — for example, a dialog box or an MMC snap-in. Your answer should describe the steps or process you would perform if you were sitting at a real machine.

When you finish the exam, check your answers with the answer key and then review those chapters that cover the questions you missed. If you get them all correct, you are ready to take the exam!

Questions

1 On a particular remote access server, you are using multilink to increase bandwidth. You want to configure the server so that it automatically drops unneeded links after any 50-percent usage reduction of at least 15 minutes. Which protocols are used for this process? (Choose all that apply.)

A ❑ IPSec

B ❑ BADP

C ❑ BAP

D ❑ BACP

2 On a particular Windows 2000 server, you have three hard drives that contain critical data. In addition to regular data backups, you want to configure a fault-tolerant solution to ensure that you can recover all data in the event of a physical disk failure. You want to conserve as much disk space as possible with the fault-tolerant solution. Which solution should you choose?

A ○ Spanned Volume

B ○ Striped Volume

C ○ Mirrored Volume

D ○ RAID-5 Volume

3 You need to back up system state data on your Windows 2000 Server. What do you need to do on this interface to start the backup of system state data?

Backup - [Untitled]

Job   Edit   View   Tools   Help

Welcome | Backup | Restore | Schedule Jobs |

Click to select the check box for any drive, folder or file that you want to back up.

- ☐ 📷 Desktop
  - ☒ 💻 My Computer
    - ☐ 💾 A:
    - ☐ 💿 C:
    - ☐ 💿 E: New Volume
    - ☐ 💾 D:
    - ☐ 🖳 System State
  - ☐ 📁 My Documents
  - ☒ 📷 My Network Places

Name	Comment
☒ 💻 My Computer	
☐ 📁 My Documents	
☒ 📷 My Network Places	

Backup destination:
File

Backup options:
Normal backup. Summary log.
Some types excluded.

[Start Backup]

Backup media or file name:
\\Csimmons\AD BIBLE\Backu   [Browse...]

For Help, press F1   File

---

4 Which of the following statements about a standalone Dfs is not true?

A ○ A standalone Dfs cannot have root-level Dfs shared folders.

B ○ In a standalone Dfs, all shared folders must fall under one root.

C ○ A standalone Dfs stores its Dfs topology in the Active Directory.

D ○ A standalone Dfs has a limited hierarchy.

5 On a particular Web server, a folder with company documents is shared on the intranet site. You later move the folder to a different location on your computer. After you move the folder, Web users cannot access it. What do you need to do?

A ○ Use the Virtual Directory tab to change the path to the new folder location.

B ○ Use the Documents tab to change the path to the new folder location.

C ○ Use the Directory Security tab to change the path to the new folder location.

D ○ Rename the folder.

6 You want to manually clean a WINS server database. After you select the server that you want to clean in the WINS console, what must you do next?

A ○ Choose Action➪Scavenge Database.

B ○ Choose Action➪Verify Database Consistency.

C ○ Choose Action➪Verify Version ID Consistency.

D ○ Choose Action➪Back Up Database.

7 You have just received an updated driver for a hardware device. What is the best way to update the driver in Windows 2000?

A ○ Use the General tab in the device's properties.

B ○ Click the Update Driver button on the Driver tab in the device's properties.

C ○ Use the Add/Remove Hardware wizard.

D ○ Manually place the driver in the appropriate directory.

8 You need to install a service for a particular NIC. After you access the connection's properties, what do you need to do next?

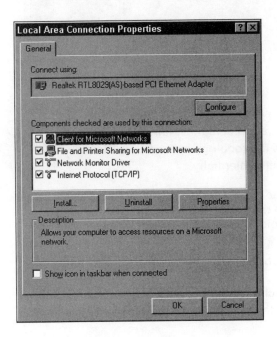

9 Secondary DNS servers within a DNS zone receive update information from the primary DNS server through what process?

A ○ Replication

B ○ DNSUpdate

C ○ Zone Transfer

D ○ Text Files

10 You install a printer on a Windows NT 4.0 server and share the printer, but the printer is never automatically published in the Active Directory. What is the problem?

A ○ The spooler is not functioning.

B ○ The print device is not functioning.

C ○ Only Windows 2000 computers can automatically publish printers in the Active Directory.

D ○ There is an object identity problem in the Active Directory.

11 Your Windows 2000 server has several legacy hardware devices installed. You are concerned that some IRQ conflicts exist between the devices. How can you easily check for IRQ conflicts in Windows 2000?

A ○ Use the device's Driver tab.

B ○ Use the device's Resource tab.

C ○ Use the device's General tab.

D ○ Use the Add/Remove Hardware wizard.

12 On a particular DNS server, you want to make certain that only DNS names that completely adhere to the DNS naming structure are resolved. What can you do on the Advanced tab to enable this feature?

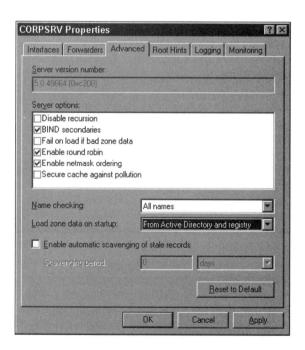

13 On a particular shared folder, you want to disconnect all connected users from the folder, but not from other folders that they may be accessing. What tool can you use to easily accomplish this task?

A ○ The folder's Properties dialog box
B ○ The Shared Folders snap-in
C ○ Network Monitor
D ○ Performance Monitor

14 You want to install Windows 2000 Server on a Windows NT 4.0 domain controller. You want to keep all your user and group accounts. What happens during setup that automatically upgrades your NT domain controller to a 2000 domain controller?

A ○ The Installation wizard runs.
B ○ The Active Directory installation wizard runs.
C ○ Setup stores your user accounts in ACCNT.TXT.
D ○ Setup cannot automatically upgrade the server to a domain controller.

15 If you want to make a profile mandatory, what do you need to do to NTUSER.DAT?

A ○ Rename it to NTUSER.MAN.
B ○ Delete it.
C ○ Store NTUSER.DAT in the MAN folder on the server.
D ○ Rename it to NTMAN.USR.

16 You want to configure an unattended installation. You need to create an answer file. Although you can manually create an answer file using any text editor, which Windows 2000 tool helps you create the answer file through a wizard?

A ○ WINNT
B ○ Setup Manager
C ○ Configuration Manager
D ○ Unattended Manager

17 On a Windows 2000 member server, you have a dynamic disk with 3.96MB of unallocated space. You want to use this space to create an additional simple volume. What do you need to do?

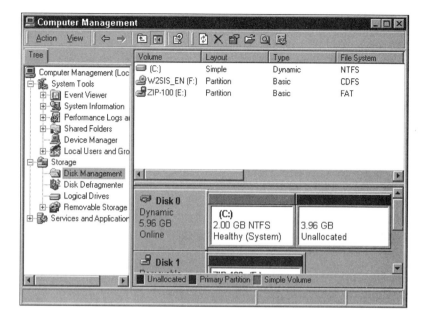

18 You notice that excessive paging seems to be occurring on your Windows 2000 member server. What is the most likely cause of this problem?

A ○ The CPU cannot handle the processing requests.

B ○ The system's DMA settings have a conflict.

C ○ You do not have enough RAM on your system.

D ○ You have too much virtual memory allocated.

19 You made some configuration changes on your server, and now the server will not start. What action should you take?

A ○ Boot into Safe Mode.

B ○ Boot into Safe Mode with Networking.

C ○ Boot using Last Known Good.

D ○ Enable Boot Logging.

20 On a domain-based Dfs, folder replicas can be automatically synchronized using which service?

A ○ FRS

B ○ TCP/IP

C ○ Directory Replication

D ○ Dfs replication driver

21 Which DHCP solution enables you to lease IP addresses for a multinet?

A ○ Scope

B ○ Superscope

C ○ Multicast Scope

D ○ Multinet Scope

22 When Windows 9*x* computers connect to a certain printer, you want to have appropriate printer drivers downloaded automatically to those machines. What do you need to do?

A ○ Nothing. This happens automatically.

B ○ Install the 9*x* drivers using the Sharing tab in the printer properties.

C ○ Install the 9*x* drivers using the Advanced tab in the printer properties.

D ○ Automatic driver download cannot occur for Windows 9*x* clients.

23 You open the Properties dialog box for a local area connection and then decide that you need to check the configuration of the NIC. How can you easily access the NIC's properties from the local area connection's Properties dialog box?

A ○ Click Install.

B ○ Click Properties.

C ○ Click Configure.

D ○ Click Remove.

24 You want to manually stop several system processes for troubleshooting purposes. Which Windows 2000 tool can you use to accomplish this task?

A ○ Performance Monitor

B ○ MSINFO

C ○ Task Manager

D ○ Disk Defragmenter

25 You need to install Windows 2000 Server on a new machine that has an unformatted hard drive. How can you make setup boot disks so you can begin the installation?

A ○ Create the disks on any Windows computer by running WINNT from the installation CD-ROM.

B ○ Create the disks on any Windows computer by running WINNT32 from the installation CD-ROM.

C ○ Create the disks on any Windows computer by running Setup from the installation CD-ROM.

D ○ Create the disks on any Windows computer by running MAKEBOOT from the installation CD-ROM.

26 Which remote access service provides a central authentication database for multiple remote access servers and collects accounting information about remote connections?

A ○ IPSec

B ○ L2TP

C ○ RADIUS

D ○ PPTP

27 Which terminal server command can you use to terminate a process?

A ○ tsdicon

B ○ tskill

C ○ tsprof

D ○ tsshutdn

28 Which file systems support the use of EFS? (Choose all that apply.)

A ❑ FAT

B ❑ FAT32

C ❑ CDFS

D ❑ NTFS

29 You need to use the Recovery console to change the attributes of a directory. What command can you use within the Recovery console to accomplish this task?

A ○ CD

B ○ Batch

C ○ Attrib

D ○ Rd

30 On a particular shared file that exists in a shared folder, you do not want the permissions of the parent folder to affect the file because you need to establish individual permissions for that file. How can you use the Security tab to configure this setup?

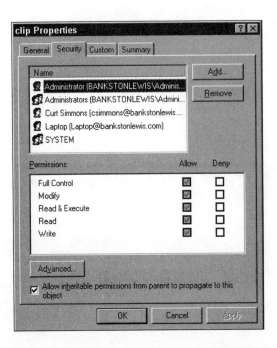

31 For a particular Web folder, you want to make certain that users of the folder have the right to browse through the folder and subfolders. What do you need to do on the Virtual Directory tab?

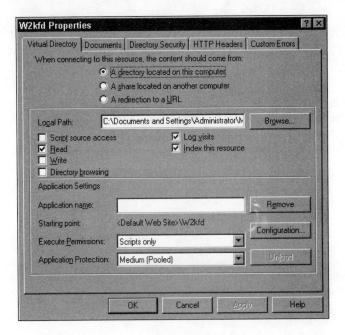

32 You want to free up as much hard disk space as possible on your Windows 2000 server. Which tool can you use to easily remove unnecessary files, including Internet files?

A ○ Disk Remove

B ○ Disk Sweep

C ○ Disk Defragmenter

D ○ Disk Cleanup

33 You want to copy a drive image so you can install that image on other new servers on your network. The new servers have exactly the same hardware configuration as the master server. Which utility can you use to help you accomplish this goal?

A ○ Sysprep

B ○ Winnt

C ○ Syspart

D ○ UDF

34 Which protocol can you use with remote access to allow the use of third-party authentication or smart-card logon?

A ○ EAP

B ○ MS-CHAP2

C ○ MS-CHAP

D ○ PAP

35 Which command can you use at the command line to encrypt files and folders?

A ○ Encrypt

B ○ Protect

C ○ Cipher

D ○ Store

36 What tool do you need to use to create the floppy disks used to install Terminal Services on client computers?

A ○ Client Creator

B ○ Client Connector

C ○ Client Connection Manager

D ○ Terminal Client

37 In Disk Management, you notice that one of your volumes is listed as Healthy (At Risk). What do you need to do to fix this problem?

A ○ Run Disk Defragmenter.

B ○ Run Disk Cleanup.

C ○ Reactivate the disk.

D ○ Regenerate the disk.

38 What prevents rogue DHCP servers from coming online and leasing inappropriate IP addresses?

A ○ DHCP

B ○ Domain Controllers

C ○ The Active Directory

D ○ Indexing Service

39 You want to use several Print Queue counters to monitor a troublesome printer. What do you need to do in this dialog box to get the Print Queue counters?

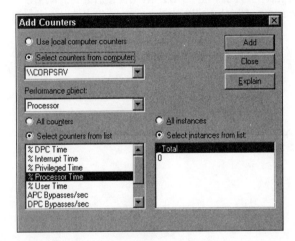

40 You decide to audit several events on your Windows 2000 server. Where does the system store the audit data?

A ○ C:\WINNT\System32\auditlog

B ○ Security log

C ○ Application log

D ○ Error log

41 How does compression affect disk quotas?

A ○ The user gains storage space by using compression.

B ○ Compression increases the number of files that a user can save under the quota.

C ○ Compression does not affect the quota.

D ○ Compression reduces the amount of storage space.

42 Your WINS server experiences severe performance problems after some changes that you made to the server's properties. You examine each tab of the Properties dialog box and realize that you may have a problem with the configuration on the Database Verification tab. Which setting should you change?

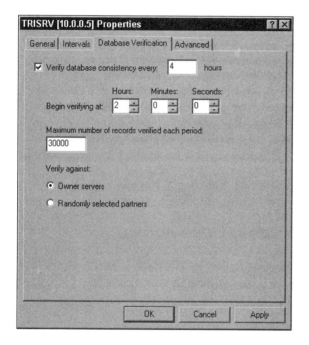

43 You want to install the Recovery console on an Alpha-based Windows 2000 server so the Recovery console is available as a startup item. You access the command prompt and change to your CD-ROM drive. What do you need to type?

A ○ \alpha\winnt32.exe\reccons

B ○ \alpha\alpha32.exe/cons

C ○ \alpha\winnt32.exe/cmdcons

D ○ Nothing. Alpha is not supported in Windows 2000.

44 Which kind of data contains information such as the registry, system boot files, and COM + Class Registration Database on a Windows 2000 member server?

A ○ User Data

B ○ System State Data

C ○ System Data

D ○ W2K Data

45 When installing Windows 2000 Server, Setup hangs during the hardware detection phase. What has probably caused the problem?

A ○ Faulty hardware device

B ○ Incompatible hardware device or driver

C ○ Conflicting IRQs

D ○ I/O disk error

46 You want to make certain that remote access clients cannot log on to the RAS server between the hours of 10:00 p.m. and 5:00 a.m. What do you need to do to create this restriction?

A ○ Create a policy.

B ○ Create a profile.

C ○ Configure the server's connection to reject calls during the desired hours.

D ○ You cannot configure this restriction.

47 You want to use Terminal Services in Remote Administration mode. How many client licenses do you need?

A ○ None

B ○ 4

C ○ 12

D ○ 15

48 Which tool can you use to configure an audit policy for your Windows 2000 member server?

A ○ Group Policy snap-in

B ○ Computer Management

C ○ Configure Your Server

D ○ You cannot do this.

49 What is the minimum password character length recommended by Microsoft?

A ○ 5

B ○ 7

C ○ 10

D ○ 12

50 Which tool can you use to configure local accounts on a Windows 2000 member server?

A ○ Group Policy snap-in

B ○ Configure Your Server

C ○ Computer Management

D ○ Active Directory Users and Computers

Answers

1 *C and D.* Bandwidth Allocation Protocol (BAP) and Bandwidth Allocation Control Protocol (BACP) are both used to automatically drop multilink connections when bandwidth utilization falls below a certain mark. *Objective: Configure, monitor, and troubleshoot remote access (Chapter 19).*

2 *D.* If you have three physical disks and you want to use a fault-tolerant solution while reducing the disk cost (in megabytes), a RAID-5 volume is your best choice. *Objective: Monitor, configure, and troubleshoot disks and volumes (Chapter 16).*

3 *Click the System State check box, browse for the appropriate backup media, and click Start Backup.* You can manually back up system state data or any other data by using the Backup tab in the Windows Backup tool. *Objective: Recover system and user data by using Windows Backup (Chapter 15).*

4 *C.* A standalone Dfs does not store its Dfs topology in the Active Directory, and therefore does not provide fault tolerance. *Objective: Configure, manage, and troubleshoot a standalone Distributed File System (Dfs) (Chapter 11).*

5 *A.* Use the Web folder's Virtual Directory tab to change the path to the Web folder so that it points to the correct location. *Objective: Monitor, configure, troubleshoot, and control access to files and folders via Web services (Chapter 10).*

6 *A.* You can manually clean old records from a WINS server database by scavenging the database. This action, which is also performed automatically, removes old records. *Objective: Install and configure network services for interoperability (Chapter 6).*

7 *B.* If you need to update a driver, click the Update Driver button on the Driver tab. This action launches the Update Driver wizard, which guides you through the process. *Objective: Configure Hardware (Chapter 13).*

8 *Click Install, select Service, click Add, select the desired service, and click OK.* Use the Properties dialog box to install network services that should run on the chosen connection. *Objective: Install and configure network services (Chapter 18).*

9 *C.* Zone transfer is the process by which the primary DNS server in a zone updates information on the secondary DNS servers. *Objective: Install and configure network services (Chapter 7).*

10 *C.* Only Windows 2000 computers can share a printer and have it automatically listed in the directory. Printers connected to down-level computers must have the printer object manually created by an Active Directory administrator. *Objective: Install and configure network services for interoperability (Chapter 8).*

11 *B.* The Resource tab lists the resources in use by a particular hardware device and will automatically tell you if any conflicts exist with other devices. From the answer list provided, this is the only way to check for IRQ conflicts. *Objective: Troubleshoot hardware devices (Chapter 12).*

12 *Click the Name Checking drop-down list and select Strict RFC.* Strict RFC names strictly adhere to the DNS RFC for naming structure. Names that are not strict RFC are treated as errors when this option is selected. *Objective: Install and configure network services for interoperability (Chapter 7).*

13 *B.* You can use the Shared Folders snap-in to disconnect users from folders or even disconnect individual users from folders. *Objective: Monitor, configure, troubleshoot, and control security on files and folders (Chapter 9).*

14 *B.* When upgrading to Windows 2000 over an NT 4.0 domain controller, Setup detects that the computer is a domain controller and automatically launches the Active Directory Installation wizard to install the Active Directory. This action upgrades the computer to a Windows 2000 domain controller and migrates your accounts into the Active Directory. *Objective: Upgrade from Microsoft Windows NT 4.0 (Chapter 3).*

15 *A.* To create a mandatory user profile, simply rename NTUSER.DAT to NTUSER.MAN, which makes the NTUSER file read-only. Any subsequent changes made by the user are not saved to the profile. *Objective: Configure and manage user profiles (Chapter 17).*

16 *B.* Setup Manager provides a wizard that helps you create an answer file or edit an existing one. *Objective: Create answer files by using Setup Manager to automate the installation of Windows 2000 Server (Chapter 4).*

17 *Right-click the unallocated space, click Create Volume, and then follow the steps in the wizard to create the simple volume.* You can create any disk volume using the Create New Volume wizard. *Objective: Monitor, configure, and troubleshoot disks and volumes (Chapter 16).*

18 *C.* The only possible answer is C. Excessive paging occurs when you do not have enough physical RAM available on your system. The computer writes memory data to the hard disk and recalls it when needed. *Objective: Monitor and optimize usage of system resources (Chapter 14).*

19 *C.* If you have system configuration changes that prevent the system from booting, boot using the Last Known Good option, which reads the last known good configuration from the registry. All configuration changes made since the Last Known Good will be lost. *Objective: Troubleshoot system restoration by using Safe Mode (Chapter 15).*

20 *A.* File Replication Service (FRS) is used on domain-based Dfs servers to synchronize folder replicas. *Objective: Configure, manage, and troubleshoot a domain-based Distributed File System (Chapter 11).*

21 *B.* Superscopes can be used to combine different DHCP scopes for multinet purposes. *Objective: Install and configure network services for interoperability (Chapter 5).*

22 *B.* Printer drivers for Windows 9*x* computers can be automatically downloaded to them from Windows 2000 computers if the 9*x* drivers are installed for the printer. Access the printer's Sharing tab and click the Additional Drivers button to add them. *Objective: Monitor, configure, troubleshoot, and control access to printers (Chapter 8).*

23 *C.* When you have the Local Area Connection Properties dialog box open, you can click Configure to open the properties for the NIC. *Objective: Install, configure, and troubleshoot network adapters and drivers (Chapter 18).*

24 *C.* You can use Task Manager's Processes tab to select and end processes that are running on your system. *Objective: Set priorities and start and stop processes (Chapter 14).*

25 *D.* You can use the MAKEBOOT utility on the Windows 2000 installation CD-ROM to make the four boot disks required to start an installation. You can create these disks on any Windows computer. *Objective: Perform an attended installation of Windows 2000 Server (Chapter 3).*

26 *C.* You can use RADIUS with remote access for a central authentication database for multiple remote access servers. *Objective: Configure, monitor, and troubleshoot remote access (Chapter 19).*

27 *B.* You use the tskill command to terminate a terminal server process. *Objective: Install, configure, monitor, and troubleshoot Terminal Services (Chapter 20).*

28 *D.* NTFS is the only file system that supports Encrypting File System. *Objective: Encrypt data on a hard disk by using Encrypting File System (Chapter 21).*

29 *C.* You can use the Attrib command within the Recovery console to change the attributes of a file or directory. *Objective: Recover systems and user data by using the Recovery console (Chapter 15).*

30 *Clear the Allow Inheritable Permissions From Parent to Propagate to This Object check box and then assign the desired permissions.* By default, inheritance is in effect for files and subfolders in a shared folder. You block inheritance on the Security tab in the properties of the desired file or subfolder by clearing the check box. *Objective: Monitor, configure, troubleshoot, and control access to files and folders in a shared folder (Chapter 9).*

31 *Click the Directory Browsing check box.* If you want users to be able to browse a Web folder, assign the directory-browsing right on the Virtual Directory tab in the Properties dialog box. *Objective: Monitor, configure, troubleshoot, and control access to Web sites (Chapter 10).*

32 *D.* Disk Cleanup is the best tool to use when you need to remove unnecessary files in order to create more disk space. *Objective: Optimize disk performance (Chapter 14).*

33 *A.* You use Sysprep to duplicate a hard disk so that the image of the disk can be copied to other computers that have the same hardware configuration. *Objective: Create and configure automated methods for installation of Windows 2000 (Chapter 4).*

34 *A.* Extensible authentication protocol (EAP) can be used to provide secure communication for smart-card logon or third-party authentication software. *Objective: Configure inbound connections (Chapter 19).*

35 *C.* You use the Cipher command to encrypt files or folders on your system using EFS. *Objective: Encrypt data on a hard disk by using Encrypting File System (Chapter 21).*

36 *A.* You use Client Creator to create the floppy disks used to install Terminal Services on client machines. *Objective: Install, configure, monitor, and troubleshoot Terminal Services (Chapter 20).*

37 *C.* If a disk is offline or a volume's status is displayed as At Risk, you can use the Reactivate Disk option to try to correct the problem. *Objective: Recover from disk failures (Chapter 16).*

38 *C.* DHCP servers must be authorized by the Active Directory, which prevents unauthorized or rogue DHCP servers from leasing IP addresses. *Objective: Install and configure network services (Chapter 5).*

39 *Click the Performance Object drop-down list and select Print Queue. Next, select the desired counters and then click Add to add them to the chart.* The Print Queue counters are an effective troubleshooting tool for printing problems. *Objective: Monitor, configure, troubleshoot, and control access to printers (Chapter 8).*

40 *B.* Audit data is stored in the security log, which you can review using Event Viewer. *Objective: Implement, configure, manage, and troubleshoot auditing (Chapter 22).*

41 *C.* Compression does not affect disk quotas. If a user has 50MB of storage space under the quota, the use of file compression does not increase the amount of storage space. *Objective: Monitor and configure disk quotas (Chapter 17).*

42 *Change the consistency check from every 4 hours to at least 24.* Database consistency check is a CPU-intensive operation. If the server runs a check every 4 hours, too much processing time is being used for the consistency check. The default setting is every 24 hours, and the check should be run during nonpeak hours. *Objective: Install and configure network services (Chapter 6).*

43 *D.* Windows 2000 does not natively support Alpha systems. *Objective: Recover systems and user data by using the Recovery console (Chapter 15).*

44 *B.* On Windows 2000 member servers, system state data includes the registry, COM + Class Registration Database, system boot files, and certificate services data if your server is a certificate server. *Objective: Manage and optimize availability of system state data and user data (Chapter 14).*

45 *B.* If Setup hangs during the hardware detection phase, you most likely have an incompatible hardware device or driver. To avoid this problem, check the HCL before beginning installation. *Objective: Troubleshoot failed installations (Chapter 3).*

46 *A.* Remote Access Service enables you to create RAS policies that can control various client access options, such as access time-and-day restrictions. *Objective: Create a remote access policy (Chapter 19).*

47 *A.* Remote Administration mode allows two concurrent connections, which do not require any licensing. *Objective: Remotely administer servers by using Terminal Services (Chapter 20).*

48 *A.* You can use the Group Policy MMC snap-in to configure an audit policy for the local machine. *Objective: Implement, configure, manage, and troubleshoot Account Policy (Chapter 22).*

49 *B.* Microsoft recommends that passwords contain at least seven characters, with a mix of letters, numbers, and keyboard symbols. *Objective: Implement, configure, manage, and troubleshoot local accounts (Chapter 22).*

50 *C.* You use the Computer Management console to configure local accounts on a Windows 2000 member server. *Objective: Implement, configure, manage, and troubleshoot local accounts (Chapter 22).*

Appendix B
Practice Exam 2

• •

Practice Exam Rules

▶ 90 minutes to complete the exam

▶ 50 questions

▶ At least 38 correct answers to pass the exam

▶ No cheating! (Don't use your book to find answers, because you won't have this luxury on exam day)

• •

*H*ere's another opportunity to practice for the Windows 2000 Server exam. If you have taken the first practice exam, you already know the rules. Read each question carefully, and make certain that you read all the answer choices before making a final decision.

In addition to the regular multiple-choice questions, this practice exam has some interface questions. On those questions, I ask you about some configuration option and then show you a picture of an element from the Windows 2000 Server user interface — for example, a dialog box or an MMC snap-in. Your answer should describe the steps or process you would perform if you were sitting at a real machine.

When you finish the exam, check your answers with the answer key and then review those chapters that cover any questions you missed. If you get them all correct, you are ready to take the exam!

Questions

1 After creating a DHCP scope and enabling the scope on a Windows 2000 member server, what must you do so that server can lease IP addresses?

A ○ Start the DHCP service.

B ○ Choose Action⇨Lease.

C ○ Authorize the server with the Active Directory.

D ○ Connect the member server to a domain controller.

2 You need to create an alias name record for a particular DNS server. What kind of resource record do you need to create?

A ○ A

B ○ CNAME

C ○ MX

D ○ All of the above

3 If you move a shared folder from an NTFS volume to a FAT32 volume, what effect does the move have on the folder's permissions?

A ○ Permissions are retained.

B ○ Permissions are inherited from the destination folder.

C ○ Read permission is assigned to the folder.

D ○ All NTFS permissions are lost.

4 For a particular backup plan, you want to perform a backup that backs up only selected files and folders that contain markers, but you do not want any of the existing markers cleared. When you configure the backup job, what do you need to select on the Backup Type tab to meet your goals?

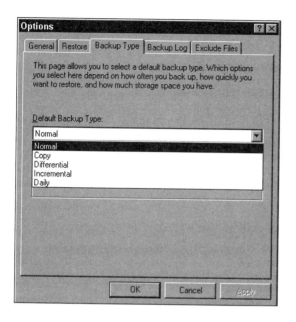

5 To ensure that your computer's hardware is compatible with Windows 2000, what resource should you check before attempting a Windows 2000 installation?

A ○ SETUP.DOC

B ○ DEVICELIST.DOC

C ○ HCL

D ○ COMPAT.TXT

6 You experience some problems with the processor on your Windows 2000 member server. You want to use Performance Monitor to see the percentage of processor usage over a period of time. In the Add Counters dialog box, what do you need to do?

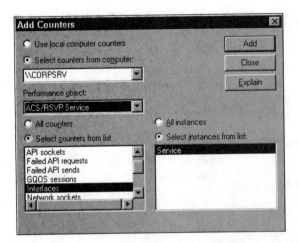

7 You have installed the NWLink protocol so your Windows 2000 server can communicate with a NetWare server. After installing the protocol, you cannot connect to the NetWare server. What is the most likely cause of the problem?

A ○ Incorrect subnet mask

B ○ Incorrect frame type

C ○ Incorrect default gateway

D ○ Incorrect IP header

8 You have shared a Web folder on an intranet site hosted by your Windows 2000 member server. The content in the folder is time-sensitive and you want to configure an expiration date for the Web folder. Where can you configure this setting?

A ○ Virtual Directory tab

B ○ Directory Security tab

C ○ HTTP Headers tab

D ○ Custom Errors tab

9 On a hard disk dual-booting Windows NT Server 4.0 and Windows 2000 Server, you upgrade the disk to dynamic. After you perform this action, you can no longer boot into NT Server 4.0. Why?

A ○ The partition was deleted.

B ○ Previous versions of Windows cannot read dynamic disks.

C ○ You need to edit BOOT.INI.

D ○ The operating system is damaged.

10 By default, what is the name of an answer file in Windows 2000?

A ○ ANSWER.TXT

B ○ UNATTENDED.TXT

C ○ DIFF.TXT

D ○ REF.TXT

11 Which VPN protocol is used with IPSec to create highly secure transmissions?

A ○ PPTP

B ○ L2TP

C ○ PAP

D ○ MS-CHAP V2

12 You want to use EFS to encrypt data on a compressed volume, but you cannot seem to do so. What is the problem?

A ○ EFS does not work with compression.

B ○ Your version of compression does not support EFS.

C ○ You need to install the EFS protocol.

D ○ The volume has errors.

13 You need to configure an auditing policy for a particular Windows 2000 member server. Which tool enables you to do this?

A ○ Event Viewer

B ○ Group Policy snap-in

C ○ Configure Your Server

D ○ Computer Management

14 What type of policy has widely replaced system policies in Windows 2000?

A ○ Local

B ○ Group

C ○ Domain

D ○ Organizational Unit

15 How many days can unlicensed Terminal Services Application Server mode clients use applications before being refused by the server?

A ○ 40

B ○ 60

C ○ 90

D ○ 120

16 Which is a major disadvantage of a standalone Dfs?

A ○ No support for Dfs links

B ○ No fault tolerance

C ○ No support for Windows 98 clients

D ○ No support for shared folders

17 You want to configure several identical printers so they appear as one printer to network users. How can you configure this setup?

A ○ On the Ports tab of the printer's properties, enable printer pooling.

B ○ On the Ports tab of the printer's properties, enable printer pooling and select the correct ports.

C ○ On the Advanced tab of the printer's properties, enable multicast printing.

D ○ On the Security tab of the printer's properties, enable printer sharing.

18 You want to make certain that no unsigned drivers can be installed on your system, and you want to ensure that this setting remains in effect, regardless of who logs on to your server. What do you need to do in the Driver Signing Options dialog box to configure this setup?

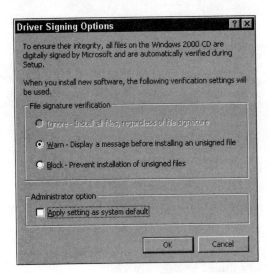

19 You experience problems starting your Windows 2000 server. You need to boot into Safe Mode with Networking, but you also want to make certain that only the basic VGA driver is loaded. Besides booting into Safe Mode with Networking, what else do you need to do?

A ○ Nothing.

B ○ Enable VGA Mode.

C ○ Enable Boot Logging.

D ○ Boot into Safe Mode with Command Prompt.

20 By accessing Performance Options on the Advanced tab of System Properties, what two performance optimization choices do you have for application response? (Choose two.)

A ❑ Applications

B ❑ Services

C ❑ Processes

D ❑ Background services

21 On the General tab in a particular dynamic disk's Properties dialog box, what can you do to reduce the amount of disk spaced used by files and folders and have the change configured immediately?

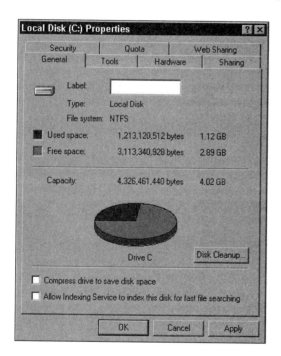

22 You experience problems with a WINS server and you want to write a detailed event log for troubleshooting purposes. How can you configure this?

A ○ Server Properties, General tab

B ○ Server Properties, Intervals tab

C ○ Server Properties, Database Verification tab

D ○ Server Properties, Advanced tab

23 You want to configure a disk quota on a FAT32 volume, but the option does not seem to be available. What is the problem?

A ○ Disk quotas are not installed on your server.

B ○ The volume is offline.

C ○ There is a general system error.

D ○ Disk quotas are supported only on NTFS volumes.

24 For a particular Remote Access server, you want to configure the server so that all clients use a smart-card to log on. In the Authentication Methods dialog box, which protocol do you need to select?

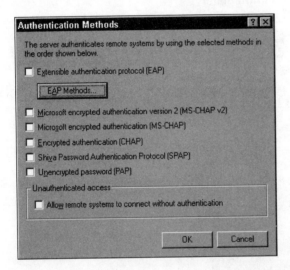

25 You have an encrypted folder encrypted by EFS. You drag and drop several documents into the folder, but they are not encrypted. What do you need to do?

A ○ Decrypt the folder.

B ○ Re-encrypt the folder.

C ○ Use the copy-and-paste method.

D ○ The files cannot be encrypted.

26 You need to configure a local account for your Windows 2000 member server. Where can you configure this local account?

A ○ Group Policy snap-in

B ○ Computer Management

C ○ Users and Groups snap-in

D ○ Active Directory Users and Computers

27 For any given remote access profile, what is the default setting used on the IP tab of the profile's Properties dialog box?

A ○ DHCP enabled

B ○ Static IP assignment pool

C ○ Server defined

D ○ There is no default setting

28 You need to copy a drive image and use it to install several servers that do not have the same hardware as the master server. Which utility do you need to use?

A ○ Winnt

B ○ Syspart

C ○ Sysprep

D ○ UDF

29 You need to use the Windows Recovery console to repartition a hard drive on your system. What command do you need to use within the console to accomplish this task?

A ○ Attrib

B ○ Batch

C ○ Mkdir

D ○ Diskpart

30 You have a small office network. Only the Windows 2000 server has a connection to the Internet through an ISDN line. You want the other Windows 2000 Professional computers to have an Internet connection as well, but you do not want to purchase the hardware. What is an inexpensive solution?

A ○ Install modems.

B ○ Share the Internet connection.

C ○ Use a proxy server.

D ○ There is no inexpensive solution.

31 You want to configure a particular DNS server so that it only listens for DNS queries on certain IP addresses. Where can you configure this setting?

A ○ Server properties, Interfaces tab

B ○ Server properties, Advanced tab

C ○ Zone properties, Name Servers tab

D ○ Zone properties, Zone Transfers tab

32 You have a shared folder that contains numerous company documents. You place a new document in the shared folder. What does this action do to the permissions configured for the documents?

A ○ The permissions remain the same.

B ○ The permissions are removed.

C ○ Permissions are inherited from the parent folder.

D ○ All permissions are changed to Read.

33 Over time, the read response for your hard disk has slowed down. What is the most likely cause of the problem?

A ○ Incorrect IRQ setting

B ○ Incorrect DMA setting

C ○ Corruption

D ○ Fragmentation

34 Which of the following is not a part of system state data on a Windows 2000 member server?

A ○ Registry

B ○ SYSVOL

C ○ COM + Class Registration Database

D ○ System Boot Files

35 Which operating systems cannot be directly upgraded to Windows 2000 Server? (Choose all that apply.)

A ❑ Windows NT 3.51

B ❑ NT versions earlier than 3.51

C ❑ Windows 9*x*

D ❑ Windows NT Terminal Server 4.0

36 By accessing Disk Management on a Windows 2000 server, you notice that a volume's status is listed as Initializing. What action do you need to take?

A ○ None.

B ○ Format the disk.

C ○ Reactivate the disk.

D ○ Recreate the volume.

37 You need to use the Recovery console to delete a directory on your Windows 2000 server. Which command do you need to use in the Recovery console to accomplish this task?

A ○ Ren

B ○ Rmdir

C ○ Set

D ○ Mkdir

38 Which system state data component applies only to Windows 2000 domain controllers?

A ○ Registry

B ○ COM + Class Registrations

C ○ System Boot Files

D ○ Active Directory database

39 You are setting up a domain-based Dfs server on your network. You have both NTFS and FAT partitions available on your server. You realize that you can install Dfs on both NTFS and FAT partitions, but what major problem will you have with the domain-based Dfs if you install it on the FAT partition?

A ○ FAT does not allow multiple Dfs links.

B ○ FAT does not support the domain-based Dfs.

C ○ Automatic replication cannot occur on a FAT partition.

D ○ All Dfs link security will be compromised on the FAT partition.

40 Your company wants to use multicasting so that all clients can view company multimedia. You want the multicast IP addresses to be assigned automatically. How can you do this?

A ○ Use DHCP.

B ○ Use MADCAP.

C ○ Use the Multicast snap-in.

D ○ You cannot do this.

41 You need to create a new Virtual Private Network (VPN). What is the easiest way to create this new connection in Windows 2000?

A ○ Use the Create Tunnel Connections wizard.

B ○ Use the Make New Connection wizard.

C ○ Use Add/Remove Programs and install the service.

D ○ You can't create VPNs in Windows 2000.

42 On a particular printer, you want to create a schedule so the printer is only available from 8:00 a.m. to 10:00 a.m. Additionally, you do not want documents spooled. How can you configure both of these items on the Advanced tab in the printer's Properties dialog box?

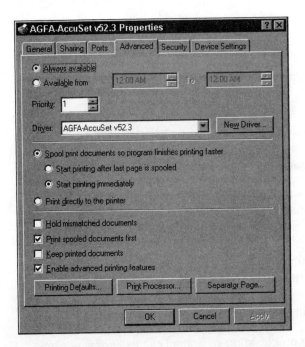

43 You want to disable a particular hardware device by using the device's Properties dialog box. On which tab can you temporarily disable the device without removing it from the system?

A ○ General

B ○ Driver

C ○ Advanced

D ○ Resource

44 You want to make certain that users can access a particular Web folder by sending their password and username in clear text. What authenticated access method do you need to allow?

A ○ NTFS

B ○ Basic authentication

C ○ Secure authentication

D ○ Clear authentication

45 You want to configure a user profile so the user can log on to any workstation and receive the same profile. What kind of profile do you need to create?

A ○ Local User Profile
B ○ Roaming User Profile
C ○ Mandatory User Profile
D ○ This cannot be done

46 Which remote access technology uses the BAP and BACP protocols?

A ○ IPSec
B ○ Multilink
C ○ Smart Card
D ○ Tunneling

47 For a terminal service connection on a particular server, you want to use encryption that encrypts data between the client and the server using the server's standard key strength. Which encryption level do you need to use?

A ○ Low
B ○ Medium
C ○ High
D ○ Maximum

48 You need to configure auditing for a particular folder. What do you need to access to configure this feature?

A ○ Folder Properties, Advanced tab
B ○ Folder Properties, Security tab, Advanced button
C ○ Folder Properties, Auditing tab
D ○ Folder Properties, Configuration tab, Advanced button

49 Which tool can you use to analyze your computer's security configuration?

A ○ Templates
B ○ Security Configuration and Analysis
C ○ Event Viewer
D ○ Active Directory Users and Computers

50 Which terminal server command can you use to disconnect a client from a Terminal Services session?

A ○ tsdisconnect
B ○ tsdisconcl
C ○ tsdisconrcl
D ○ tsdiscon

Answers

1 *C.* Before a Windows 2000 member server can lease IP addresses to clients, it must be authorized by the Active Directory. *Objective: Install and configure network services (Chapter 5).*

2 *B.* An alias record (CNAME) enables you to create an alternate name for a DNS server and is often used to combine several DNS servers to appear as one server. *Objective: Install and configure network services for interoperability (Chapter 7).*

3 *D.* If you move a folder from an NTFS volume to a FAT32 volume, you lose all NTFS permissions because FAT32 volumes do not support NTFS permissions. *Objective: Monitor, configure, troubleshoot, and control security on files and folders (Chapter 9).*

4 *Select the Differential option.* A differential backup backs up selected files and folders that contain markers, but it does not clear the existing markers. *Objective: Recover system and user data by using Windows Backup (Chapter 15).*

5 *C.* The Hardware Compatibility List (HCL) tells you which hardware devices are compatible with Windows 2000. The HCL is available at www.microsoft.com or on your installation CD-ROM. *Objective: Perform an attended installation of Windows 2000 Server (Chapter 3).*

6 *Select the Processor performance object and the % Processor Time counter and then click Add.* To use Performance Monitor to view the percentage of processor usage time, use this counter. *Objective: Monitor and optimize usage of system resources (Chapter 14).*

7 *B.* When using NWLink, the most common troubleshooting problem is an incorrect frame type, which prevents communication. *Objective: Install, configure, and troubleshoot network protocols (Chapter 18).*

8 *C.* On the HTTP Headers tab, you can assign an expiration date and time for Web folder content by clicking the Content Expiration check box and entering the desired values. *Objective: Monitor, configure, troubleshoot, and control access to files and folders via Web services (Chapter 10).*

9 *B.* Previous versions of Windows cannot read dynamic disks, so you should not upgrade them until you are running only Windows 2000. *Objective: Monitor, configure, and troubleshoot disks and volumes (Chapter 16).*

10 *B.* UNATTENDED.TXT is the default name of answer files in Windows 2000. You can use different names, however, so you can create additional answer files for different installations. When running WINNT, point to the correct answer filename. *Objective: Create answer files by using Setup Manager to automate the installation of Windows 2000 Server (Chapter 4).*

11 *B.* Layer 2 Tunneling Protocol (L2TP) is supported in Windows 2000 with the use of IPSec. Together, they ensure highly secure transmissions. *Objective: Install, configure, and troubleshoot a virtual private network (VPN) (Chapter 19).*

12 *A.* EFS does not work with compression in Windows 2000. In order to use encryption, the compression must be removed. *Objective: Encrypt data on a hard disk by using Encrypting File System (Chapter 21).*

13 *B.* Use the Group Policy snap-in to configure audit policies for the local machine. *Objective: Implement, configure, manage, and troubleshoot account policy (Chapter 22).*

14 *B.* Group Policy is the preferred method for implementing policies in Windows 2000, but system policy is still supported for backward compatibility. *Objective: Implement, configure, manage, and troubleshoot system policy in a Windows 2000 environment (Chapter 21).*

15 *C.* Terminal Services Application Server mode clients can access applications for 90 days without a license. *Objective: Configure Terminal Services for application sharing (Chapter 20).*

16 *B.* From the answer choices provided, the only possible answer is no fault tolerance. A standalone Dfs does not store the Dfs topology in the Active Directory, so if the Dfs server goes down, Dfs is not available to network clients. *Objective: Configure, manage, and troubleshoot a standalone Distributed File System (Dfs) (Chapter 11).*

17 *B.* On the Ports tab of the printer's properties, you can select the Enable Printer Pooling check box and then select the ports for the printer pool. *Objective: Monitor, configure, troubleshoot, and control access to printers (Chapter 8).*

18 *Click the Block radio button and then select the Administrator Option check box.* You can stop all unsigned drivers from being installed on a system by clicking the Block radio button. The Administrator Option makes this setting effective, regardless of who is logged on. You must be logged on as an administrator to configure this setting. *Objective: Configure driver signing options (Chapter 13).*

19 *A.* When you choose to boot into Safe Mode with Networking, only the minimal VGA driver is loaded, so in this situation, you do not need to do anything else. *Objective: Troubleshoot system restoration by using Safe Mode (Chapter 15).*

20 *A and D.* For application response, you can choose to optimize performance for applications or background services. By default, the background services option is selected. *Objective: Set priorities and start and stop processes (Chapter 14).*

21 *Click the Compress Drive check box and then click Apply.* Compression is available in Windows 2000 on dynamic volumes to help reduce the amount of disk space used by files and folders. *Objective: Configured data compression (Chapter 16).*

22 *D.* You can write a detailed event log to the Windows event log by accessing the WINS Server properties and clicking the log check box option on the Advanced tab. This action should only be used for troubleshooting purposes because it degrades system performance. *Objective: Install and configure network services (Chapter 6).*

23 *D.* Disk quotas are supported only on NTFS volumes, not FAT or FAT32. *Objective: Monitor and configure disk quotas (Chapter 17).*

24 *Select EAP.* Extensible Authentication Protocol provides secure logon for clients using smart cards and also supports third-party authentication methods. *Objective: Configure, monitor, and troubleshoot remote access (Chapter 19).*

25 *C.* To place files into an encrypted folder, you need to use the copy-and-paste method, rather than drag and drop, so the files will be encrypted. *Objective: Encrypt data on a hard disk by using Encrypting File System (Chapter 21).*

26 *B.* The Computer Management console on a Windows 2000 member server is used to create and manage local accounts. *Objective: Implement, configure, manage, and troubleshoot local accounts (Chapter 22).*

27 *C.* For remote access policies, the IP configuration is set to default to the server's settings. Whatever settings you have made on the server define how clients receive an IP address. You can, of course, override the default setting on the IP tab of the profile's properties. *Objective: Configure a remote access profile (Chapter 19).*

28 *B.* Syspart can be used to copy disk images to computers that do not have the same hardware configuration as the master. Syspart is available as a utility and as a command parameter under WINNT32. *Objective: Create and configure automated methods for installation of Windows 2000 (Chapter 4).*

29 *D.* The Diskpart command enables you to partition your hard drive while using the Recovery console. *Objective: Recover system and user data using the Recovery console (Chapter 15).*

30 *B.* You can share dial-up or ISDN connections in Windows 2000 so that other computers can access the share and connect to the Internet. This feature is designed for small-office or home networks. *Objective: Install, configure, and troubleshoot shared access (Chapter 18).*

31 *A.* The Interfaces tab in the Server Properties dialog box enables you to restrict a DNS server's listening by specifying certain IP addresses that it will respond to for resolution queries. *Objective: Install and configure network services (Chapter 7).*

32 *C.* By default, inheritance is in effect for shared folders and the files and subfolders contained in the folder. All files and subfolders inherit the permissions of the parent folder. *Objective: Monitor, configure, troubleshoot, and control access to files and folders in a shared folder (Chapter 9).*

33 *D.* Fragmentation occurs when files are written in a noncontiguous manner on your hard disk. This causes a slower read response time. Run Disk Defragmenter to correct the problem. *Objective: Optimize disk performance (Chapter 14).*

34 *B.* SYSVOL is a part of system state data on Windows 2000 domain controllers — not member servers. *Objective: Manage and optimize availability of system state data and user data (Chapter 14).*

35 *B and C.* You cannot directly upgrade previous versions of NT earlier than 3.51 or Windows 9x to Windows 2000. *Objective: Perform an attended installation of Windows 2000 Server (Chapter 3).*

36 *A.* Volume initialization is an internal process and not an error. The status will change to healthy after initialization is complete. No action should be taken. *Objective: Recover from disk failures (Chapter 16).*

37 *B.* Rmdir is a command you can use within the Recovery console to delete a directory. *Objective: Recover systems and user data by using the Recovery console (Chapter 15).*

38 *D.* System state data is the same for Windows 2000 domain controllers and Windows 2000 member servers, with the exception of the Active Directory database (and the SYSVOL folder), which applies only to domain controllers. *Objective: Recover system and user data by using Windows Backup (Chapter 15).*

39 *C.* On domain-based Dfs, automatic replication with other Dfs servers can occur automatically, but only on NTFS partitions. When setting up a domain-based Dfs, you should always use NTFS partitions. *Objective: Configure, manage, and troubleshoot a domain-based Distributed File System (Dfs) (Chapter 11).*

40 *B.* MADCAP can automatically lease multicast IP addresses to DHCP clients. *Objective: Install and configure network services for interoperability (Chapter 5).*

41 *B.* The Make New Connection wizard is the easiest way to establish new connections in Windows 2000. *Objective: Configure the properties of a connection (Chapter 18).*

42 *To create the desired schedule, click the Available From radio button and then enter the starting and ending times. To avoid spooling documents, click the Print Directly To The Printer radio button. Objective: Monitor, configure, troubleshoot, and control access to printers (Chapter 8).*

43 *A.* You can use the General tab in a hardware device's Properties dialog box to disable the device. Click the drop-down list and select Disable. You can re-enable the device in the same manner. *Objective: Configure hardware devices (Chapter 12).*

44 *B.* Basic authentication allows users to log on to a Web folder with a clear-text password. You can enable this feature on the Directory Security tab of the folder's Properties dialog box. *Objective: Monitor, configure, troubleshoot, and control access to Web sites (Chapter 10).*

45 *B.* A roaming user profile is stored in the Active Directory and follows a user, regardless of which workstation the user employs for logging on to the network. *Objective: Configure and manage user profiles (Chapter 17).*

46 *B.* Multilink enables you to combine several links to create more bandwidth, such as combining several modem connections. BAP and BACP can dynamically manage multilink connections by dropping unneeded links if bandwidth falls below a certain utilization. *Objective: Configure, monitor, and troubleshoot remote access (Chapter 19).*

47 *B.* The Medium encryption setting encrypts data between the client and the server using the server's standard encryption key. *Objective: Install, configure, monitor, and troubleshoot Terminal Services (Chapter 20).*

48 *B.* You can configure a file or folder for auditing by accessing its properties, clicking the Security tab, and then clicking the Advanced button to configure auditing. *Objective: Implement, configure, manage, and troubleshoot auditing (Chapter 22).*

49 *B.* The Security Configuration and Analysis tool can check your security configuration and log errors or problems. *Objective: Implement, configure, manage, and troubleshoot security by using the Security Configuration Tool Set (Chapter 22).*

50 *D.* You can use the tsdiscon command to disconnect a terminal server client session. *Objective: Install, configure, monitor, and troubleshoot Terminal Services (Chapter 20).*

Appendix C

About the CD

● ●

*H*ere's some of the great stuff you'll find on the CD-ROM:

- ✔ The QuickLearn game, a fun way to study for the test
- ✔ Practice and Self-Assessment tests, to make sure you are ready for the real thing
- ✔ Practice test demos from Transcender, QuickCert, and Super Software

System Requirements

Make sure that your computer meets the minimum system requirements listed in this section. If your computer doesn't match up to most of these requirements, you may have problems using the contents of the CD:

- ✔ A PC with a 486 or faster processor.
- ✔ Microsoft Windows 95 or later.
- ✔ At least 16MB of total RAM installed on your computer. For best performance, you should have at least 32MB of RAM installed.
- ✔ A CD-ROM drive — double-speed (2x) or faster.
- ✔ A sound card for PCs.
- ✔ A monitor capable of displaying at least 256 colors or grayscale.
- ✔ A modem with a speed of at least 14,400 bps.

Important Note: To play the QuickLearn game, you must have a 166 or faster computer running Windows 95 or 98 with SVGA graphics. You must also have Microsoft DirectX 5.0 or later installed. If you do not have DirectX, you can install it from the CD. Just run D:\Directx\dxinstall.exe. Unfortunately, DirectX 5.0 does not run on Windows NT 4.0, so you cannot play the QuickLearn Game on a Windows NT 4.0 or earlier machine.

Using the CD with Microsoft Windows

To install the items from the CD to your hard drive, follow these steps:

1. **Insert the CD into your computer's CD-ROM drive.**

2. **Click Start⇨Run.**

3. **In the dialog box that appears, type** D:\IDG.EXE.

   Replace *D* with the proper drive letter if your CD-ROM drive uses a different letter. (If you don't know the letter, see how your CD-ROM drive is listed under My Computer.)

4. **Click OK.**

   A license agreement window appears.

5. **Read through the license agreement, nod your head, and then click the Accept button if you want to use the CD — after you click Accept, you'll never be bothered by the License Agreement window again.**

   The CD interface Welcome screen appears. The interface is a little program that shows you what's on the CD and coordinates installing the programs and running the demos. The interface basically enables you to click a button or two to make things happen.

6. **Click anywhere on the Welcome screen to enter the interface.**

   Now you are getting to the action. This next screen lists categories for the software on the CD.

7. **To view the items within a category, just click the category's name.**

   A list of programs in the category appears.

8. **For more information about a program, click the program's name.**

   Be sure to read the information that appears. Sometimes a program has its own system requirements or requires you to do a few tricks on your computer before you can install or run the program, and this screen tells you what you might need to do, if necessary.

9. **If you don't want to install the program, click the Back button to return to the previous screen.**

   You can always return to the previous screen by clicking the Back button. This feature enables you to browse the different categories and products and decide what you want to install.

10. **To install a program, click the appropriate Install button.**

    The CD interface drops to the background while the CD installs the program you chose.

11. **To install other items, repeat Steps 7–10.**

12. **When you've finished installing programs, click the Quit button to close the interface.**

    You can eject the CD now. Carefully place it back in the plastic jacket of the book for safekeeping.

In order to run some of the programs on this *MCSE Windows 2000 Server For Dummies* CD-ROM, you may need to keep the CD inside your CD-ROM drive. This is a Good Thing. Otherwise, the installed program would have required you to install a very large chunk of the program to your hard drive, which may have kept you from installing other software.

What You'll Find

Shareware programs are fully functional, free trial versions of copyrighted programs. If you like particular programs, register with their authors for a nominal fee and receive licenses, enhanced versions, and technical support. *Freeware programs* are free, copyrighted games, applications, and utilities. You can copy them to as many PCs as you like — free — but they have no technical support. GNU software is governed by its own license, which is included inside the folder of the GNU software. There are no restrictions on distribution of this software. See the GNU license for more details. Trial, demo, or evaluation versions are usually limited either by time or functionality (such as being unable to save projects).

Here's a summary of the software on this CD.

Dummies test prep tools

QuickLearn Game

The QuickLearn Game is the *...For Dummies* way of making studying for the Certification exam fun. Well, okay, less painful. OutPost is a DirectX, high-resolution, fast-paced arcade game.

Answer questions to defuse dimensional disrupters and save the universe from a rift in space-time. (The questions come from the same set of questions that the Self-Assessment and Practice Test use, but isn't this way more fun?) Missing a few questions on the real exam almost never results in a rip in the fabric of the universe, so just think how easy it'll be when you get there!

Please note: QUIKLERN.EXE on the CD is just a self-extractor, to simplify the process of copying the game files to your computer. It will not create any shortcuts on your computer's desktop or Start menu.

You need to have DirectX 5.0 or later installed to play the QuickLearn Game; and it does not run on Windows NT 4.0.

Practice Test

The Practice test is designed to help you get comfortable with the certification testing situation and pinpoint your strengths and weaknesses on the topic. You can accept the default setting of 60 questions in 60 minutes, or you can customize the settings. You can choose the number of questions, the amount of time, and even decide which objectives you want to focus on.

After you answer the questions, the Practice test gives you plenty of feedback. You can find out which questions you answered correctly and incorrectly and get statistics on how you did, broken down by objective. Then you can review the questions — all of them, all the ones you missed, all the ones you marked, or a combination of the ones you marked and the ones you missed.

Self-Assessment Test

The Self-Assessment test is designed to simulate the actual certification testing situation. You must answer 60 questions in 60 minutes. After you answer all the questions, you find out your score and whether you pass or fail — but that's all the feedback you get. If you can pass the Self-Assessment test regularly, you're ready to tackle the real thing.

Links Page

I've also created a Links Page — a handy starting place for accessing the huge amounts of information on the Internet about the certification tests. You can find the page at D:\Links.htm.

Screen Saver

Here's a spiffy little screen saver that the Dummies team created. Maybe, like sleeping with the book under your pillow, this can help you learn subliminally! Screen shots of test questions will fill your screen, so when your computer is not doing anything else, it can still be quizzing you! And if you'd like to visit the *Certification ...For Dummies* Web site, all you have to do is press the space bar while the screen saver is running — your default browser will be launched and send you there! (You might want to keep this in mind if you're the kind of person who hits the space bar to get rid of your screen saver.)

Commercial demos

QuickCert Exam Simulator, from QuickCert, Inc.

This package from QuickCert offers practice tests for several Certification exams. Run the QuickCert IDG Demo to choose the practice test you want to work on. For more information about the Exam Simulator, visit the QuickCert Web site at www.quickcert.com.

Self Test MCSE Windows 2000 Server Demo

This demo, designed to help you prepare for the Windows 2000 exam, gives you another 10 practice questions. Get lots more by ordering the software. Learn more by visiting the Web site: www.selftestsoftware.com.

Transcender Windows 2000 Server Flash, from Transcender Corporation

Another demo from the good folks at Transcender, this one is designed to help you learn the fundamental concepts and terminology behind Windows 2000 Server. You provide short answer-type explanations to questions presented in a flash card format, and grade yourself as you go. To learn more about what Transcender has to offer, check out their Web site at www.transcender.com.

Transcender Demo Sampler, from Transcender Corporation

Transcender's demo tests are some of the more popular practice tests available. The Certification Sampler offers demos of many of the exams that Transcender offers.

W2000 Server MCSEprep, from Super Software

This demo, designed to help you prepare for the Windows 2000 Server exam, gives you another 20 practice questions. Get lots more by ordering the software. Learn more by visiting the Web site, www.mcseprep.com.

If You've Got Problems (Of the CD Kind)

I tried my best to compile programs that work on most computers with the minimum system requirements. Alas, your computer may differ, and some programs may not work properly for some reason.

The two likeliest problems are that you don't have enough memory (RAM) for the programs you want to use, or you have other programs running that are affecting installation or running of a program. If you get error messages like Not enough memory or Setup cannot continue, try one or more of these methods and then try using the software again:

✔ **Turn off any antivirus software that you have on your computer.** Installers sometimes mimic virus activity and may make your computer incorrectly believe that it is being infected by a virus.

✔ **Close all running programs.** The more programs you're running, the less memory is available to other programs. Installers also typically update files and programs; if you keep other programs running, installation may not work properly.

✔ **In Windows, close the CD interface and run demos or installations directly from Windows Explorer.** The interface itself can tie up system memory, or even conflict with certain kinds of interactive demos. Use Windows Explorer to browse the files on the CD and launch installers or demos.

✔ **Have your local computer store add more RAM to your computer.** This is, admittedly, a drastic and somewhat expensive step. However, adding more memory can really help the speed of your computer and enable more programs to run at the same time.

If you still have trouble installing the items from the CD, please call the IDG Books Worldwide Customer Service phone number: 800-762-2974 (outside the U.S.: 317-572-3342).

Index

• X •

• Z •

Notes

IDG Books Worldwide, Inc., End-User License Agreement

Installation Instructions

To install the items from the *MCSE Windows 2000 Server For Dummies* CD to your hard drive, follow these steps:

1. **Insert the CD into your computer's CD-ROM drive.**

2. **Click Start⇨Run.**

3. **In the dialog box that appears, type** D:\IDG.EXE.

   Replace *D* with the proper drive letter if your CD-ROM drive uses a different letter.

4. **Click OK.**

5. **Read through the license agreement that's displayed and then click Accept.**

   The CD interface Welcome screen appears.

6. **Click anywhere on the Welcome screen to enter the interface.**

   The interface displays a list of categories for the software on the CD.

7. **To view the items within a category, just click the category's name.**

   A list of programs in the category appears.

8. **For more information about a program, click the program's name.**

9. **To install a program, click Install. If you don't want to install the program, click Back.**

   The CD interface drops to the background while the CD installs the program you chose.

10. **After you install the programs you want, click Quit and then eject the CD.**

For more information, see the "About the CD" appendix.

IDG BOOKS WORLDWIDE
BOOK REGISTRATION

Register This Book and Win!

We want to hear from you!

Visit **http://my2cents.dummies.com** to register this book and tell us how you liked it!

- Get entered in our monthly prize giveaway.

- Give us feedback about this book — tell us what you like best, what you like least, or maybe what you'd like to ask the author and us to change!

- Let us know any other *For Dummies*® topics that interest you.

Your feedback helps us determine what books to publish, tells us what coverage to add as we revise our books, and lets us know whether we're meeting your needs as a *For Dummies* reader. You're our most valuable resource, and what you have to say is important to us!

Not on the Web yet? It's easy to get started with *Dummies 101*®: *The Internet For Windows*® *98* or *The Internet For Dummies*® at local retailers everywhere.

Or let us know what you think by sending us a letter at the following address:

For Dummies Book Registration
Dummies Press
10475 Crosspoint Blvd.
Indianapolis, IN 46256

™
...FOR DUMMIES

BESTSELLING
BOOK SERIES